Making the Connection

Making the Connection

Practical Steps in ESG Management

Peter Sammons

BEP

BUSINESS EXPERT PRESS

Leader in applied, concise business books

Making the Connection: Practical Steps in ESG Management

First published in 2024 by
Business Expert Press, LLC
222 East 46th Street, New York, NY 10017
www.businessexpertpress.com

ISBN-13: 978-1-63742-598-5(paperback)
ISBN-13: 978-1-63742-599-2(e-book)

Business Expert Press Environmental and Social Sustainability for
Business Advantage Collection

First edition: 2024

10 9 8 7 6 5 4 3 2 1

Description

In finance, investments, and insurance, "ESG" refers to a series of perceived risks of material interest to investors, which must be reported as such. Beyond this, "ESG" is a response to increasingly intrusive governmental and regulatory demands for *greater sustainability in corporate operations.*

In the world of business, private or public sector, ESG is a set of *practical challenges*—how do we improve performance across the three key areas of natural environment, corporate social responsibility, and internal–external governance? Superficially, these three disciplines are distinct and disparate, but they can be actively managed by adopting a project management style and benefit from a common methodology and "language."

This book enables a logical evaluation of the component parts of the ESG task and how they fit together. *Part 1* sets the scene on the big picture of what ESG is and the sustainability impetus behind it. *Part 2* speaks into corporate strategy and where ESG fits into this. *Parts 3 to 5* look in detail at "E," "S," and "G," respectively, using a common "roadmap" to approach each task, adopting a similar methodology and project management style. *Part 6* explores the neglected area of third-party relationships and how ESG "wins" are achievable in concert with third parties up and down our value chain. *Part 7* looks at the technical area of *data* and how we need to master this discipline, again managing this in concert with our key third-party counterparts. Seven appendices provide useful additional material.

Keywords

defining ESG; ESG strategic positioning; ESG roadmap; 3PM third-party management; ESG data; ESG materiality assessment; Scope 1, 2, and 3 emissions; ESG taxonomy; double materiality; ESG data management; ESG in the value chain; regulatory compliance; sustainability strategy; ESG corporate values and mission

Contents

Elevator Pitch—ESG

Sixty Seconds .....

Sustainability is a political and social imperative. How can our world advance and thrive in a sustainable way, that is, a way that enables us to live within the planet's resources and hand over to future generations a viable socioeconomic "ecosphere"?

ESG is the broadly accepted set of evolving mechanisms that will best enable modern complex societies to work toward sustainable outcomes as evinced by the United Nations' 17 *Sustainable Development Goals.*

"E," "S," and "G" are separate, but overlapping, specialisms. Addressing them requires sound planning and deliberative ongoing management.

Rome was not built in a day; ESG outcomes will develop over time. Our generation is "investing" for the next. Businesses—and public sector organizations—need to embark on a journey and build a robust "business case" for action. After that, they must deliver on their promises!

We need to achieve ESG .... without bankruptcy.

PART 1

Setting the Scene

CHAPTER 1

Extended Elevator Pitch

Defining ESG

ESG will not "solve" all of society's ills or eliminate all risks, but it represents a measured and precautionary approach that seeks to minimize risks and potential harms, while maximizing opportunity to create sustainable outcomes. ESG is neither a "movement" nor a "philosophy."

ESG-embedding is a rational, proactive, RAM[1] organizational response to society's need to work toward a sustainable world, that is, one where humans can maximize the opportunity to live fruitful lives in reasonable social, economic, and physical security, in an otherwise uncertain world.

ESG is a tool or, more correctly, a *toolbox*, of interconnected policies, processes, and practical remedial actions, for organizational leaders (and their teams) to enable and facilitate contribution toward, and achievement of, sustainable goals. It also facilitates responding to government regulation and enhances visibility of such responses.

ESG should usefully be segregated into its constituent parts, that is, "E", "S", and "G", to focus meaningfully on outcomes.

Sustainability is the lodestar that guides ESG efforts. In Figure 1.1 (which is further explored in Chapter 20), we note that sustainability is at the center of our puzzle, with some tasks being essentially outwards-looking and others focused inwards. What motivates us to take strong action will differ across varying businesses and local circumstances, but we can say that self-interest, our sense of social purpose (or social responsibility), and the sheer desire to "treat others as we would want to be treated" will underpin our endeavors to respond proactively to ESG-type demands.

---

[1] RAM = realistic, achievable, and measurable = we set ourselves tasks and targets that can be documented and tracked. This implies we have an agreed and auditable "baseline" from which we move and measure progress.

Outward   Inward

Agenda
2030 (SDGs)

Social impact   Governance

S list   3PM   G list

SUSTAINABILITY

E list   (Self-interest
motivator)   EU
taxonomy

Environmental
impact   (Social dynamic
motivator*)

* Treat others as
you would want to
be treated

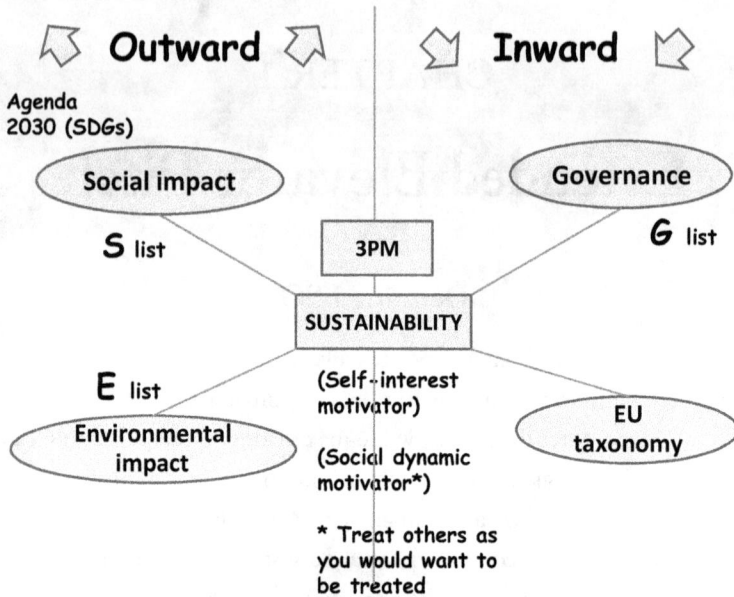

Figure 1.1 Sustainability at the core

The outward focus suggests that we shall interact more with the "outside world," while the inward focus suggests that what we achieve shall be largely in-house and (perhaps) of less visibility to our varying stakeholder communities. The "E" list, "S" list, and "G" list referenced in Figure 1.1 are highlighted in Appendix 1, while strategic high-level responses are "road-mapped" in Parts 3 to 5 of this book.

Defining Sustainability—Technical Definition

Sustainability refers to the objective of maintaining or supporting a process continuously over time. In the 21st-century business and policy contexts, Sustainability seeks to prevent the depletion of natural or physical resources so that they will remain available in the long term. Sustainable policies emphasize the future effect(s) of any given policy or business practice on humans, ecosystems, and the wider economy. The concept often corresponds to the insight that without significant amendments to the routine way the planet is managed, it is likely to encounter major, and possibly irreparable, damage.

Defining Sustainability—Environment

The natural environment is under considerable pressure as an indirect result of the world's noble ambition of lifting the bulk of its global population out of poverty toward a higher standard of living. Rapid industrialization and significant population shifts (migration and population growth generally) have led to major adverse impacts in:

- Water depletion
- Biodiversity and habitat reduction
- Climate change
- Land contamination
- Energy consumption
- Pollution
- Waste management

Here, sustainability implies integrated efforts to reduce, mitigate, and reverse environmental degradation.

Defining Sustainability—Social

Sustainability is the objective of living, working, and prospering in a way that ensures not only that we can thrive indefinitely but also that we can do so in collaboration with all relevant stakeholders. Sustainability suggests a commitment to the *circular economy* and *recognition that our actions may adversely affect others*. All actions are therefore planned to minimize adverse impacts, and where these impacts cannot reasonably be avoided, mitigating or compensating actions are taken to offset such impacts. Within all this, there is an underlying motive of "do unto others as you would have them do unto you" and a clear recognition of the reality of interdependency.

Here, sustainability implies prioritizing social benefits of corporate activities, such as social enterprise partnering. Social benefits will feature as a subsection of the associated business case for investment—social impacts will not be ignored.

Defining Sustainability—Governance

The way we govern organizations (and countries) has a direct impact on social and environmental outcomes. Under financial regulation, there have long existed demands for good quality, dependable and transparent governance practices, and effective ongoing management. The U.K. Financial Reporting Council's 2018 *Corporate Governance Code* is a well-structured, modern statement of best practice. Other countries have broad equivalents.

In terms of sustainability, *governance* supplements and systemizes responses to "environmental" and "social" challenges. In addition, it implies that organizations hold themselves to high standards of ethical behavior and competent modern management, particularly in:

- Data protection
- Cybersecurity
- Supply chain
- Stakeholder relations
- Ethics including antibribery
- Staff and management remuneration and reward
- Financial management

ESG

In this book, where we refer to sustainability in the specific ESG context, we capitalize this as Sustainability.

ESG is the focal point for organizations to make a practical difference in the broad area of Sustainability. It is not a philosophy. Rather, it is a mechanism (or a series of mechanisms). At its best, ESG is a toolbox of *practical* activities and measures that are applied to help improve organizational performance across diverse operations, but with a special focus on the *E*nvironment (minimizing adverse impacts in the natural environment), *S*ocial performance (maximizing positive contribution to social well-being), and *G*overnance (self-governance; ensuring we meet all legal requirements and can *demonstrate* compliance thereto). ESG motivates us to "understand where we are today," so we can map our journey to "where we want to be tomorrow." We are deliberate in seeking to advance and place RAM targets around specific objectives. ESG as a concept recognizes the need for improvement—without bankruptcy—and energizes us to develop practical tools to help achieve clear objectives.

Agenda

ESG is rapidly ascending the senior manager's to-do list. Regulatory demands and public opinion insist that ESG standards be improved over time, especially to meet the UN's 2030 sustainable developmental goals (SDGs) and the COP[2] process commitment to reduce greenhouse gas emissions. These ambitions must be translated into clear targets with potential penalties[3] for noncompliance.

There is a growing consensus that when we get our ESG policy and process right, we build brand value and can also use the ESG agenda as a mechanism to drive out cost over the long term, so ESG is both a compliance question and a potential value-driver.

Initial regulatory targets are focused on big businesses, but these larger enterprises will inevitably "flow down" their ESG response into their value chain, especially via suppliers and contractors. In the same way, our customers will almost certainly exert pressure on us to "improve our game" in the ESG arena, so we need to have a good story to tell.

ESG is no longer a tactical response. It is a strategic imperative.

Unique Selling Proposition

This book is markedly different from most material "published" on ESG. There is certainly good material "out there," especially on the Internet, and much of it is freely available. The "beating heart" of this book is its four "roadmaps" that are designed to provide a suitable "launch pad" for further action, especially for organizations that are at the beginning of their ESG journey. These high-level roadmaps are comprehensive and

---

[2] Conference of the Parties—see Appendix 2.
[3] Penalties might be self-imposed, of course. But, equally, these might be imposed by the market, by investors, and by regulators. On these bases, ESG is not "an optional extra," as it may once have been perceived!

designed to spur internal discussion and further research. The interrelated "way-points" of these "roadmaps" represent a creative approach to the whole subject. Material on the Internet is often linked to specific data-driven solutions which tend to ignore the "bigger picture" of ESG management.

What is unique about this book is its recognition of "3PM" (third-party management) as a distinct management discipline and an absolutely vital *delivery mechanism* for effecting "wins" in the ESG sphere. Third parties are more than "just" suppliers and are encountered throughout your value chain. How to engage with, influence, partner, and move in concert with these third parties to deliver practical ESG solutions is something we explore in Part 6 of this book.

The United States, Europe, and the World

This book is written in Britain and reflects the positive experience here. Britain, in turn, has been influenced by European (especially EU) practice, and there remains a broad policy alignment as regards ESG, even though Britain today operates a *lighter touch* regulatory regime.

The United States is in a different place at the time of writing and can be characterized as being four years behind the broad European thinking in the sustainability arena. It may use European policy and regulatory instruments as inspiration for federal regulatory initiatives. Likewise, U.S. businesses may adopt or adapt some European innovations to create an analogous U.S. model. At the time of writing, the United States is moving from a largely voluntary disclosure regime (as regards sustainability reporting) toward a mandated and regulated model. This development enjoys broad political support and will build over the period 2025–2029.

Nations elsewhere are developing local and regional approaches to sustainability and ESG initiatives, but are likely to want to align to, if not fully adopt, regulatory and reporting approaches already trialed successfully in British, EU, and U.S. regimes. International standardization in the ESG or Sustainability arena makes much sense, especially within the broadly accepted desire to achieve the UN's "SDGs" (see Chapter 6). Expect increasing international alignment over time, and monitor developments in your own domicile.

CHAPTER 2

Review and Understand

A Wide Perspective

In many of our diagrams ("schematics"), you will see the image in Figure 2.1.

Figure 2.1 reminds us that whatever we seek to achieve under the broad heading of "ESG" must be informed by, and linked to, our wider organizational strategy. Any initiative or "target" not so informed must be declared as "suspect" and should be open to challenge. A soundly run organization *continually* reviews its business context to ensure it is pursuing the right strategy, overall.

This book is not limited to private sector organizations. "Business" is a broad term. Public sector organizations face the same ESG challenges as those of the private sector, and overall solutions will be analogous—if not identical—in many circumstances. This book is suitable, therefore, for public sector managers.

Where the text speaks of "markets," our public sector readers should consider these as their public mission or public charter and "downstream activities" as the tasks they undertake on behalf of their stakeholder communities.

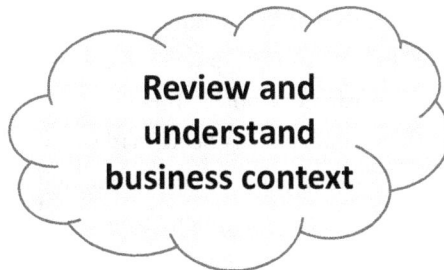

Review and understand business context

Figure 2.1 Context cloud

There is an *elephant-in-the-room* type question here about whether "the ESG tail" is beginning to wag "the corporate dog!" Is the advancement of ESG outcomes the primary purpose of any business and does such activity flow naturally from a proper, well-considered, review of our business context?

Such review is the lifeblood and *raison d'etre* of senior management and is probably conducted on a continuous basis. Everything we do should flow from an insightful appreciation of what makes our business, and our sector, "tick." This is the "real world" of business, and it implies a good strategic appreciation of *context*. This is true for public bodies as well as for commercial organizations.

It is unlikely that we shall effectively decipher the ESG puzzle without a thorough appreciation of our business context, including its broad "direction of travel." Throughout this book, where you see a "cloud image" as above, this represents some *activity* leading toward a discrete task to be completed and an associated thought process to be undertaken. We hope readers will appreciate this and will "interpret" each cloud symbol (and its short "descriptor") within their own business context.

Watch the Clouds!

In terms of Figure 2.2, key tasks for our senior management team are suggested in four of the five "cloud" symbols. The fifth is "how to read this book." The author sees this book as a series of self-help "pointers," enabling management to move quickly through various agendas and, hopefully, to reach speedy conclusions that leave us facing in "the right direction" for our next steps.

Not everything in this book will apply in your situation. You choose what's important. So, please use the "roadmaps" to identify high-level tasks within the separate "E," "S," and "G" puzzles. Associated with each "roadmap" are a series of explanatory notes. These help advance your thinking and internal discussion, serve as benchmarks to anything you have already achieved, and encourage further discussion and creative debate.

Beyond this, as a senior management team, you will monitor the corporate horizon to address new opportunities, new threats, and new

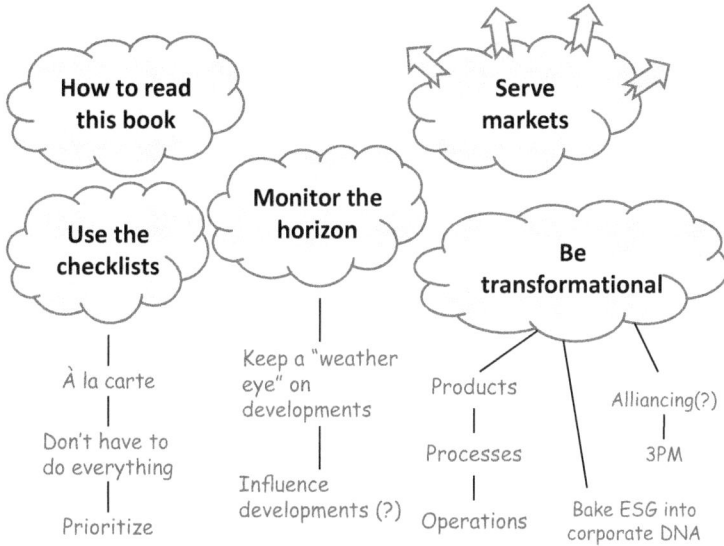

Figure 2.2 Executive briefing

demands. Wrapped in with this will be your high-level appreciation of those background "E," "S," and "G" risks. This is all part-and-parcel of reviewing and understanding your business context, a task that never ends! Your biggest objective and day-to-day challenge is, of course, to *serve your markets*, a generally outward-facing activity. We hardly need to add (but, for clarity, I shall) that if you are a public sector organization, the analogy to serving markets is to deliver on your *charter in public service* and so serve the tax-paying public.

Being *transformational* is the other aspect of all this. No business stays the same for long, and change is constant. Business cycles are shortening. Fresh risks and opportunities emerge all the time. ESG is just one of many pressing considerations for senior managers. Accordingly, we should wrap in ESG considerations into our strategic thinking and planning. We may well find that, spurred by such environmental, social, and/or governance considerations, new and radically different opportunities arise. Plainly, we would want to take advantage of those that best meet our strategic objectives. Where our competitive situation is favorable, we may determine to be early adopters of change rather than laggards.

CHAPTER 3

The Challenge

Not a Panacea

The core challenge in ESG management for all organizations, whether public or private sector, is to embed *effective* management processes that create sustainable change without losing sight of the main purpose of our organization. Elsewhere, we call this "ESG without bankruptcy."

ESG-embedding is a rational, proactive, RAM[1] organizational response to society's need to work toward a sustainable world, that is, one where humans can maximize the opportunity to live fruitful lives in reasonable social, economic, and physical security in an otherwise uncertain world.

Some ESG enthusiasts promote their concept as a panacea. For a few, their zeal borders on the obsessional. Yet, organizational managers must take due notice of ESG demands while also "delivering" on a huge range of additional (competing?) agendas, not least to ensure the continuity of their organization—and the jobs that they provide—in a world of shortages, supply disruptions, energy price spikes (and shortages), political instability, technological revolution, and media intrusion. It is not an easy task.

ESG will not "solve" all of society's ills or eliminate all risks. Yet, when implemented properly, it can be characterized as *a measured and precautionary approach that seeks to minimize risks and potential harms, while maximizing opportunity to create sustainable outcomes.*

ESG is not a "movement," nor is it a "philosophy." *ESG is a tool* (or more correctly, a *toolbox*) of interconnected policies, processes, and practical remedial actions for organizational leaders and for managers (and their teams) to *enable and facilitate contribution toward, and*

---

[1] Realistic, achievable, measurable.

achievement of, sustainable goals. It also enables adequate response to government regulation while enhancing the visibility of such responses.

As we suggest throughout this book, ESG should optimally be segregated into its constituent parts, that is, "E," "S," and "G," to focus meaningfully on outcomes. *Sustainability is the lodestar that guides ESG efforts.*

Senior Manager Agenda

Sustainability refers to the objective of maintaining or supporting a process continuously over time. In the 21st-century business and policy contexts, Sustainability seeks, first, to prevent the depletion of natural or physical resources so that they will remain available in the long term. Sustainable policies emphasize the future effect(s) of any given policy or business practice on humans, ecosystems, and the wider economy. The concept corresponds to the insight that without significant amendments to the routine way the planet is managed, it is likely to encounter major, and possibly irreparable, damage. Sustainability increasingly encompasses the need for fair and decent employment practices, which is actualized by the "S" part of ESG, and an overriding need for good corporate governance, which is reflected in the "G" aspect of ESG.

For these reasons, ESG has ascended the senior manager agenda and *might be described as the organizational response* (both public and private sectors) *to the broader "Sustainability" agenda*. Today's managers are assailed by a range of demands for "compliance" to standards that are set by third parties (see schematics on pages 35 and 36). Managers need to know how much time, effort, and energy to devote to meeting compliance requirements. This is, perhaps, the major challenge to modern business management.

We can say that *true* "compliance" is focused on meeting legal or regulatory demands. As these have increased, so has the need for formal compliance monitoring (often via an internal "Compliance Department," so favored by large organizations). Small- and medium-sized businesses must determine how much overhead to apply to Sustainability, ESG, and compliance generally. Increasing compliance = increasing overhead = increased cost of sales = decreasing competitiveness = decreasing market share = decreasing viability. A balance has to be struck, and this is a key part of the challenge to senior managers, in particular.

Managers cannot focus everywhere. As regards ESG, they need good, solid, accessible, and (ideally) easy-to-implement solutions. Failing that, they need user-friendly guidance with scalable responses *as a starting point* toward developing their own bespoke solutions within their particular business context. This book provides a number of "roadmaps" that help focus practical efforts. In addition, it encourages organizations to achieve as much as possible using in-house resources and expertise, developing and investing these in preference to handing over strategic guidance to external "specialists."

True, "no man is an island" and we shall have to work with external parties to optimize Sustainability outcomes. But, we should not abdicate management or strategy formulation to others for two compelling reasons: (1) we lose a measure of control, and risk becoming reactive rather than proactive and (2) external advisers can be remarkably expensive and represent a considerable *opportunity cost* in a business environment that is making numerous and diverse financial demands on all organizations.

The challenge, then, to organizations and to their management teams is considerable. *The good news remains that there is a great deal that we can achieve with in-house resources and we can develop our own responses to varying ESG demands.*

CHAPTER 4

Corporate Values and Mission

Creative Dialogue

ESG is generally described as an organizational response (both private and public sectors) to the broader Sustainability agenda. As we listen to people discussing ESG, we can get the impression that it is considered a panacea—a cure to all the world's problems. Inevitably, there will be a "pushback" to this agenda, which sometimes comes across as a zealous mission far removed from the day-to-day hurly-burly of modern corporate life.

It is not our purpose, here, to question or challenge the broad Sustainability, or ESG, agendas. Almost inevitably, direct challenges will emerge from business people, governmental practitioners, and a range of professionals from the compliance and legal areas, not to mention others who find increasing ESG-type pressures[1] bearing down upon them. Organizations need creative dialogue and constructive disagreement and to avoid "groupthink." One comment we do wish to make, however, is that ESG is often perceived as a bandwagon upon which everyone must jump. Those promoting ESG most loudly are often NGOs[2] that do not carry responsibility for securing a return on investment, and also software

---

[1] Interestingly, the U.S.-based consultancy firm McKinsey published a valuable keynote article titled "Does ESG Really Matter—And Why?" in summer 2022. This raised some uncomfortable questions, albeit McKinsey seeing itself as dedicated to the ESG world and an advisor in this sphere. Their candid questioning, however, was refreshing and, at the time of writing, this remains a useful resource to reflect upon potential shortcomings of the ESG mission.

[2] Nongovernmental organizations.

firms and other nonindustrials that have "product to sell." Some of these latter firms seem to be saying "here is an ESG problem, and here is the software solution to all your needs!"

Worse, at the time of writing, ESG developments and responses can seem more interested in *reporting* "progress" than actually making a difference in the three broad areas of social performance, good and transparent governance, and superior environmental stewardship. At the time of writing, executives and other professionals may lie awake at night worrying, but probably not about social disparities within their value chains or environment degradation, but more likely about "reporting" and avoiding poor publicity. One wonders whether the current ESG projection via nongovernmental campaigners is driving optimum responses and behaviors. It may even promote the very "greenwashing" response it tries to overcome.

Yet, ESG is presently "the only game in town" to respond to major (and potentially existential) globalized crises in an integrated way, so we must play to its strengths while eliminating its weaknesses.

As will be suggested in Chapter 5, the most profound boardroom decision relating to ESG is to define your corporate stance on the matter. In the next chapter, we will introduce ESG Laggard > First Base > Follower > Leader > Transformer, as characterizations of corporate stance. In part, this decision will be governed by your existing stated vision and the mission of the organization. Generally, a *mission statement* communicates the purpose of the organization. The *vision statement* provides insight into what the company hopes to achieve or become in the future. A *values statement* reflects an organization's core principles and ethics. True, not all organizations publish such "statements." Yet, this approach of projecting a clear brand image brings with it many significant benefits that we do not need to rehearse here.

By placing a *sustainable* purpose at the heart of an organization, ESG criteria potentially help investors, and others, to screen companies in which they may consider investing. The standards reviewed include *environmental impact* of a company's activities and *social relationships* in the geographical area(s) in which they operate; this particularly includes relations with employees, suppliers, customers, and the wider community. Similarly, they review an organization's leadership and governance and how this impacts the way it is run, with focus on:

- Vision, purpose, and values
- Sustainable business strategy
- Transparency on executive pay
- Shareholder rights
- Internal controls

These ideas can be *summarized* in appropriately considered and articulated values and mission statements. The publisher *IT Governance Publishing* has a number of "template" policy documents[3] available, including corporate policy statements on:

- Environmental issues
- Antibribery and antimoney laundering
- Corporate social responsibility
- Modern slavery
- Unconscious bias
- Antiharassment and antidiscrimination

These templates may prove, for some organizations, to be a creative and inexpensive spur to commence a fresh approach to "vision" and "mission" *statements* or to benchmark existing corporate materials. Today, it might be considered that a consolidated statement on ESG policy may suffice, but your author counsels against this and recommends, instead, keeping the three subject areas of "E," "S," and "G" distinct. That is the approach adopted in this book, in any case, and we are likely to find, in the years 2024 to 2034, further divergence in these agendas. We will also encounter the need for differing professional disciplines and competencies in the three interrelated areas to "take the lead" in driving optimized responses and, therefore, to make the greatest practical impact.

---

[3] This is in its "ESG Toolkit" series.

Corporate Responsibility

The statements below represent a common approach across many modern organizations and, as written, may be a creative way to characterize an organization's overall response to broad social pressures. As such, they may make a useful starting point for reflection and discussion:

Corporations assess and take seriously their *responsibility* across a number of dynamics: staff, customers, social impact (of operations), broader stakeholders (including governmental agencies), investors and shareholders, and the environment. They seek to ensure, wherever possible, that social impacts are *positive* to communities and/or to a wider society. CSR has a wide remit and focuses on *positive* activity and measurable outcomes.

Corporations assess and take seriously *social* impacts of operations generally measured in terms of reduction of and/or avoidance of *adverse* social impacts. They focus on a range of initiatives generally around environment (sustainability), ethics, good working practices for themselves and key business partners (especially suppliers), volunteering, and philanthropy. They focus on creation of "policy" and "operational guidance" to set expectations and secure clear PR-type messages as part of internal or external communications and marketing efforts.

Good corporate *governance* is about effectively supervising the management of corporations to uphold the organization's integrity, achieve transparent and rigorous policies and procedures, and ensure legal compliance. It should, in addition, promote good relations with stakeholders, including shareholders and employees. Leadership teams and boards need to demonstrate clear oversight of corporate culture and actively engage with relevant stakeholders, again including employees. Executive pay and a lack of diversity on boards (and in top leadership teams) are emerging as key issues in corporate governance.

What the above means in terms of practical hands-on work must, of course, be the subject of *ongoing* thought and scrutiny. In this book, we recommend using "roadmaps" with checklists of activities (see Appendix 7 and also Chapters 12, 15, and 18) to properly focus our activities across ESG. In turn, there will be a degree of ongoing skills enhancement and organizational learning to improve performance across the three distinct arenas of "E," "S," and "G."

Only a clear statement of corporate values and mission can help in this nonstatic task. Expect to learn over time. While this is an ongoing informal task, it is suggested you *formally* review your vision, mission, and values statements every three years.

PART 2

Strategy

CHAPTER 5

Positioning ESG

Vive la Difference….

Pundits conflate the separate disciplines of "E," "S," and "G" as though they are one subject. Responses to "E," "S," and "G" pressures, and (increasingly) to regulatory demands, will share certain common components, but the three areas of "E," "S," and "G" are quite different disciplines, albeit being linked to the broader social theme of sustainability. This book tackles "E," "S," and "G" questions as three distinct subjects. In addition, we recognize that *third-party relationship management* also has a profound role to play in responding to ESG pressures. So, the sixth part of this book focuses on this area and we use the moniker "3PM" (third-party management) to describe this discipline.

By segregating "E," "S," and "G," senior managers can address each as a separate "opportunity" and, where resources permit, delegate corporate response to different teams or individuals. At a more basic level, splitting the problem into separate workstreams makes the question more manageable and results in better-tailored guidance material. We use simple "schematics" (diagrams) wherever relevant, for several good reasons:

- A picture is worth a thousand words!
- They help "lock" into our mind's eye interrelated questions.
- They aid and speed comprehension.
- They provide a common starting point for discussion and problem solving.

Public or Private?

In this book, we use the terms "company," "corporate," "business/es," and "organization/s" interchangeably, which may suggest that the material is addressed to private sector firms. Readers are encouraged to think *across* public and private spheres. All public sector organizations are run (in a sense) as "businesses" and certainly on businesslike lines. ESG challenges and challenge–response for both public and private enterprises are similar and, in many cases, identical. This book is of equal value and applicability across public and private sector organizations. The "checklists" in Chapters 11, 14, and 17 are applicable across both sectors.

Referring to Figure 2.2 on page 11, the sections immediately below provide more insight.

How to Read This Book

The author envisages this book being used as a starting point for further discussion as well as providing some very practical material for taking concrete steps to make rapid progress. Any manager will benefit from taking time out and reading the entire material, but this is not the author's intention. *This is a manual for action rather than a literary exercise.* It provides a common language and a common mindset to aid comprehension and establish baselines. As such, it provides a valuable "foundation" on which to build.

Readers can "dip in" to the material and "zero in" on particular subjects. Some managers will want/need to absorb the material in greater depth, while others will only use it cursorily. Either way, it should be used as a practical tool to assist in building the *business case* for action.

Use the Checklists

In four places in this book, we provide practical checklists, and readers will certainly add their own specific priorities to speed and enhance target-setting and then to progress to achieving the objectives.

In the three areas of "E," "S," and "G," we provide a roadmap with 39 substages, each of which is described in detail elsewhere in the book. Detailed notes are tailored specifically toward each subdiscipline. Some readers will identify that they have already embarked on their "journey" and addressed certain stages. Other readers may form the view that they do not need to adopt each and every stage of the checklists and may even have developed a very different "roadmap" to reach their own specific goals. If so, then that is splendid! The key point is that you have a plan, recognizable as such, which is meaningful to your own employees as well as to your external stakeholders.

This book's high-level "roadmaps" should then be used as an *à la carte* menu of options. You can expand on, ignore, or refashion to meet your own particular needs. There is no thought that we should use them slavishly! Furthermore, we must prioritize tasks to ensure that we meet our own particular needs most effectively. It is expected then that senior managers (in particular) will use the checklists to verify that the basic elements have been satisfactorily addressed by their teams.

Monitor the Horizon

For company seniors, an increasingly complex and urgent concern is regulatory compliance coupled with public pressure/market expectations. We must continually monitor the horizon to make sure we know what is going on and what additional pressures may emerge. We do this not as passive observers in "reactive" mode, but rather as active participants responding to need and ensuring our organization continues to meet emergent regulatory demands head-on, rather than being buffeted by each fresh development.

Furthermore, it is entirely possible to *influence developments* by taking an active part in them. How much time, effort, and energy should be applied to external influencing is a board-level matter. We note, though, that organizations can proactively influence and guide developments through engaging in public discussion, working within trade associations and stakeholder groups, with *standards* organizations, through active technological research and development and through legitimate lobbying. We do not have to be passive observers. As subject matter experts *in our own sphere*, we can bring a degree of realism and common sense to discussions that will affect our long-term interests and objectives.

Serve Markets

Irrespective of any other consideration, our first and foremost task is to serve our markets and meet the needs and wants of our customers.

We forget this at our peril and at our employees' peril. Two universal truisms reflect this:

- *When a business forgets that it exists to serve the needs of its customers, it is on the "final approach" to oblivion.*
- *When a public sector enterprise forgets that it exists to meet the direct needs of the tax-paying public, it has become an organizational wastrel.*

In Figure 2.2, we depict the task of serving markets as being thoroughly outward-focused. Markets, of course, are "third parties" to our own organization and so the area of *third-party relationship management*[1] is part of the "big picture" in achieving our "E," "S," and "G" objectives.

Be Transformational

Figures 5.1 and 5.2 remind us that we have the option of taking a "transformational" approach to the whole question of ESG management. At its most basic, is our objective "business as usual" (today's model translated into tomorrow's uncertain world) or is it to "transform" our business to better meet tomorrow's challenges?

In responding to ESG pressures, we must inevitably take a good hard look at our "products" (howsoever we define that term). Do these "products" burnish our ESG credentials? Do they help us optimally meet ESG targets? Do they serve the needs of today's market—and, more crucially, will they continue to meet the needs of tomorrow's marketplace? In precisely the same way, we must keep under review our business "processes"[2] to ensure that these match our corporate values and mission statement. Finally, our day-to-day business "operations" must support value creation (to use an economist's term) and, *over time*, must be achieved in ever

---

[1] In this book, we generally use the moniker "3PM," for third-party management, to describe this.

[2] A business process, business method, or business function is a collection of related, structured activities or tasks carried out by people or equipment in which a *specific sequence* produces a service or product for a particular customer, or customers.

more efficient and effective ways. Tomorrow's business will not look like today's business. We need, over time, to *transform* our businesses to meet tomorrow's needs and pressures.

Within this transformational paradigm, we can say that ESG is a focal point and is expected to become increasingly relevant over the period 2024–2034. We hope it is not too much of a cliché to suggest (as we do in Figure 2.2) that we "bake" ESG considerations into our corporate DNA, yet this is not too far from the truth. Increasingly, we must "think" "E," "S," and "G" as we develop business plans and new products and processes and enter new markets. ESG is moving from a "nice to have" consideration to a fundamental one.

On the right side of Figure 2.2, as we explore being "transformational" in our approach, we flag up 3PM (see Chapter 20), recognizing that it is within and through a range of third parties that we will actually implement the bulk of our ESG responses. If "3P" relationships are important today, they will become more important tomorrow.

The question of *alliancing* must also be considered. Can we engage in any formal or informal alliancing with customers, "suppliers," and even competitors to move our ESG responses further forward? This approach area can yield direct benefits and should always be within the purview of company seniors. In a genuinely *commercial* environment, however, the counter-consideration of antitrust/competition law may intervene, so alliancing must always be handled appropriately and in line with business realities. That's why in our Figure 2.2 schematic, we include a question-mark in parentheses.

ESG Stance/ESG Positioning

Following on from the preceding discussion, a clear and profound decision must be made as to how an organization will "position" ESG considerations/responses within its business model. This will be reflected in whether our stance is essentially a tactical one (minimalist response) or truly strategic (immersive response). Figure 5.1 opens this out.

This schematic posits the idea of a corporate journey with distinct waypoints. A company may determine to move from a purely tactical response to a "transformational" one—from tactical to strategic. Readers

**TRANSFORM
BUSINESS MODEL**

**BUILD E–S–G
REPUTATION AND
BRAND IMAGE**

**EMPHASIZE
PREVENTION
TO ELIMINATE
WASTE**

**COMPLY WITH
REGULATIONS**

**TODAY'S
BUSINESS AS
USUAL**

Tactical	Strategic

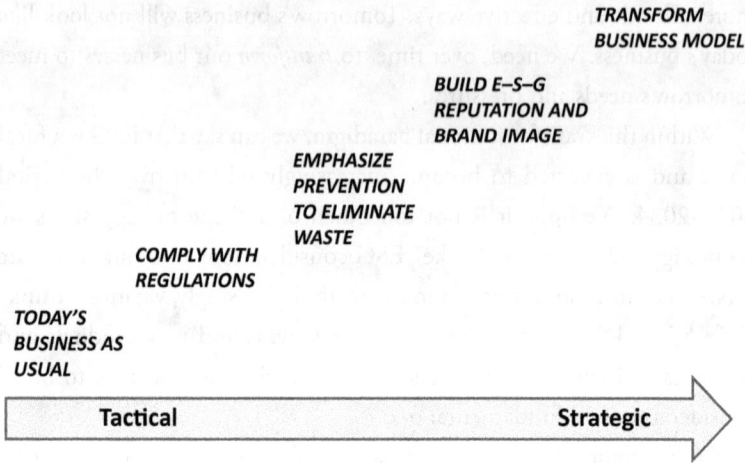

Figure 5.1 Corporate stance (1)

may want to pause for a moment to assess where presently their business stands in this continuum. On the left, we suggest that a business decides to carry on business more or less as today's model, meeting legal requirements but with no strategic investment. Depending on the business size, market penetration, extent of regulatory involvement, and resources available, this may be a fully rational approach. It marks a *minimalist* approach to ESG.

On the right of Figure 5.1, we recognize a "transform" stance where ESG has become a key driver of value; between left and right is a continuum of progression toward ESG maturity. In the sections that follow, below, we add some details to characterize these differing corporate postures.

Today's Business as Usual (1)

Stance:
- Corporate social responsibility (CSR) focus
- Community relations explored and leveraged
- Engage in philanthropy
- Say the right things

React to events

Ad hoc "quick fix" approach to incidents and new requirements

Crisis management if things go wrong

For some businesses, we repeat, *this may be a rational stance to adopt.* In terms of ESG realities, however, this is a "laggard" stance as opposed to a "leader" response. Some businesses have been accused of "greenwashing" (pretending to achieve more in terms of reducing environmental impact than is actually the case). Where a business adopts the minimalist stance as in Figure 5.1, it is possible that greenwashing may be a factor. For any business positioned on the left of this continuum, the question becomes "why?" and "for how long" (is this sustainable over time)? Moving on …

Comply With Regulations (2)

Stance:
- Compliance only
- Peripheral to business
- Silo thinking

Set policies and processes

View as cost-driver

Maintain low profile

This can overlap with the "business as usual" stance discussed earlier. The key difference may be that this particular business sector is heavily regulated and that *compliance* has become a major factor in thinking—on all questions. Compliance is viewed generally as a cost-driver, perhaps as an unwelcome necessity. These businesses tend to be "followers" of sector-relevant innovation and think more tactically. Moving on…

Emphasize Prevention to Eliminate Waste (3)

Stance:
- Corporate quality initiative
- Improved financial performance
- Standards and enforcement

Target cost reductions

Define/reinforce desired behaviors

Pursue "low-hanging fruit"

Sustainability reporting = burden

In corporate stance (3) above, the emphasis is on "efficiency." This may not be an unreasonable stance for a variety of sensible reasons. It places our business very much in the field of meeting all direct requirements and doing so effectively and efficiently. Quality is upheld and customer needs are met at the most basic levels. ESG is a factor, but the emphasis remains on *de minimis* responses (as little as we can efficiently accommodate). This stance still tends toward the view that ESG is a cost-driver. Businesses adopting this approach are still *following* where others have led. Moving on...

Build E–S–G Reputation and Brand Image (4)

Stance:
- Source of competitive advantage
- Company imperative
- Exec team responsible

Emphasize:
- Clear ESG vision
- Vision leads objective setting
- ESG part of company strategy
- Clear accountability for results
- Develop core competencies—see ESG within this

Engage in effective outreach:
- Employees
- Customers
- Value chain (e.g., suppliers)
- Regulators
- Stakeholder communities

Firms adopting the aforementioned stance have made a full transition to perceiving ESG in a thoroughly positive light. ESG responses are genuine product differentiators and are seen to add value (probably reasonably quickly in terms of payback (*return on investment*)). These firms build on the foundation of efficiency (cost minimization) but determinedly added ESG *value creation* in terms of brand, market positioning, and innovation. Successes are celebrated. Such organizations can genuinely be considered as *leaders* in their field. Moving on…

Transform Business Model (5)

Stance:
- Perceive ESG as a source of long-term viability
- Core to entity
- CEO responsible
- Best application of ESG investments

Empower entrepreneurial behavior through systems thinking and focus on innovating
- Processes
- Products
- Services

Support partnering initiatives to preserve health and vitality of future generations:
- Multiple stakeholders, including public sector
- Industry-wide initiatives
- Global viewpoint (global footprint?)

View sustainability reporting as essential to *telling the story.*

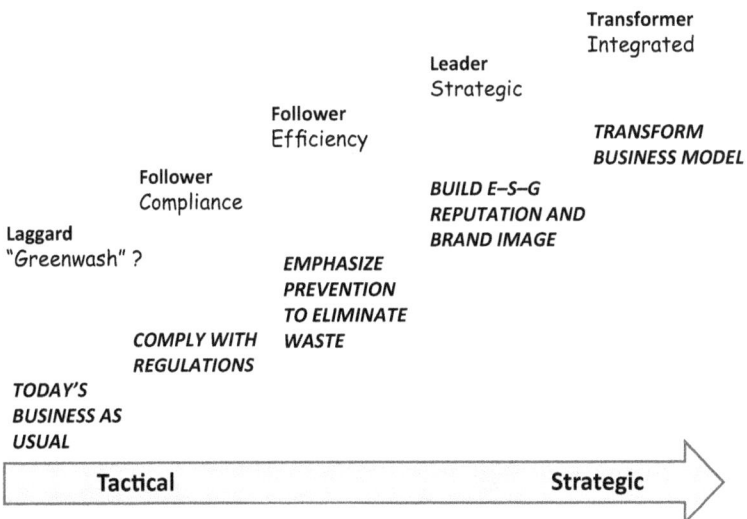

Figure 5.2 Corporate stance (2)

The question for senior managers (in particular) is, *what is your current stance as regards ESG imperatives?* Is your stance fixed or do you have an ambition (business need) to move to a different stance? Are you in the tactical or strategic sphere? Where do you expect to be in five years? Crucially, can you use ESG as a lever for value generation? We reflect on this briefly in Chapter 7, Executive Outputs.

Please take some time to consider/discuss these questions.

CHAPTER 6

Senior Manager Briefing

A Response .....

ESG is a key organizational response (both public and private sectors) to the wider "Sustainability" agenda. It encapsulates a range of initiatives that are deemed, by broad consensus, to represent the most likely *coordinated* program to lead to lasting change that optimizes the life opportunities for present and future generations.

Modern managers are assailed by a range of demands for "compliance" to standards that are set by third parties (see Figure 6.1). Businesses must determine, as a strategic question, to which *voluntary* standards they will subject themselves. In turn, managers need to know how much time, effort, and energy to devote to meeting the compliance requirements. Interestingly, there is a specific ISO standard in our three areas of immediate concern (top left area of Figure 6.1—ISOs 14001, 26000, and 37000).

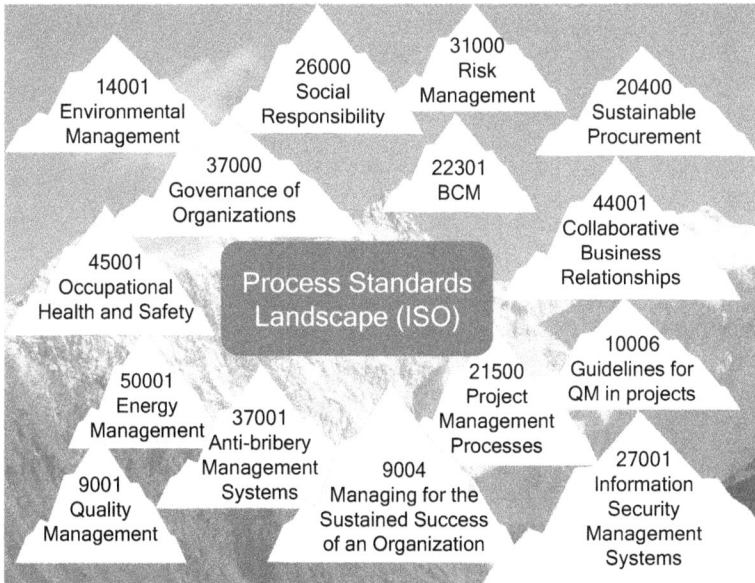

Figure 6.1 Process standards landscape

But many standards feature in our broad management agenda, as suggested in the nonexhaustive selection of ISOs above. Of course, *true* "compliance" is focused on meeting legal and regulatory demands. As these have increased, so too has the need for formal compliance monitoring (often via an internal "Compliance Department").

Small- and medium-sized businesses must determine how much overhead to apply to Sustainability, ESG, and compliance generally. Increasing compliance = increasing overhead = increased cost of sales = decreasing competitiveness = decreasing market share = decreasing viability. A balance has to be struck.

Figure 6.2 locates "ESG" as a major current focus. But, our topography illustrated above highlights differing—and overlapping—organizational concerns, each of which will find its way onto our agenda. We must curate and manage data of all sorts (think General Data Protection Regulation (GDPR) in Europe), while net zero has become a societal target in its own right. *Modern slavery* is a growing social issue, and businesses are required to make varying "disclosures" as to performance and progress across differing concerns. Figure 6.2 seeks to capture the "flavor" of this task. There are many mountains to climb!

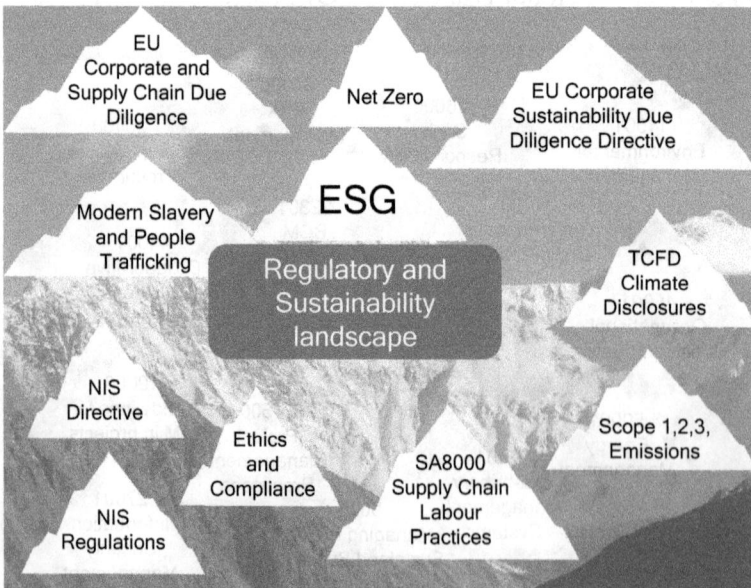

Figure 6.2 Regulatory and sustainability landscape

ESG Without Bankruptcy

Some pressure groups and special-interest parties promoting ESG and setting the agenda (at the time of writing) seem quite oblivious to financial on-costs and other opportunity costs, associated with fresh and ever-rising compliance demands. Furthermore, the fact that western businesses are expected both to "lead the way" and to set the highest standards in the absence of matching, or reciprocal, measures by direct competitor nations in the non-OECD world seems an unintelligible and unreasonable objection—to at least some promoters of ESG.

Is it possible, however, to achieve much of what is sought in terms of ESG advances generally, without incurring excessive on-costs? Within existing corporate structures and modus operandi, we can go a long way to raise standards and achieve defined outcomes without making our "business" nonviable. We should be able to achieve *ESG without bankruptcy*!

In the future, governments may recognize the real overhead burden of ESG and provide suitable financial incentives to ease the pain—time will tell! But, for all organizations, the challenge right now is to embed ESG thinking into routine operations in such a way that it becomes standard practice and part of our "corporate DNA." Change to operating procedures does not have to entail additional overhead expense. Reinvestment in capital equipment and facilities can "onboard" ESG requirements without substantially altering overall investment costs. Principally, organizations need genuine "joined-up-thinking" to, incrementally, drive up ESG performance without excessively driving up overheads.

Insights on the Big Picture ...

Those questions that now travel under the acronym "ESG" are linked to the ambitious UN Agenda 2030. The *Agenda for Sustainable Development* was launched by the UN in September 2015 and aimed at ending poverty in all its forms. It envisages *"a world of universal respect for human rights and human dignity, the rule of law, justice, equality and non-discrimination."* Grounded on the Universal Declaration on Human Rights, it emphasizes the responsibilities of all states to promote human rights. There is

a particular emphasis on the empowerment of women and of vulnera-
ble groups such as children, young people, people with disabilities, older
persons, refugees, internally displaced persons, and migrants.

Many large businesses and trade groups signed up proactively to the
2030 Agenda. The public sector in its myriad forms can be assumed to be
"on board" by virtue of their symbiotic relationship with central governments, which were national signatories to the Sustainable Development
Goals. For the record, the specific goals are (1) elimination of poverty,
(2) zero hunger, (3) good health and well-being, (4) quality education,
(5) gender equality, (6) clean water and sanitation, (7) affordable and
clean energy, (8) decent work and economic growth, (9) industry, innovation and infrastructure, (10) reduced inequality, (11) sustainable cities and
communities, (12) responsible consumption and production, (13) climate
action, (14) life below water, (15) life an land, (16) peace, justice, and
strong institutions, and (17) partnership for the goals.

At a summary level, however, and where "ESG" becomes a central
concern, we can summarize the regulatory backdrop as in Figure 6.3.

We can see, from Figure 6.3, how the SDGs link to the associated
strategy for financing agenda. Financing is perceived as a key mechanism to

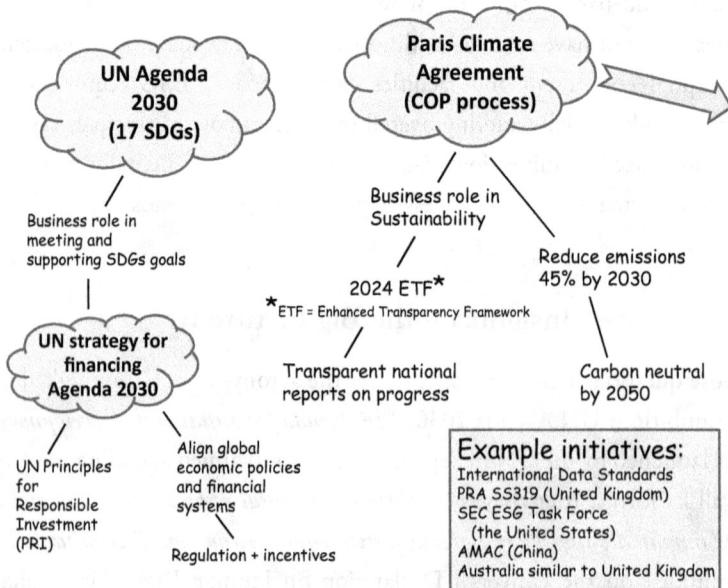

Figure 6.3 Regulatory backdrop

bring about change. In turn, these link to the UN *Principles for Responsible Investment*. Along the left side of Figure 6.3, we "see" how businesses are indirectly impacted through global alignment of economic policies. The right side reminds us that the linked agenda called "net zero" is seen as the most pressing, immediate, question. The Paris Agreement is a *legally binding international treaty on climate change*. Adopted by 196 parties at COP 21 in Paris (December 2015), it entered into force in November 2016. The goal is to limit global warming to below 2°C, preferably to 1.5°C, compared to pre-industrial levels.

To achieve the ambitious COP 21 goals, there are a number of major national and international initiatives underway, each spawning subprojects and/or subagendas. Within this, and starting in 2024, is an Enhanced Transparency Framework ("ETF") which requires signatory nations to provide transparent reports on progress toward net-zero goals. Part of that involves individual organizations to provide reports on their own progress. The immediate goal is to reduce GHG emissions by 45 percent by 2030 and then achieve full carbon neutrality by 2050. To make all this work in practice, it is Europe that has set the pace, principally through the EU and EFTA (European Free Trade Association). In Figure 6.3, the big arrow stretching to the right is picked up

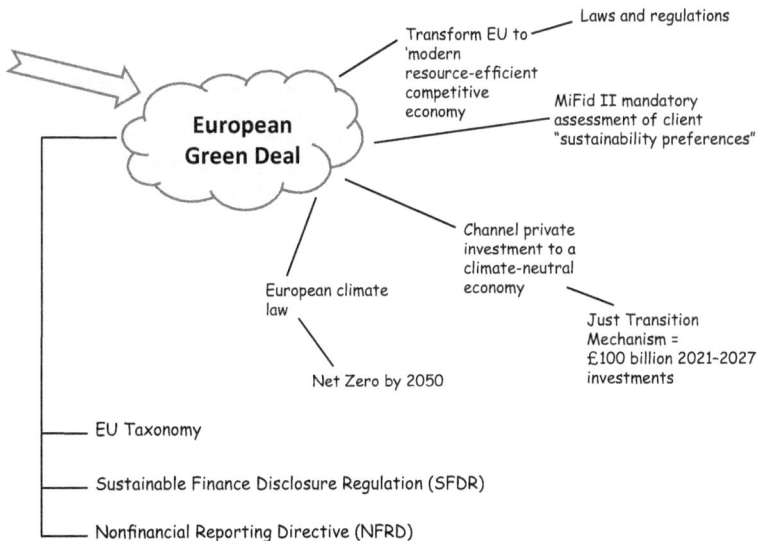

Figure 6.4 Regulatory backdrop—European Green Deal

in Figure 6.4, representing the broad "European" program under the "European Green Deal."

This reminds us that European climate law enshrines net-zero achievement by 2050. At the highest level, there is an ambition to transform the EU into a "modern resource-efficient economy" and back this with associated laws and regulations. MiFID II is the EU legislative framework regulating financial markets in the bloc and improves protection for investors[1]. Its underlying aim is to standardize practices across the EU and enhance confidence in the industry. Under MiFID II, there is a mandatory assessment of client "sustainability preferences." The gist of this is that any investment client, new or existing, must be asked about their sustainability preferences. They have three options to choose from: a *taxonomy alignment* (read below for an explanation of EU Taxonomy), a *percentage in sustainable investments* as defined by the Sustainable Financial Disclosure Regulation (SFDR), or a quantitative or qualitative consideration of *principal adverse impacts* (PAIs), which aim to capture any *material* negative effects that investments have on the environment and/or society. Once a client chooses one, or a combination of these options, a financial adviser must ensure that a product offered matches the client's sustainability preferences. If not, the product cannot be sold unless the client changes their sustainability preferences.

Looking again at the schematic above, we can see that under the European Green Deal, the intention is to channel private investment toward a climate-neutral economy. Supporting this, the EU itself promises £100 billion positive investment over six years, although whether this is truly "new money" is a moot point. Irrespective of this, the environmental ambition in all this is quite clear.

The EU taxonomy[2] is a classification system that establishes a list of environmentally sustainable economic activities. It is expected to play an important role helping the EU scale up sustainable investment and implement the European Green Deal. The EU taxonomy provides companies,

---

[1] USA equivalent legislation is contained in the 1934 Securities Exchange Act, the 1998 Regulation Alternative Trading System, and the 2005 Regulation National Market System.

[2] See Appendixes 4 and 5 for more insight.

investors, and policymakers appropriate definitions of economic activities considered environmentally sustainable. In this way, it should create security for investors, protect private investors from "greenwashing," help companies become more climate-friendly, and help shift investments where they are most needed.

At a practical level, the taxonomy provides a listing of what might be argued as "good guys" and "bad guys" in terms of economic activities vis-à-vis environmental impacts, even though this is not how it is intended to be interpreted. But, it does provide a useful "snapshot" of economic "macro sectors," broken down into subsectors, a DNSH assessment, and mitigation factors. Useful for investment specialists and environmentalists, it also has value in the field of 3PM activities (see Chapter 20).

Governance of ESG Questions

The executive team sets the strategic direction of the organization; this direction will be impacted by ESG as much as any other pressure or external concern. In the next chapter, we put in place a "high-level roadmap" to suggest the immediate practical tasks for the exec team. Here, however, we simply consider who the key "players" or player groups steering this agenda are. Given the public relations and reputational aspects as well as the macro risks, the CEO will have an involvement. Considering the emerging data and data-handling requirements, arguably the CIO might have a direct involvement in setting strategy, even though data handling might also be considered a legal or compliance question. Given the financial pressures and potential investments, the CFO will also sit

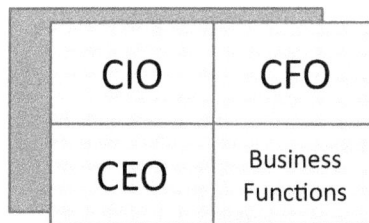

CIO	CFO
CEO	Business Functions

Key responsibilities .....

Figure 6.5 ESG governance—key responsibilities

at the high table in understanding ESG issues and helping to establish practical measures to advance our high-level responses.

Besides these three key executives, there are likely to be other senior managers with a direct involvement, as suggested in Figure 6.5 above. We argue later in this book that, to advance our agenda across the whole ESG piece, *third-party relationships* (or 3PM) are "key" to helping us meet our commitments and targets, which suggest that the head of Sales and Marketing and the CPO (chief procurement officer) will be involved. See Part 6 for more details on this. Sitting in the background, for many organizations, will be the non-executive directors, bringing a range of practical experience, usually from diverse backgrounds. Their task, as always, is to provide an independent view on the running of our business, its governance, and boardroom best practice. They oversee and constructively challenge management in the implementation of strategy within the organization's system of governance and the risk appetite set by the board. As regards 3PM, we would expect the nonexecutives to bring some genuine independence in insight and practical hands-on experience. Let's leverage best practice and positive experience from wherever we can ...

CHAPTER 7

Executive Outputs

Stance

The purpose of this short chapter is not to tell senior managers how to run their businesses; rather, it is to focus on the key outputs for the senior team with regard to the broad ESG question. In this book, we highlight three separate workstreams, that is, "E," "S," and "G," with differing specialisms deployed and differing timeframes and risks encountered. Our high-level (executive-level) "roadmap" below suggests 16 relatively straightforward tasks that need to be formalized, but are sometimes missed as definitive steps.

Before looking at these 16 tasks, we spend a moment on what is perhaps, for senior managers, the most important single decision in this book, and arguably one that will set the pace and effort invested in achieving "E," "S," and "G" objectives. What is to be your organization's ESG "stance"? Will it be to "lead" or "follow" the initiatives of other organizations? Are you on the front foot or back foot or somewhere in between? Will you set the pace to achieve some competitive advantage through all this or will you simply comply with legal and ethical require-ments, leaving others to do the "heavy lifting" in advancing this area of corporate management? Will your stance be "tactical" or "strategic?"

Having more fully explored this in Chapter 5, we summarize this in Figure 7.1. Moving from left to right, we recognize five different (and overlapping) corporate postures on ESG that move from purely "tactical" response (left) to fully strategic (right). On the far left is the >*laggard* who will simply persist in doing "what we are doing today." Essentially, there is no change to current practices, objectives, and methods—tomorrow looks like today. This stance may, in reality, be borderline illegal as it may not even seek to meet regulatory requirements *in full*. There is something minimalistic in response on the far left side of our illustration.

Laggard	First base	Follower	Leader	Transformer
"Greenwash"?	Compliance	Efficiency	Strategic	Integrated
				TRANSFORM BUSINESS MODEL
			BUILD E–S–G-REPUTATION AND BRAND IMAGE	
				Stance:
		EMPHASIZE PREVENTION TO ELIMINATE WASTE	Stance: *Source of competitive advantage *Company imperative *Exec team responsible	*Source of long-term viability *Core to entity *CEO responsible *Best application of ESG investments
		Stance: *Corporate quality initiative *Improved financial performance *Standards and enforcement	Emphasize: *Clear ESG vision *Vision leads objective setting *ESG part of Corp strategy *Accountability for results *Develop core competencies	Empower entrepreneurial behavior through systems thinking, focus on innovating: *Processes *Products *Services
TODAY'S BUSINESS AS USUAL Stance: *CSR *Community relations *Philanthropy	**COMPLY WITH REGULATIONS** Stance: *Compliance only *Peripheral to business *Silo thinking	Target cost reductions Define/reinforce desired behaviors	Engage in effective outreach: *Employees *Customers *Value-chain (e.g., suppliers) *Regulators *Stakeholder communities	Support partnering initiatives to preserve health and vitality of future generations: *Multiple stakeholders • Public sector *Industry *Global
Say right things React to events Ad hoc "quick fix" Crisis management	Set policies and processes View as cost-driver Maintain low profile	Pursue "low hanging fruit" Sustainability reporting = burden		View sustainability reporting as essential to *telling the story*

Tactical ➤ Strategic

Figure 7.1 Corporate stance (3)—tactical to strategic

Can there ever be sound business justification for sitting on the far left of this spectrum? However unpalatable, the answer must be, tentatively, "yes," there can be. If an industry is facing only a short-term future leading toward closure or complete diversification, then a minimalist ESG approach may be right. One example in the western world right now might be (perhaps perversely) coal extraction. If the expectation is that *this coal firm will no longer exist in five years* and we are managing proactively toward closure, then a rational stance in all of this will be a *minimal* response.

Such an organization will, then, be a *laggard* in terms of where direct competitors or analogous companies may "stand." There are soon to be (2024 +) legal challenges associated with "greenwashing," so "today's business as usual" may actually become illegal for some firms. Caution is advised, and specialist legal input will be essential. Moving to the right of our illustration, *compliance* with regulations (only) is the next recognizable stance with our >*first base* company. The reasoning for this may be similar to that of the *laggard* above, and there may be a desire to invest little money or time, rather this >*first base* firm may be happy to "freeload" on the efforts of others. Compliance alone is their objective, certainly with the letter—if not the spirit—of relevant regulations. In the middle of our schematic stands the >*follower*. Even though these are not "investing to win" the ESG battle, they seek to link all compliance responses to efficiency measures. There is nothing irrational in this stance. While the *laggard* and the *first base* stance both tend to see ESG as a cost-driver, the *follower* is looking more toward efficiency and even to target cost reductions.

Would it be fair to say that most organizations are somewhere in the middle? If so, in many cases, they may be doing precisely the right thing in terms of their business context and strategic plans. What may be "problematic" in this middle positioning is that *Sustainability reporting* is still perceived as a burden, rather than an opportunity to move in a more innovative direction. Moving to the right in our schematic above, those organizations that "see" ESG as a strategic question are more likely to be >*leaders* in their field. They perceive the whole question as one of seeking competitive advantage. Certainly, this advantage will help to drive out cost over the long term, but there may be intervening investments to make in order to achieve that longer-term benefit. On the right side of our illustration lies the >*transformer*, which seeks to transform their business model and processes toward a 21st-century model which fully recognizes ESG questions (along with other considerations, such as technology and consumer shifts) as being at the heart of building a "USP" (unique selling proposition), which integrates technology, market, supply, and ESG considerations as a single package. It could be said that for these firms, ESG becomes a part of corporate DNA.

Where does your company stand today? Where should it stand tomorrow? You may want to pause at this point and consider that question for yourself. It may also be a creative way to advance discussion within your organization.

Assuming clarity about your corporate stance on ESG and assuming senior managers have a good overall grasp of business context, we can now characterize some of the key high-level ("H") outputs from the executive team (Figure 7.2).

This high-level roadmap should be read as necessary alongside the detailed "E," "S," and "G" roadmaps elsewhere in this book. Our next chapter provides detailed notes on the 17 steps below.

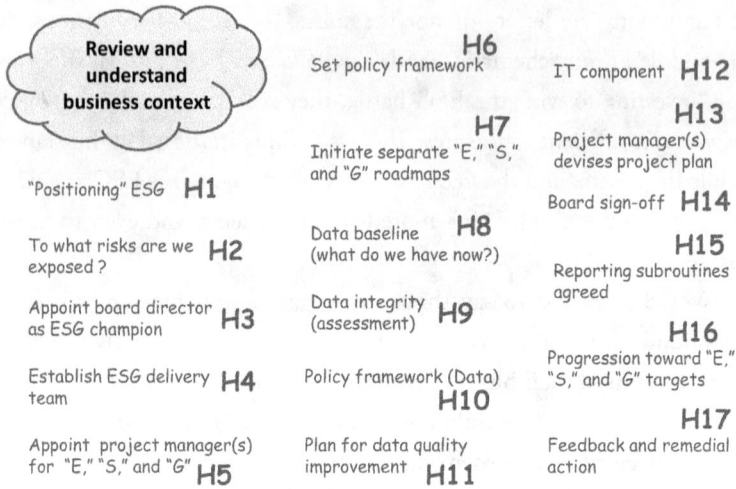

Figure 7.2 ESG—executive-level roadmap

Business as Usual ("BAU")

How do we move from high-level decisions into making a practical difference in day-to-day operations? How do we "operationalize" things, moving from planning to *business as usual* (BAU)? The optimum approach, plainly, is to "embed" ESG considerations into operational plans: What are the opportunities and how do we take advantage of them? What are the risks and how do we avoid (or mitigate) them? Figure 7.3 highlights the idea that ESG becomes a *distinct* consideration as we develop operational plans and "inform" these plans at high level. By consciously adopting a methodology that incorporates ESG into investment business cases (as well as operational business cases, for example, to enter into new markets or to spend money on a significant "capital" or "revenue" project), we achieve two "wins": (1) we ensure ESG-type questions are not missed and (2) we create a learning opportunity via review–report–feedback. Figure 7.3 summarizes these ideas.

Review and
understand
business
context

BOARD

ESG stance ......

BOARD

OPERATIONS

| E | S | G |

H6

Operational plan(s)

Stakeholder input and buy-in

Project established + implemented   H12

Targets set/agreed/implemented

Project feedback = tangible progress   H15

Review/Reporting   H16

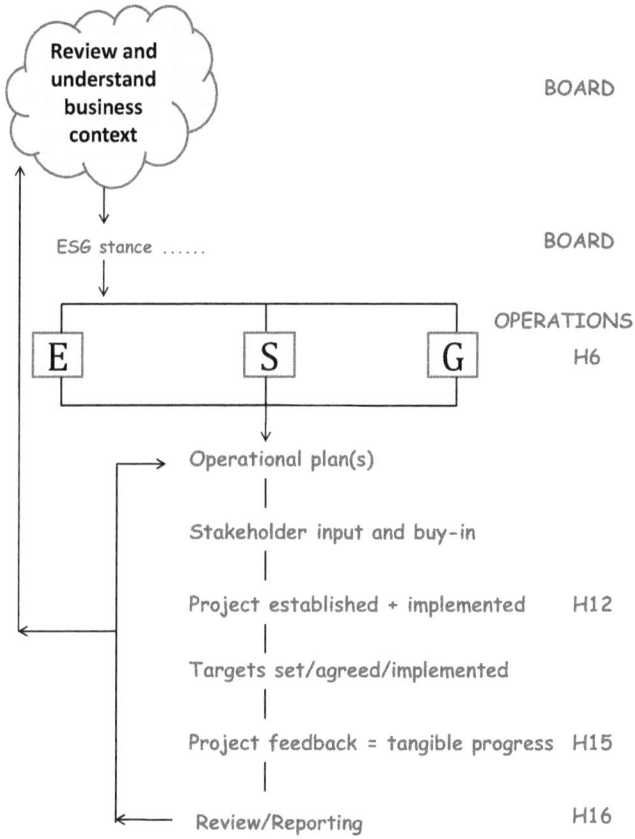

Figure 7.3 Roadmap—board expression to BAU

Readers may want to ponder at this point, to what extent do you capture these approaches in your decision-making process?

CHAPTER 8

Executive-Level Roadmap—Notes

Explanatory Note

This chapter adds detail and context to the "executive-level" roadmap in Figure 7.2.

In common with other *roadmaps* in this book, stage H0 (not cited below, where we begin at H1) indicates that there will have been—and continues to be—a thorough-going business context review, leading to effective *business strategy* development and associated detailed *business plans*. A soundly run organization, and an effective senior manager, will have a good grip on the overall business environment, how its own organization interacts within its own business sector, and the way it relates to other business sectors.

With an in-depth contextual insight undergirding our strategic direction, we can confidently factor-in the responses required for the broad ESG agenda. For senior executives, this is plainly not about immersion in practical detail; rather, it is about setting the scene corporately and ensuring that ambition becomes reality. It is about effective delegation ....

The notes below add further insight into the executive tasks. Be clear, however, that we do not "slavishly" follow each step, and the list of tasks is not intended to be exhaustive. The purpose of the 17 steps is to *initiate* our organizational response to ESG demands such that the major early decisions are tailored to our business context and the major "subcomponents" of our corporate response are suitably "owned" from the earliest time.

The executive focus here will be via the board (and its equivalent in public sector organizations) and the people doing the work will be the senior management team (or "SMT").

The executive challenge is to move ESG requirements from external pressure points (such as regulatory involvement) into corporate "business as usual" subroutines. Unlike the separate "E," "S," and "G" high-level roadmaps, the SMT response indicated in these 17 steps should be essentially a one-time task which then devolves down to *operational director* control, management, and feedback.

Stage	Description	Detailed Notes
H1	Positioning ESG	This was explored in Chapter 7 (Executive Outputs). The "positioning" of ESG is not a static, one-time decision and it is likely to change over time. Rome was not built in a day; ESG embedding is a journey from initial exploration to maturity. Expect this journey to take time
		At stage H1, however, some clarity about how we "position" ESG is valuable. It helps us secure consensus and suggests the level of senior management support and their ongoing involvement. H1 and H2 may be iterative tasks
		Further, an ESG *materiality assessment* will help us to best understand our stakeholders' insights and so to determine our optimum corporate "stance" and how this impacts our strategy. Chapter 25 looks at the question of *materiality*
H2	To what risks are we exposed?	This conversation is high level. Given our overall business context, we intuitively sense which areas of our business are likely to be most impacted and where there is associated risk
		If our organization is a *heavy manufacturing* organization, then the "E" questions may represent the clearest challenge (and potential threat)
		If we are a *multinational conglomerate* that owns many subdivisions across varying geographies, "G" questions can be very challenging. In addition, labor standards in different countries present their own challenges and nuances. To such a business, "S" questions may also loom large
		If we are an *extractive industry* or *trader* and our supplier base is principally on the other side of the planet, our impact on *local communities* may be considerable, so "S" factors potentially represent a concern

Stage	Description	Detailed Notes
		The objective here is not to consider nor answer every possible permutation of risk, but it may be possible to reach an early consensus as to the likely *direction of travel* in dealing with the present ESG paradigm and to collocate our responses within the broader corporate strategy
		If we perceive supply risk and political instability (recent history reflects supply-chain bottlenecks and disruption), the response to ESG demands may lie partly in near-shoring or re-shoring certain operations. If we perceive we are dependent on conflict zone materials, our best response may be to re-engineer product and utilize newer technology, rather than seek to micro-manage partners in other parts of the world
		This early H2 discussion does not preclude engagement with other threats and opportunities as our ESG focus sharpens. Indeed, we will expect greater clarity and more information to arise as we shift into the high-level response tasks suggested by our 39 step "roadmaps" for the "E," "S," and "G" challenges
		The "output" of H2 is to secure broad executive consensus to the issues *as presently understood*
H3	Appoint board director as ESG champion	"Championing" is a key task of the executive suite. Where organizational politics need to be deftly managed, where response inertia is a real possibility, and where burnout and task distraction is a possibility, a champion who can guide, mentor, challenge, and "open doors" (and possibly "close doors" as well!) is extremely valuable
		It is possible that one executive director can champion all three responses. A subdivision of tasks may also be desirable; we need joined-up thinking but this does not mean one exec must handle the entire task
		The output from H3 is to get a name in the frame— someone becomes personally accountable
H4	Establish ESG delivery team	Linked with H1 and H2, at this early stage, the senior management team should be able to "frame" a delivery team
		Plainly, this is not a one-time answer to the question. The team may change (even rapidly). But it will initiate the task and provide a reporting mechanism

(Continued)

(*Continued*)

Stage	Description	Detailed Notes
H5	Appoint project manager(s) for "E," "S," and "G"	Depending on your corporate approach to project management, this may be the right time to put a name in the frame
		Will this be a generalist PM or a subject matter specialist? At this stage, we may have confidence that the person named will handle this throughout the project timeframe to a successful conclusion (which is likely to mean moving out of the *project phase* and into the *business-as-usual* phase)
		It may, however, be that we deliberately appoint a manager we know will later yield the job to another manager yet to be identified. The reason is to get the project underway in the shortest timeframe rather than to settle the ownership once and for all
H6	Set policy framework	This remains high level as the detailed project plan stages 8 to 10 may supersede this task. At this relatively early stage, however, we know that the framework is likely to involve typical *policy development* subroutines
		In addition, as this is focused through the senior management team, the task is to set the *framework to determine the policy* rather than set the policy itself. As at H2, it may be reasonably clear as to what our broad policy shall be, but there will be a range of detail to be considered and incorporated. Having established the framework, policy drafters have a guideline as to how to undertake their task
		The output of H6 is broad SMT consensus about the policy objective and the likely *direction of travel*. This might be a board minute. The follow-on activity will likely be picked up at project plan stages 8 to 10
H7	Initiate separate "E," "S," and "G" roadmaps	We have provided a 39 step roadmap for the three areas of corporate focus, "E," "S," and "G," (see Appendix 7) together with bespoke notes for each area. (See chapters 12, 15 and 18.) These are broadly similar, giving operational teams a "pattern" within which to work. There are subtle differences, so you are encouraged to consult the specific "roadmap" for your particular interest
		The output of H7 is that there is a date when the task of detailed research and investigation essentially commences and the task devolves down to operational-level managers

Stage	Description	Detailed Notes
H8	Data baseline (what do we have now?)	The question of data is a potentially complex one. At the most basic in each of the three arenas, "E," "S," and "G," we already have some information provided in a data-centric format. We are reducing information down to measurable "numbers" so we can track the current situation ("baseline") and progress toward a demonstrably improved future situation
		The broad task is to establish what data is required to be sought or recorded, its accuracy, and its relevance
		Many organizations, especially in the *small to medium enterprise* ("SME") sector, presently collect little meaningful ESG data. The H8 task is to search what we presently have so we can state, with a high degree of confidence, that we have a "measure(s)," giving a clear enough indication of "where we are today." From this baseline we can then measure or demonstrate progress. Data measures will become more sophisticated or granular in the future and, indeed, we shall likely move to a new, improved baseline in the foreseeable future. *But we have to start somewhere …*
		H8 output is a summary of data sources and information routinely collated now, as well as a high-level statement as to what data we anticipate we shall need in the future. From these baselines, we can track progress, change, and—crucially—improvement
H9	Data integrity (assessment)	This is a more technical task and will not be carried out by the SMT. What we need to know at this point is how "robust" our present data is and what "market-pull" or regulatory pressures may demand that we supply in the future
		In the broadest terms, we are likely to be looking at these sorts of questions: **E** As regards the EU taxonomy, how is our business characterized? What 3PM relationships materially impact this characterization? What data do we have or need on: • GHG emissions • Energy consumption • Location and transportation • Materials • Pollution • Water use, etc. How robust is the current data and how do we collect? What more do we need to know in the future?

(Continued)

(Continued)

Stage	Description	Detailed Notes
		S
		What social impacts does our business typically impose on stakeholder groups:
		<ul><li>Community development</li><li>Health and safety</li><li>Human rights, including modern slavery</li><li>Social enterprise partnering</li><li>Employer amenities, showers, changing rooms, etc.</li><li>Controversial tenants</li></ul>
		Here, the "story" will be as much narrative as hard statistical data. How robust is the current data and how do we collect? What more do we need to know in the future?
		G
		In terms of governance, what is our approach (beyond policy statements and associated Public Relations (PR)) to factors such as:
		<ul><li>Cybersecurity</li><li>Data protection</li><li>Regulatory fines and history</li><li>ESG clauses in existing leases</li><li>ESG clauses in procurement-type contracts (and associated contract management)</li><li>Stakeholder relations</li><li>Antibribery policy</li><li>Controversial tenants</li></ul>
		How do we collect data, and is it our present insight that the data collected is robust and dependable?
		Here, the "story" will be as much narrative as hard statistical data. What additional information, narrative, or insight will we likely require in the future?
H10	Policy framework (data)	What are our present policies (if any)? How do we 'police' policy compliance and how do we deal with noncompliance?
		As regards data specifically, are there data protection questions? Is there presently any expectancy that data protection + confidentiality will be enhanced via regulatory demands?
H11	Plan for data quality improvement	At this early stage, the SMT imparts a clear "direction of travel," but data will be a separate workstream in any ESG project
		SMT's early involvement will give a clear "steer" regarding the organization's attitude to investments to improve data quality

Stage	Description	Detailed Notes
H12	IT component	Linked to H11, is there a specific ICT aspect? Are our current systems future-proof? Do we need to reinvest in hardware, or software, to better track or control data?
		At this early stage, it is the *principle* that we are setting out. Individual workstreams on "E," "S," and "G" will probably generate additional insight into this specific question
H13	Project manager(s) devises project plan	The assumption here is that three separate project plans emerge, focusing on "E," "S," and "G" subcomponents of the ESG question. This is by no means essential, however. In some circumstances, a single plan may be adequate
		Generating such a project plan will follow normal project management planning subroutines
		Flexibility and a recognition of growth or development of the plan itself will be valuable. We need to be realistic— "Rome was not built in a day." Our ESG responses will take time to develop and mature
		The output here will be a plan, or series of plans, that the SMT can get behind and will also provide a believable and defendable statement to our stakeholder communities
H14	Board sign-off	In whatever way that the board signs-off on important issues
H15	Reporting subroutines agreed	At this initial phase, we build in appropriate reporting subroutines that will become a key focal point in ongoing management
		Report metrics and timeliness should be detailed
H16	Progression toward "E," "S," and "G" targets	There is an in-built understanding that there are no "quick-fixes"; the ESG world will itself develop and mature over time. But our own short, medium, and long-term corporate objectives must be deliberatively worked toward
H17	Feedback and remedial action	In one sense, this is the most important element for the SMT. Given today's growing regulatory intrusion and pressure from stakeholder groupings, our corporate ability to report accurately, and to show real progress, is essential. Beyond this, moves across the ESG arenas to make directors *personally* liable for some aspects of performance mean that feedback is more of a focal point than it was in previous eras. Achievement of exacting targets represents a "success story" that we shall want to celebrate. Faltering progress demands deliberative remedial action to get us back on track
		The SMT is not involved day-to-day in the minutia of ESG management, but these broad areas of concern need to remain on their collective "SMT radar screen," with regular reports generated

CHAPTER 9

The Subcomponents

"All Things Work Together"

It is helpful to break ESG down into its component parts: "E" for environmental responses, "S" for social, and "G" for governance responses. This book adds a fourth dimension, being TPRRM[1] (or "3PM") responses, which completes the picture, noting that ESG cannot be *properly* managed without *direct* reference to 3PM.[2] In the briefest terms, these are as follows.

E

It recognizes that the natural environment is under pressure from generally man-made factors and that current practice is broadly unsustainable. Few argue about this, although there is a view that "the science is not settled," in the sense that neither risks nor remedies are properly understood. Be that as it may, the broad consensus is that environmental degradation whether through greenhouse gas (GHG) emissions, pollution, resource depletion, or biodiversity loss is, quite simply, unsustainable— and something has to "give." At the time of writing this book, the key "E" agenda item was GHG reduction with a broad target of "net zero" by 2050. But, other "E" problems are pressing. Ocean pollution, in several major forms, follows close behind "global warming." All environment questions seem to be interlinked.

---

[1] Third-party risk and relationship management.
[2] Third-party management.

S

In a globalized world with constant media focus and burgeoning non-governmental organization (NGO) activity, there is growing awareness of the "social" cost of our modern way of life. Political instability leading to major population movements has only exacerbated the problems—there are more potential "victims" today. Social costs and impacts of organizational operations (and policies) have long been a matter of concern. We can think of *child labor* and *acid rain* issues in the 1980s. Globalization from the 1990s and greater governance focus through organizations like the ILO[3] have led to greater awareness. In addition, consumer sentiment increasingly demands good (or at very least fair) outcomes for workers and communities on which consumers depend for supply of manufactures at affordable prices and for supply of food.

Not only can organizations cause adverse social impacts but they can also make positive social contributions, often with relatively little effort and investment. Today's sentiment is that organizations (whether public or private sector) should play their part in working toward more sustainable *social* outcomes.

G

This is probably the more difficult subcomponent to define. Today, boards and their directors are under increased scrutiny. Incompetent boards and directors enjoy reduced public sympathy, and corporate governance qualifications are increasingly required of directors. That is no bad thing! Good governance has a positive impact on society and the planet. Poor governance leads to negative outcomes for organizations and the communities in which they operate.

We tend to think of governance as principally a *private sector* domain. Yet, public organizations must be held accountable to high governance standards, and poorly run public organizations are as much a menace as poorly run private ones.

---

[3] International Labour Organization.

"Governance" goes beyond the mechanics of running organizations. Sound corporate governance has long been considered the bedrock of an open free society and of the "market" method of economic distribution. So, in well-developed market economies, we already have powerful and institutionalized "high-level" governance, much of it underpinned by legislation, convention, and case law. Yet, beyond these mechanisms, we must "govern" our environmental ("E") and "social" ("S") outcomes. Increasingly, these are part of the governance equation. And governance itself must be subject to a degree of internal as well as external scrutiny.

Is governance itself changing? In the private sector, *shareholder-based governance* predominates in the Anglosphere (the United States, the United Kingdom, New Zealand, Australia, and arguably India), as these are market-based economies with dispersed ownership (via shareholders). But this is not, however, the global norm where a majority of firms are family owned and with centralized ownership. Socioeconomic factors, such as strong labor unions, business groups, government-owned banks, and even institutionalized corruption, significantly impact business strategies and decision making. In these societies, it is more correct to speak of *stakeholder-based governance*. The broad ESG agenda may be pushing toward a greater convergence toward *stakeholder-based* governance, which raises many interesting questions beyond the scope of this book.

Governance is linked to "compliance." The advance of standards in governance has led to a far more professionalized compliance operation.

During the late part of the last century, both public and private organizations focused on "outsourcing" *noncore* operations. For the early part of the present century, this approach was extended to *core* operations. This became a major feature of market-based economies (Anglosphere, once again), but made fewer advances in *stakeholder-based economies* (as defined above). Nevertheless, increased dependence on third parties to enable organizations to deliver meant that compliance operations and influence were ramped up in many big organizations, setting the pace for smaller ones.

Third-Party Management (3PM)

TPRRM has become a bigger item on the board's agenda in the past 10 years from 2014. "Third-party management" or "3PM" aims to achieve consistency and dependability in all relationships with third parties, not just "suppliers." It provides consistency through:

- Proactive management
- Appropriate risk controls
- Materiality assessment
- A common corporate language and stance on managing third-party relationships
- More scientific "contract management" with greater emphasis on achieving key performance indicators (KPIs)
- Greater recognition as to who "third parties" are

We can characterize third parties, with whom we may have contractual relationships, as:

- Key customers
- Consultants
- Contractors or suppliers
- Agents
- Distributors
- Joint ventures

Beyond these, other entities might be "managed" on a similar basis, even though the legal relationship is less clear-cut. Relations with certain regulatory bodies and investor groups, even NGO groups, lend themselves to more deliberative management. "3PM" is a major activity in its own right and has spawned its own management theory and software-based management tools. Our interest in this book focuses around the reality that, to achieve ESG advances or benefits, we must work with third parties, *especially* contractors, vendors, or suppliers, to define, measure, and meet our key ESG targets. "No man is an island!"

In Part 6 of this book and especially Chapter 20, we look at 3PM issues and opportunities. Right now, however, we can make some high-level generalizations as suggested in Figure 9.1.

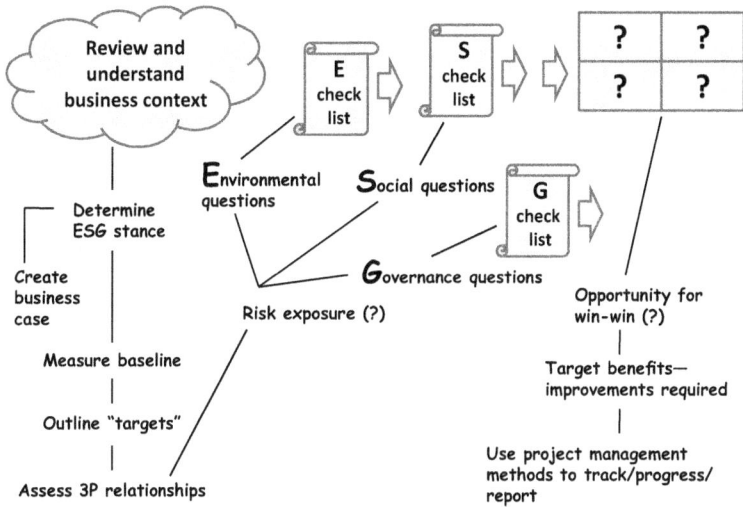

Figure 9.1 ESG + 3PM—leveraging relationships

The ideas suggested in Figure 9.1 remind us that, as always, everything we do must be planned and undertaken in the context of our overall corporate strategy ("business context"). Within this, we determine our overall ESG "stance" (see Figures 5.2 and 7.1) and create corporate consensus around it ("build business case," above). Having established "where we are today" in terms of our ESG credentials ("measure baseline"), we can move on to outline RAM[4] targets. Once we have done that, we can begin to see where and how our third-party relationships can help us achieve goals and where risk may lie, both to ourselves and to our key third-party relationships.

From risk assessment, we then move toward using our "E," "S," and "G" checklists and how we progress those both internally and via our different third-party relationships. That idea is suggested in the four "?" boxes in Figure 9.1. As we review our third-party relationships, we can also begin to see opportunities for win–win outcomes and how we might mutually and beneficially work toward achievement of the goals. That will require deft negotiation and team-building skills. We consider more of this in Chapter 21.

---

[4] Realistic, achievable, and measurable.

ESG and Product Development

At a practical level, "E," "S," and "G" considerations should be embedded in any business case for entry to *new markets* and development of *new products*, especially the latter. We use the term "product" here in a very loose sense. It may imply the idea of a manufacturing type of business, but we can "stretch" our definition if we consider that all organizations, whether private or public sector, "make" something. A hospital performs operations (literally!) that have a preplanned outcome, the "product" being restoration to good health of a patient. An airport provides landing and take-off slots and ground-handling facilities. Its "product" is dependable turnaround for many airlines.

In terms of our own business, we sit at the heart of a series of interconnected activities as our organization (in Figure 9.2, it is "YOU!") prepares to develop and market a new "product." Depending on the nature of the "product," we may engage with engineering, design, R&D, and distribution as key *internal* stakeholders. But our activities, more broadly, are directed by our overarching business context, our key "third parties" (3PM in the schematic), and the concept of taxonomy. Our "markets" will also be informing us of wants and concerns. Within

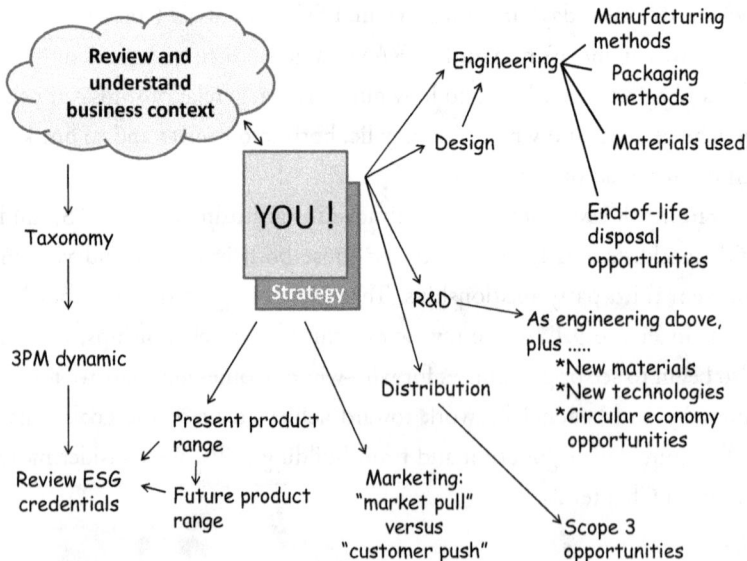

Figure 9.2 ESG and product development

all this, the "E" and "S" dynamics of ESG loom large (or should loom large, if we are doing this correctly). The "G" element may be a lesser concern.

As a business reports its strategy to investors and other stakeholders, a part of its "good story" will be the ability to state, categorically, that ESG issues have been factored-in to new product development and that our new products incorporate incremental (and perhaps, even transformational) benefits that positively contribute toward meeting ESG concerns. In this, *the tail does not wag the dog*! Rather, we simply address, in a systematic way, *relevant* ESG concerns as we simultaneously factor-in other legitimate matters such as product quality, product safety, and after-sales support.

PART 3

"E"

CHAPTER 10

Environment—The Rationale

Footprint

The environment, especially climate change aspects, is considered the most pressing immediate concern in the "ESG world." Indeed, if climatologists' predictions are correct, there could be knock-on environmental implications (e.g., crop failure and habitat reduction) that lead directly to adverse social ramifications. So the "E" and "S" parts of ESG are, in principle, intertwined.

Many organizations have well-embedded environmental policies and associated action programs. This has been best known, and most identifiable, via "corporate responsibility" policies, which have been a feature of corporate *mission statements* since well before the turn of the century[1]. Much of this began with pollution control and avoidance of direct adverse environmental impacts on locales in which organizations operate. Today, the primary emphasis is on climate change.

Movement beyond localized environmental impacts to a broader sense of "shared ecosphere" does not imply that other enviro-concerns are ignored, but rather that they are rolled in to our broad enviro-programs. Many organizations, then, will have experience dating back years in taking localized adverse impacts into account, measuring them, and reporting[2] on them. The bigger question of climate change can be built upon such earlier experience; usually, businesses are not "starting from scratch." What *has* changed in recent years is that we now need to account for carbon footprint in *measurable* ways using standard measures, with some of which we may be unfamiliar.

---

[1] Social impact was a key aspect of Quaker-owned businesses from the early 19th century, so a history of *social impact* is precisely that—a history!
[2] "Impact assessments."

Irrespective of business sector, organizations today are getting used to terms such as *carbon neutral, netzero, climate positive*, and so on. With limited knowledge, our organization might feel obliged to "jump on the climate commitment bandwagon," but before we make promises that we cannot honor and inadvertently start greenwashing, we must set a *baseline* by measuring present emissions and other impacts. The old adage, "what gets measured gets managed," is especially relevant when it comes to GHG emissions. Before we reduce and mitigate, we need to learn how to measure accurately.

Measurement and tracking help break sustainability goals into smaller, manageable steps. With *accurate* measures, we can identify strategies and interim targets to support our bigger ambitions. Our stakeholders, including key customers, shareholders, and our own employees, increasingly expect us to make a public commitment to good environmental progress and to take action, so we need to measure accurately our carbon footprint in order to demonstrate progress.

At the highest level, we subdivide emissions into those activities our business controls (direct emissions) and activities that support our business operation but are outside our control (indirect emissions).[3] Direct emissions include energy and fuel used in operations (manufacturing, facilities, and distribution). Indirect emissions include all value-chain activities both upstream and downstream, a potentially more complex set of values, including everything from employee commutes to the overhead emissions of cloud-based software services. Unless we own significant real estate, it is our *indirect* emissions that typically comprise the bulk of our GHG profile. These are the most nebulous to identify and then to calculate.

Units of Measure

Carbon, measured in MT CO_2 (metric tons of carbon dioxide), has become the standard unit of measure for GHG sustainability targets, but is not the only measure we need. Other factors such as water consumption, waste management, or land contamination, can be equally important.

---

[3] See Appendix 3 on scope emissions.

In terms of GHG, however, there is an "equalizing" conversion for such activities: carbon emissions equivalent (CO_2e). This enables universal measurement that can capture other GHGs like methane, nitrous oxide, and fluorinated gases. For example, 1 metric ton of methane has a warming effect 25 times that of CO_2 and would be measured as 25 metric tons of CO_2 equivalent. By using MT CO_2e, we quantify our organization's impacts across a diverse range of activities: vehicle emissions, purchased electricity, business travel, employee commutes, and so on.

Measuring CO_2e makes it possible to see where our business has the greatest environmental impact and consequently highlights where we can find meaningful reduction opportunities. Once we have a better understanding of MT CO_2e, we can engage with emission scopes (Scope 1, 2, and 3), which is increasingly the standard framework helping organizations segregate emissions into subcategories. See Appendix 3 for more insight on scopes. These help us identify, report on, and address GHG emissions across everything we do in operating our business.

Needless to say, there are today specialist software providers that can assist in making these calculations, often under SaaS (*software as a service*) arrangements. Even large companies continue (at the time of writing) to rely principally on spreadsheets to track their CO_2e emissions and other environmental impacts. While there is nothing intrinsically wrong with this, there are more sophisticated measurement "solutions" available on a SaaS basis, and for many organizations, switching to bespoke measurement systems will be a part of their "E" journey. Over the long term, such solutions may well ease and speed tracking, but we should not underestimate the practical challenges of identifying good software packages or service providers and then the *change management* task of on-boarding new software and adjusting operating practices to achieve best value from them.

In our next two chapters, we suggest a "roadmap" to benchmark your present "E" approach and/or to help you get started if your approach to date has been disjointed.

CHAPTER 11

ESG High-Level Roadmap—Environmental

Using This Chapter

Please refer to Appendix 7—The 39-Step ESG Roadmap. The "steps" required to project manage ESG activities are similar for "E," "S," and "G" subcategories. Cross refer each "step" with the associated "notes" in Chapters 12, 15, and 18, respectively.

Where in the "roadmap" in Appendix 7 you see, for example, *step 12*, the associated notes for each "E," "S," and "G" subcategory will be, respectively, E12, S12, and G12. Please navigate through the 39 steps in this way.

CHAPTER 12

ESG High-Level Roadmap—Environmental—Explanatory Notes

Explanatory Note

This chapter adds detail and context to the high-level "environment" roadmap in Appendix 7.

In common with the other places in this book, stage E0 (not cited below, where we begin at E1) indicates that there will have been—and continues to be—a thorough-going business context appreciation and ongoing review. In turn, these lead to effective *business strategy* development and associated detailed *business plans*. A soundly run organization and an effective senior manager will have a good grip on the overall business environment and how their own organization interacts within its business sector and how it relates to other business sectors. Bluntly, "we know our onions!" as previous generations might have put it. We know our business, and we know what we're doing!

With that an in-depth insight undergirding strategic direction, we can confidently factor-in our broad ESG response and develop detailed plans to progress, deliberatively, in this area. The notes below add further insights into the tasks. Be clear, however, that we do not "slavishly" follow each and every step, and these are not necessarily assembled in a chronological order. Rather, it is likely that subsections of the roadmap will be undertaken in parallel, at the same time. There may also be a periodic revisiting of earlier steps to improve outcomes. Within these "39 steps," we should find the critical responses necessary to research, define, and, finally, execute our overall plan.

Step 33, *Action Phase*, may seem a little cryptic. What this step indicates is that after planning and research, we mobilize to carry out "concrete actions," upon which we can later report in accordance with regulatory demands and stakeholder requirements.

Stage	Description	Detailed Notes
E1	"E" objective(s) documented	It may be that our business already has a clear "environmental policy." At this early stage, we will reconsider our *present* stance in the light of emerging requirements associated with the UN's 17 SDGs
		Beyond this, we require clear insight into our Scope 1, 2, and 3 GHG emissions and other direct environmental impacts caused by our operations. If an EU-based firm, we shall take due note of the *European Green Deal* provisions (risks and opportunities)
		Further, we will carry out a simple *materiality assessment* in terms of our normal operations and geographic footprint. Do our "normal" business operations impact the environment or the natural ecosphere directly? To what extent might these impacts be "adverse"?
		We may be able to perceive quick win opportunities as well as longer term challenges associated with present, or planned future, business developments
E2	What does this mean in practical terms?	We may well be able to perceive quick win opportunities as well as longer term challenges associated with present or planned future business developments
		Review the existing environmental "policy" (if any) and brainstorm possible changes. This is only exploratory at this stage, yet we may be able to devise some fairly "obvious" changes that will be needed, even at this early stage
E3	Board exec nominated	As we consider the wider "ESG" picture, we can determine to what extent board-level support and backing will be required *to really make things happen*
		Will we appoint one board member to oversee "ESG" or will we subdivide this, possibly involving three directors?
		And, in your context, are "E," "S," and "G" of equal materiality, or does one predominate given your business situation?
		The materiality question will best be considered in the light of the EU's taxonomy which remains (at the time of writing) the most comprehensive appreciation of risk and materiality, sector by sector
		One, two, or even three board-level champions may be required

Stage	Description	Detailed Notes
E4	Stakeholder engagement	Given that we are here considering the "environment" dynamic of our operations within the emerging heightened awareness in this arena, your organization may already have established extensive stakeholder management strategies in place. These may be fully adequate to give expression to formal communication and consultation with relevant stakeholders
		There is, today, a growing *body of knowledge* and associated *protocols* and *methods* around stakeholder management. Is this a hard skill, a soft skill, or an amalgam of both?
		How good are you presently at stakeholder management?
		Your purpose right now is to establish who are the right (legitimate) stakeholders and what is their required level of involvement?
		Dependent on your precise operational and business context, these are the types of stakeholder you may need to engage with:
		• Employees generally • Operational directors • Environmental specialists • Communities adjacent to operations • Investor groups • Specialist NGOs (non-governmental organizations*)
		* An organization that, generally, is formed independent from government. Typically nonprofit entities, many are active in environmental concerns. They can also include clubs and associations that provide services to their members and others
		Having identified potential stakeholders, the next step is formally to "engage" with them. Prepare a stakeholder engagement plan with specific objectives including:
		• Informing, exploring • Seeking (clarifying) perceptions • Seeking buy-in • Seeking active cooperation, where appropriate • Agreeing future communications approach

(Continued)

(*Continued*)

Stage	Description	Detailed Notes
H7 to H10	Data integrity	Please refer to the high-level "map" in Figure 7.2
		The broad task is to establish what data is required to be sought or recorded, its accuracy, and relevance
		In the "environmental" aspect of ESG, we expect heightened concern and must avoid any perception of "greenwashing" or a *negligent misrepresentation* of facts
E5	3-year horizon targeted (with metrics)	At this relatively early stage, we should be able to outline a rationale for our next steps in the "environmental" arena of ESG. This gives us a "direction of travel" and some clear relevant targets. While such targets may be modified as time goes by, and especially in the light of practical experience, we should be able to assess approximate timeframes and tasks
		Within this, we shall want to put in some measures ("metrics") that we consider relevant, even if we have to modify those metrics at a later stage
E6	Project manager appointed	It is recommended that a project management style is adopted to manage each of the "E," "S," and "G" subelements of our ESG task. In turn, this suggests appointment of a dedicated manager
		Considerations will be:
		• Can we have one project manager handling the entire "E," "S," and "G" question? • Is this a full-time task or is it a subelement of an FTE role? • Is this a task for a general manager or a task for a specialist? • Will special training be required?
		Larger firms may already have a dedicated environment manager. Smaller firms may consider a general manager or a project manager to be the natural skill-set and then "back-fill" environmental skills to bring then up to speed on relevant environmental technicalities
E7	Project management protocols enabled	In adopting a project management style, associated protocols and methodologies will be required. Do they already exist? Is your organization, for example, already certified to ISO 21500? Do you use PRINCE2 or equivalent?

Stage	Description	Detailed Notes
E8	"E" policy draft tabled	E8 to E10 may be considered as a single step
		In the light of emerging ESG challenges and reporting requirements (think regulation), does our existing policy need modification? In fact, your existing statement may be perfectly adequate and require no modification at all. Beware the temptation to devise policy statements that use today's faddish language or respond to activities or lobbying of pressure groups (that may, or may not, be legitimate stakeholders)
E9	"E" policy draft socialized	Internal stakeholders certainly should be consulted. What about external stakeholders? Where do you "draw the line"?
		Socialization may result in an iterative document development process, with several drafts before securing agreement and senior manager buy-in
E10	"E" policy draft published	Following general internal agreement, the policy document must be presented to senior management and then formal "sign-off" achieved
		Diary-in policy review steps
E11	Communications (internal and external)	Communications will be an ongoing task. In a project management environment, communications will typically be a separate workstream. Link this to your communications policy, if you have one
		Beware making environmental "promises" that have not been properly thought through and stress tested. Remember that communications will be both internal and external —possibly they are handled as two separate work streams? Irrespective of that, they need to be harmonized. Avoid the potential for internal and external communications containing conflicting messages
		What is to be communicated and in what format? Our year 1, 2, and 3 plans (see E12) may suggest the content of at least some communication messaging
E12	Year 1 plan Year 2 plan Year 3 plan	This is likely to be a mixture of narrative and data information. Treat this as you would any formal business plan
		Remember that the added dimension (difficulty?) in the ESG arena is that, today, we live in an era where *greenwashing* is under active scrutiny and, in some situations, can constitute a tort (a civil wrong)
		Your own house style will be observed in the presentation of the plan, but you may consider it useful to keep the format consistent across the years of the plan itself

(Continued)

(Continued)

Stage	Description	Detailed Notes
E13 Internal	Communications messages (website) (marketing)	The realities here are likely to be similar to those for E11 and E12, and there may be direct linkage
		The core difference is that website and marketing messages are essentially public domain, may be very widely distributed or accessible, and can be argued as being a key factor in potential customers making purchasing decisions (or otherwise to engage with us commercially)
		It is important, therefore, that we stay on-message and avoid accusation of "greenwashing." Our messages need to be proportionate and truthful
E14 Internal	Associated filing systems created (audit trail)	An area often forgotten. Too many organizations have ad hoc filing "systems"
		Given increasing regulatory intrusion in the ESG arena and the associated demand for data integrity and avoidance of *greenwashing* and also given that staff turnover is (at the time of writing) experiencing increased velocity, it is vital that we can both preserve and access records. We need to leave a sound audit trail and one that does not over depend on individuals being "good" at preserving information in their private "filing system"
		You required a company wide system that everyone understands and is suitably backed up. Generally, records are stored electronically, but manual record keeping must equally be robust and dependable
E15 Internal	Managerial and team targets devised and promulgated	These may have been articulated as step E12, but more likely, this will be linked directly to performance appraisal and job role or description. Plainly, staff members need to know what is expected of them
		Given the growing importance of ESG, individuals need to have a genuine sense of "ownership" of the task and clear targets to achieve
E16 Internal	Review loop embedded	Not only linked to E15 but also, more broadly, we need to review our plans and be able to actively manage progress as well as spot deviation from objectives
		From here, we move away from internal review and into external action (roadmap stage E33)
E17 External	3PM workstream	This is linked to the 3PM (or third-party risk and relationship management) aspect of this book

Stage	Description	Detailed Notes
		The key point we make here is that commercial relationships for all organizations are "two-way," that is, we buy and sell. Our ESG obligations and interests can be impacted in both directions, even though we can recognize that we have more leverage with our suppliers than with our customers
		Within this workstream (which may in practice be simple and straightforward), we look candidly at pre-existing and emerging ESG requirements and opportunities, to establish, at high level, whether direct implications arise from our commercial relationships. Link this to E18 and E19
E18 External	Know your customer (sales)	Is our market "customer pull" or "supplier push"? Do we principally respond to customer demand (e.g., FMCG sector) or do we introduce innovative products and services that change customer behavior?
		In terms of ESG considerations, can we achieve some of our targeted outcomes by working with our customers? What conversations will be required and what preparation do we need to undertake?
		Working with our customers, what ESG "benefits" might we target and how much effort will be required to achieve them? Will the effort be worth the practical outcome?
		There may be a mutuality of interest ("win–win") in working with suppliers to meet Scope 1, 2, and 3 reductions, as this is deemed the most urgent area of ESG management
E19 External	Know your supplier (procurement)	In the field of "procurement," we need to understand with clarity: • Where are we exposed to direct or indirect "E," "S," or "G" risks (and opportunities)? • In the "E" arena specifically, do we understand GHG Scope 1, 2, and 3 emissions? (See Appendix 3 for detail) • What is the geographic footprint of our suppliers? Are certain regions of the planet (or specific countries) known to represent high or low risk in terms of "E," "S," or "G"? • Do we have a good insight into our supplier base (e.g., Kraljic *supplier positioning* technique)? • What is our relative bargaining position with our suppliers (and especially our strategic suppliers; Kraljic definition)?

(Continued)

Stage	Description	Detailed Notes
E20 External	Risk reviews	As regards our supply base, we should undertake risk reviews within our "normal" business operations
		Various techniques are available to help assess risk. Among these will be Porter's Five Forces and PESTLE analysis at the "strategic" level. Beyond these, there will be varying elements to an overall risk appreciation:
		Operational Distribution or logistics Suppliers Product or service quality Employee issues Fraud Projects Natural events IT Fire
		Strategic Markets Competitors Technology Economy Consumer needs Legal: contracts, litigation, and IPR Merger Acquisition
		Financial Exchange rates Interest rates Liquidity Profitability Credit Costs
		Compliance Stock exchange rules Taxation requirements Environmental legislation (ESG) Accounting standards Internal controls Ethics (ESG)
		From here, we move away from internal review and into external action (roadmap stage E33)

Stage	Description	Detailed Notes
E21 Procurement	Category management approached agreed	To add insight into the likely tasks that follow on from E19 and E20, above, many organizations use a procurement approach known as category management
		What type of procurement operation does your organization utilize?
		If your organization is relatively small, then your "procurement" activity may be purely tactical and offer few opportunities to achieve ESG advances. If you operate a strategic procurement strategy, then opportunities are likely to be greater
		Where organizations want to achieve a more "strategic" approach to procurement, then category management may be a part of this.
		As regards ESG within a *category management* approach, we may be able to agree at E21 how we leverage the *category strategy* to specifically achieve ESG advantages
E22 Procurement	Category plan(s)	These may be updated specifically to achieve ESG advantages
		Where heavy investment is required to meet higher environmental standards, your supplier base may demand greater commitment over time from yourselves as customer. This is always a difficult area in procurement, but may be a *quid pro quo* to achieve greater action and commitment in, for example, Scope 3 reductions
E23 Procurement	Terms and conditions (review)	Terms of trading (for purchasing) may require amendment to better reflect ESG requirements being "down-flowed" to suppliers
E24 Procurement	Review progress at (periodicity)	Having set up the procurement response to ESG demands (never forgetting that procurement must broadly respond to a range of *other* demands to secure quality, value, and supply security), we can now diary-in progress reviews
		If we diary-in reviews, let's ensure we observe them!
E25 Procurement	Feedback	Within E24. there needs to be a process to feed back information and adjust plans accordingly
E26 Procurement	Remedial action	E24 to E25 lead directly to the opportunity to take corrective action where we may be failing to achieve expected benefits

(*Continued*)

(*Continued*)

Stage	Description	Detailed Notes
E27 Procurement	Comms messages (with suppliers) (with stakeholders)	Communications are vital to the whole ESG task As regards specifically the ESG implications of procurement activity and 3PM subroutines, we need to be aware that communications can be a powerful element of "relationship management." If we are to secure mutual (win–win) outcomes with our supplier base, then "good stories" will need to be aired and shared Beware "*greenwashing*," however. Your good stories need to be true stories. Where specifically ESG implications are involved, there is a possibility of fines and reputational damage if it transpires that our "story" is misleading. This may include the legal concept of *negligent misrepresentation* Caveat emptor!
E28 Marketing	See step E18 plus ...	At this stage, we should be in a position to say that we recognize our sales market and the context in which we operate (step E0). We ought also to be in a position to say that: • "Customers X, Y, and Z represent the greatest potential for finding 'wins' in terms of ESG risks" • "Customers P, Q, and R represent the biggest risk in terms of environmental shortfall" • "Customers J, K, and L represent the clearest opportunity to help us meet our obligation to reduce *Scope 3* emissions (and will probably be happy to work with us as this will present a win–win outcome)" We may need to undertake additional research to scope-out the opportunities, but we now know the "direction of travel" and where "wins" might be secured If we do not have strong *ongoing* customer relationships (e.g., FMCG or retail outlet), the idea of "working with" customers will be somewhat different. Here, our narrative might be: • "We recognize that products A, B, and C can all be reengineered so as to reduce environmental impact, and we can target 'wins' within a given timeframe of ..." • "We recognize that product lines D, E, and F represent opportunities to reengineer via bought-in goods that in turn can secure Scope 3 emissions reduction"

Stage	Description	Detailed Notes
		• "We recognize that product lines G, H, and J are undergirded by supplies from [N] country which is known to be a source of social conflict. Should we re-source from [M] country we can secure a definite 'win' in terms of our social obligations" At this stage E28, we still have more work to do, but the picture is becoming clearer and the direction of travel more obvious
E29 Marketing	Sales (customer) materiality review	"The customer is King!" … Except when he isn't! Not all customers are of equal value to your organization. Sophisticated selling organizations have some sort of formalized "customer account management" which may include "key account managers" A simple customer account matrix will help to clarify with which customers you need to invest time, effort, and energy. Many call this a *customer materiality* approach, which recognizes that some customers are "material" to our success and our future In the same way, there will potentially be some customers that are material in the way we (your organization, specifically) address the "downstream" concerns raised via ESG
E30 Marketing	Sales (customer) risk review	There are inevitably a range of risk reviews undertaken relating to existing, and potential new, customers Within this activity, we explore specific concerns raised via the "E," the "S," and the "G" arenas. It is recommended that your organization first "brainstorm" internally to "surface" any practical risks and what additional controls and information may be required. In addition, you can compare and contrast elements of this via your trade organization and/or equivalent companies operating in (or adjacent to) your particular business sector Where you are working with direct or indirect competitors, there may be antitrust implications. Take legal advice as necessary, but transparency may be a clear line of defense—try to keep discussions and decisions in the public sphere

(*Continued*)

(Continued)

Stage	Description	Detailed Notes
E31 Marketing	Sales— determine whether to enter dialogue with potential customer to remedy or address identified risks	There may be opportunities to engage directly with potential customers (and existing customers) where there is opportunity to work collaboratively to reduce or eliminate ESG-type adverse impacts. You may find customers very willing to talk with you and to perceive these discussions as a potential mechanism to make advances in their own ESG journey *Customer materiality* (E29) may suggest the managerial level at which exploratory dialogue is first engaged in. Nevertheless, at some point, you will need to field the right technical or professional expertise in both organizations, which suggests support from middle managers and other technically qualified personnel
E32 Marketing	Remedial action	Having entered discussions via steps E28 to E30, we can now address problem areas. There may be "quick wins" available that we shall want to secure. Nevertheless, at this point, we can factor-in practical steps to "remedy" identified deficiencies
E33	**Action Phase**	In our high-level roadmap in five sub-"steps," we inserted a "flag"→ to move to "Action Phase." It is hugely important that we move beyond the theory and the "white-collar" activity of planning and research, and all the senior to middle management activity suggested in this book, *into doing things at a practical level that will directly and favorably impact our ESG requirements* An action plan, or project plan, is essential. This was suggested at step E12, but it is plain that there is so much work to do that any plan will be a "living document," continually updated to reflect experience, practical progress, and new learnings or new challenges Such plans and all that arises from them will require to be securely evidenced in your corporate filing system (audit trail maintained) as suggested at step E14
E34 "3PM"	Determine link to corporate strategy and policy objectives (E5, E17, E21 to E27, E28 to E32)	This step ensures consistency and "joined-up thinking" as well as "joined-up action" relating to our ESG challenges It also ensures we do not embark upon strategic initiatives that do not contribute to achieving our corporate goals

Stage	Description	Detailed Notes
		Allowing that most organizations have greater leverage with their suppliers than with their customers, a key plank in our earliest "wins" is likely to be achieved via our suppliers. This is true across "E," "S," and "G" subcomponents of the ESG challenge. Our contract management competencies will enable us to reflect ESG tasks into the contractual relationship and then to "manage" them throughout the life of the commercial contract. Our broad "3PM" methodology and competencies will assist here
		Even with our key customers, however, there is a contractual element to the relationship that must be proactively managed. Likewise, our broad "3PM" methodology and competencies will assist here. *Remember that your customers may "flowdown" ESG demands to you and specify the achievement of these as a contractual deliverable under the commercial relationship.* If so, you must manage and provide the supporting practical evidence of successful "delivery"
E35 "3PM"	Explore potential mutual interests and "wins" with 3P	As noted (E34), we can work with our commercial partners, be they suppliers or customers, to achieve wins. Beyond that, in a truly strategic relationship, we may be able to work collaboratively with both customers and suppliers to deliver benefits at various "layers" of the value chain
E36 "3PM"	Establish whether specific ESG targets are best achieved in combination with 3P	(*via contract*)
		As indicated at E35, there are opportunities at different links of the value chain. The key question becomes: do we want to make this a contractual requirement, specified in the "terms of reference" or the "technical specification" or the "service-level agreement" or "key performance indicators"? This requires careful thought and may depend on the specific demands of any regulatory requirements to which your organization is subjected
		Incorporating ESG requirements as contract deliverables ensures that both parties are focused on outcomes and it is recognized that (in some way) this requirement is an essential feature of the commercial relationship. A failure to "deliver" outcomes will give rise to the potential to pursue the counterparty for financial damages under the terms of the agreement

(*Continued*)

(Continued)

Stage	Description	Detailed Notes
		(via non contract commitments)
		There may be a compelling argument that the requirements are not made subject to the contract that governs the relationship, but rather becomes a noncontractual commitment. Depending on the dynamics of the relationship, it may be quicker, easier, or less contentious to make progress in a noncontract deliverable. Progress here may be more dependent on mutual, coinciding, business interests rather than a straight master–servant-type contract relationship. Provided both parties are achieving valuable benefits, this ought to be enough. The "beauty" of the emerging ESG paradigm is that it impacts all sectors of the organizational world in the same way and almost demands a collaborative and collegiate approach throughout the value chain
		If we determine on a noncontract relationship, a memorandum of understanding (MoU) style of record may be a suitable one. This really is a case of "horses for courses" and readers will have to evaluate what will work best in their business context
E37 "3PM"	Codify objectives	The point here is that irrespective of the decisions at E36, we need to record and monitor our decisions and ensure follow-up or remedial *action* where progress is below what we legitimately expect
		This will link to our audit trail (E14)
E38 "3PM"	Establish RAM measures RAM = *realistic, achievable, and measurable*	E38 overlaps with E37. The key difference is that we are seeking realistic, achievable, and measurable outcomes. Attainment of (or failure to achieve) such outcomes becomes a matter of specific interest between ourselves and our counterparty (whether customer or supplier)
		"What you cannot measure, you cannot manage." To demonstrate our contribution across the ESG task, we need hard evidence that is meaningful to our varying stakeholder groups, especially regulators

Stage	Description	Detailed Notes
E39 "3PM"	Establish "project" plan(s) (E6, E7)	Remember we are here speaking about establishing 3PM links. For procurement (focusing on the downstream activities of our value chain), *project plans* as regards "E," "S," or "G" can easily be wrapped into our category strategy—or whatever way we style our approach to managing our supply chain
		The environmental dimension of the ESG challenge is likely to be focused around our direct impact upon, and interaction with, suppliers and communities from which we procure, and thence downstream from that, subsupplier and then sub-subsuppliers. At the time of writing this book, Scope 1, 2, and 3 emission reduction is the obvious starting point in discussion, but other environmental impacts may quickly suggest themselves
		For sales, the thought process is analogous. With which customers can we, should we, work? What are the issues around key customers and to what extent might adverse environmental issues indirectly impact us as a supplier to this customer?
		We will then either (1) create a project plan to deal directly with the customer or (2) wrap such considerations into our broader marketing plan(s)

PART 4

"S"

CHAPTER 13

Social—The Rationale

"Doing Unto Others"

The social dynamic of ESG is the easiest to relate to and has the longest history. Social and employment legislation has progressed in the past half century and moved right across the planet, but especially in the western world and in those places where the International Labour Organization ("ILO" founded in 1919, and the oldest specialist advocacy organization of the United Nations) has secured real traction. In Britain, the *Health and Safety at Work Act* of 1974 was a landmark legislative achievement, as was the *Modern Slavery Act* of 2015.

The Sustainable Development Goals ("SDGs") are a collection of 17 interlinked global goals designed to be a "shared blueprint for peace and prosperity for people and the planet, now and into the future." Established in 2015 by the United Nations General Assembly, they are intended to be achieved by 2030, albeit there being genuine practical obstacles. Of these 17 goals, certainly 8 have direct social implications, as noted here:

Goal 1. End poverty in all its forms everywhere.

Goal 2. End hunger, achieve food security and improved nutrition, and promote sustainable agriculture.

Goal 3. Ensure healthy lives and *promote well-being* for all, at all ages.

Goal 4. Ensure inclusive and equitable *quality education* and promote lifelong learning opportunities for all.

Goal 5. Achieve *gender equality* and empower all women and girls.

Goal 8. Promote sustained, inclusive, and *sustainable economic growth*, full and productive employment, and decent work for all.

Goal 11. Make cities and human settlements inclusive, *safe, resilient, and sustainable.*

Goal 15. Protect, restore, and *promote sustainable use of terrestrial ecosystems*, sustainably manage forests, combat desertification, halt and reverse land degradation, and halt biodiversity loss.

Businesses, which broadly acceded to these objectives, can incorporate the ideals into concrete plans at least in their own direct operations, including (to a limited extent) those of their suppliers. For many years, there have been "CSR" objectives that businesses have sought to incorporate into their ethos. Charitable donations, social volunteering on company time, social enterprise partnering, and latterly "social performance" departments (see below) have each played a part in giving social expression to corporate operations. While not detracting from the necessary and (?) mundane business of returning a profit on capital employed and securing long-term business, it is fair to say that CSR-type activities have a broad degree of acceptance, especially among employees. In one sense, we might think of ESG as sitting under CSR in many organizations' approach to their *business values*.

Plainly the rationale for the "S" part of ESG is that, apart from the external pressures we are considering throughout this book, most societies have some concept of fairness or equity and are trying to achieve win–win outcomes in all that we do—perhaps, the concept is best summarized by the term "fair dealing." Others speak of a social "golden rule" more or less recognized internationally or "do unto others as you would have others do unto you" in traditional language. As a rationale, this is powerful and seems to be achieving more traction because of Sustainability concerns.

Businesses generally are not "social enterprises", nor are they often a part of the "third sector." They must return a profit and secure their future in a competitive and often unforgiving marketplace. Likewise, public sector organizations have core objectives that they must achieve, and they too are not "charities." Yet, all organizations are accountable to stakeholders and must recognize sustainability questions. Finally, there is the concept of the "triple bottom line" (TBL). In economics, TBL concept suggests that organizations should commit to focusing as much on social and environmental concerns as they do on profits. TBL theory posits that instead of one bottom line, there should be three: profit, people, and the planet.

What Is Social Performance?

All organizations in general, but particularly transnational businesses, will "impact" the locales in which they operate. We suggested immediately above that neither businesses nor public sector organizations are "charities" and that they are obligated at a number of levels to focus upon corporate objectives, and not to undertake work that is *ultra vires* (company law definition) to their corporate charter. The long-accepted political settlement in free societies is that voters elect governments which, in turn, set out and implement social policy. Social issues are first and foremost a government agenda, and the pursuit of social objectives is funded via general taxation (broad definition). Corporations (including public sector) in terms of social objectives operate only at the margins of this, reducing harm while legitimately pursuing corporate objectives. Providing good employment is the number-one social benefit brought about by organizations, whether private or public sector.

Despite this general *settlement* as described above, there has long been a powerful insight that corporations (private or public sector) can go one step further[1] and make positive and lasting impacts to the benefit of the locales and communities where they operate, and this is doubly true where such businesses are making significant investments (*project finance* investments) for specific "projects" in which they are engaged. Where such activities are undertaken, it is relatively straightforward and relatively inexpensive to incorporate positive social objectives and outcomes to the benefit of host communities. Today, that is what is meant by social performance, and a sound business case for investment would describe, and cost, these types of outcome as part and parcel of the investment case.

Social performance is here defined as *the effective translation of an institution's vision and values so as to positively benefit host societies at the points of their greatest social needs particularly in terms of healthcare and education and the avoidance of local "harms" such as pollution and displacement of local businesses or destruction of high-grade farming land. Where such outcomes are absolutely unavoidable, then some form of effective long-term compensation is*

---

[1] One step beyond the legitimate activity of paying taxes to the governing authorities in the domains in which they operate.

inbuilt into the project plans and especially into project finance. For example, the displacement of local businesses might be consciously offset by the provision of jobs within the new investment and associated local training to make this ambition a reality. We repeat, such activities are *relatively* inexpensive and can be readily inbuilt into corporate processes.

The link to ESG is easy enough to see. Not every business can afford a Social Performance Department, but most can build into their plans appropriate focus on labor standards, stakeholder engagement, health and safety, and so on. Social performance does not become "the tail that wags the dog," but rather a useful and affordable facet of business case development. Transnational corporations that operate in economically and socially disadvantaged societies (think especially of extractive industries and some heavy engineering) will often have social performance personnel working for them, and these can make a notable contribution to achieving valuable "social" wins in host communities.

In our next two chapters, we suggest a "roadmap" to benchmark your present "S" approach and/or to help you get started if your approach to date has been disjointed.

CHAPTER 14

ESG High-Level Roadmap—Social

Using This Chapter

Please refer to Appendix 7—The 39-Step ESG Roadmap. The "steps" required to project manage ESG activities are similar for "E," "S," and "G" subcategories. Cross refer each "step" with the associated "notes" in Chapters 12, 15, and 18, respectively.

Where in the "roadmap" in Appendix 7 you see, for example, *step 12*, the associated notes for each "E," "S," and "G" subcategory will be, respectively, E12, S12, and G12. Please navigate through the 39 steps in this way.

CHAPTER 15

ESG—High-Level Roadmap—Social— Explanatory Notes

Explanatory Note

This chapter adds detail and context to the high-level "social" roadmap in Appendix 7.

In common with the other places in this book, stage S0 (not cited below, where we begin at S1) indicates that there has been—and continues to be—a thorough business context appreciation and ongoing review. In turn, these lead to effective *business strategy* development and associated detailed *business plans*. A soundly run organization and an effective senior manager will have a good grip on the overall business environment and how their own organization interacts within its own business sector and how it relates to other business sectors. Bluntly, "we know our onions!" as previous generations might have put it. We know our business and we know what we're doing!

With that in-depth insight undergirding strategic direction, we confidently factor-in our broad ESG response and develop detailed plans to progress, deliberatively, in this area. The notes below add further insights into the tasks. Be clear, however, that we do not "slavishly" follow each and every step, and these are not necessarily assembled in a chronological order. Rather, it is likely that subsections of the roadmap will be undertaken in parallel, at the same time. There may also be periodic revisiting of earlier steps to improve outcomes. Within these "39 steps," we should find the critical responses necessary to research, define, and, finally, execute our overall plan.

Step 33, *Action Phase*, may seem a little cryptic. What this step indicates is that after planning and research, we need eventually to move to carry out "concrete actions" upon which we can later report in accordance with regulatory demands and stakeholder requirements.

Stage	Description	Detailed Notes
S1	"S" objective(s) documented	It may be that our business already has a clear "CSR"-type policy. At this early stage, we will reconsider our present stance in the light of emerging requirements associated with the UN's 17 SDGs
		Further, we will carry out a simple *materiality assessment* in terms of our normal operations and geographic footprint. Do our "normal" business operations impact individuals or communities directly? To what extent might these impacts be "adverse"?
		We may be able to perceive quick win opportunities as well as longer term challenges associated with present or planned future business developments
S2	What does this mean in practical terms?	We may perceive quick win opportunities as well as longer term challenges associated with present or planned future business developments
		Review the existing CSR "policy" (if any) and brainstorm possible changes. This is only exploratory at this stage, yet we may be able to devise some fairly "obvious" changes that will be needed, even at this early stage
S3	Board exec nominated	As we consider the wider "ESG" picture, we can determine to what extent board-level support and backing will be required *to really make things happen*
		Will we appoint one board member to oversee "ESG" or will we subdivide this, possibly involving three directors?
		And in your context, are "E," "S," and "G" of equal materiality, or does one predominate given your business situation?
		The materiality question will best be considered in the light of the EU's taxonomy, which remains (at the time of writing) the most comprehensive appreciation of risk and materiality, sector by sector. While the taxonomy is focused on environmental issues (not social), it still provides some clues as to identification, understanding, and mitigation. Also, we should note that it is possible that a social taxonomy will be developed by 2027—possibly earlier
		One, two, or even three board-level champions may be required

Stage	Description	Detailed Notes
S4	Stakeholder engagement	Given that we are here considering the "social" dynamic of our operations within the emerging heightened awareness in this arena, your organization may already have established extensive stakeholder management strategies in place. These may be fully adequate to give expression to formal communication and consultation with relevant stakeholders
		There is, today, a growing *body of knowledge* and associated *protocols* and *methods* around stakeholder management. Is this a hard skill, a soft skill, or an amalgam of both?
		How good are you presently at stakeholder management?
		Your purpose right now is to establish who are the right (legitimate) stakeholders and what is their required level of involvement?
		Dependent on your precise operational and business context, these are the types of stakeholder you may need to engage with:
		<ul><li>Employees generally</li><li>Operational directors</li><li>HR (human resources or personnel)</li><li>Communities adjacent to operations</li><li>Investor groups</li><li>Specialist NGOs (nongovernmental organizations*)</li></ul>
		* An organization that, generally, is formed independent from government. Typically nonprofit entities, many are active in social concerns; they can also include clubs and associations that provide services to their members and others
		Having identified potential stakeholders, the next step is formally to "engage" with them. Prepare a *Stakeholder engagement plan* with specific objectives including:
		<ul><li>Informing, exploring</li><li>Seeking (clarifying) perceptions</li><li>Seeking buy-in</li><li>Seeking active cooperation, where appropriate</li><li>Agreeing future communications approach</li></ul>

(Continued)

(Continued)

Stage	Description	Detailed Notes
H7 to H10	Data integrity	Please refer to the high-level "map" in Figure 7.2

The broad task is to establish what data is required to be sought or recorded, its accuracy, and relevance

In the "social" arena of ESG, we expect heightened concern and must avoid any perception of "social-washing" or a *negligent misrepresentation* of facts |
| S5 | 3-year horizon targeted (with metrics) | At this relatively early stage, we should be able to outline a rationale for our next steps in the "social" arena of ESG. This gives us a "direction of travel" and some clear relevant targets. While such targets may be modified as time goes by, and especially in the light of practical experience, we should be able to assess approximate timeframes and tasks

Within this, we shall want to put in some measures ("metrics") that we consider relevant, even if we have to modify those metrics at a later stage |
| S6 | Project manager appointed | It is recommended that a project management style is adopted to manage each of the "E," "S," and "G" subelements of our ESG task. In turn, this suggests appointment of a dedicated manager

Considerations will be:

- Can we have one project manager handling the entire "E," "S," and "G" question?
- Is this a full-time task or is it a subelement of an FTE role?
- Is this a task for a general manager or for a specialist?
- Will special training be required? |
| S7 | Project management protocols enabled | In adopting a project management style, associated protocols and methodologies will be required. Do they already exist? Is your organization, for example, already certified to ISO 21500? Do you use PRINCE2 or equivalent? |
| S8 | "S" policy draft tabled | S8 to S10 may be considered as a single step

In the light of emerging ESG challenges and reporting requirements (think regulation), does our existing policy need modification? In fact, your existing policy statement may be perfectly adequate and require no modification at all. Beware the temptation to devise policy statements that use today's faddish language or respond to activities of or lobbying by pressure groups (that may, or may not, be legitimate stakeholders) |

Stage	Description	Detailed Notes
		IT Governance Publishing publishes various template policy documents that are well considered, modern, and adaptable. These may make a useful reference point
S9	"S" policy draft socialized	Internal stakeholders certainly should be consulted. What about external stakeholders? Where do you "draw the line"?
		Socialization may result in an iterative document development process, with several drafts before securing agreement and senior manager buy-in
S10	"S" policy draft published	Following general internal agreement, the policy document must be presented to senior management and then formal "sign-off" achieved
		Diary-in policy review steps
S11	Communications (internal and external)	Communications will be an ongoing task. In a project management environment, communications will typically be a separate work stream. Link this to your communications policy, if you have one
		Beware making social "promises" that have not been properly thought through and stress tested. Remember that communications will be both internal and external—possibly, they are handled as two separate work streams? Irrespective of that, they need to be harmonized. Avoid the potential for internal and external communications containing conflicting messages
		What is to be communicated and in what format? Our year 1, 2, and 3 plans (see S12) may suggest the content of at least some communication messaging
S12	Year 1 plan Year 2 plan Year 3 plan	This is likely to be a mixture of narrative and data information. Treat this as you would any formal business plan
		Remember that the added dimension (difficulty?) in the ESG arena is that today we live in an era where *greenwashing* (or even "socialwashing") is under active scrutiny and, in some situations, can constitute a tort (a civil wrong)
		Your own house style will be observed in the presentation of the plan, but you may consider it useful to keep the format consistent across the years of the plan itself

(Continued)

(Continued)

Stage	Description	Detailed Notes
S13 Internal	Communications messages (website) (marketing)	The realities here are likely to be similar to those for S11 and S12, and there may be a direct linkage The core difference is that website and marketing messages are essentially public domain, may be very widely distributed or accessible, and can be argued as being a key factor in potential customers making purchasing decisions (or otherwise to engage with us commercially) It is important, therefore, that we stay on-message and avoid accusation of "greenwashing." Our messages need to be proportionate and truthful
S14 Internal	Associated filing systems created (audit trail)	An area often forgotten. Too many organizations have ad hoc filing "systems" Given increasing regulatory intrusion in the ESG arena and the associated demand for data integrity and avoidance of *greenwashing* and also given that staff turnover is (at the time of writing) experiencing increased velocity, it is vital that we can both preserve and access records. We need to leave a sound audit trail and one that does not over-depend on individuals being "good" at preserving information in their private "filing system" You require, ideally, a companywide system that everyone understands and is suitably backed-up. Generally, records are stored electronically, but manual record keeping must be equally robust and dependable
S15 Internal	Managerial and team targets devised and promulgated	These may have been articulated as step S12, but more likely, this will be linked directly to performance appraisal and job role or description. Plainly, staff members need to know what is expected of them. Given the growing importance of ESG, individuals need to have a genuine sense of "ownership" of the task and clear targets to achieve
S16 Internal	Review loop embedded	Not only linked to S15 but also, more broadly, we need to review our plans and be able to actively manage progress as well as spot deviation from objectives From here, we move away from internal review and into external action (roadmap stage S33)
S17 External	3PM workstream	This is linked to the 3PM (or third-party risk and relationship management) aspect of this book

Stage	Description	Detailed Notes
		The key point we make here is that commercial relationships for all organizations are "two-way," that is, we buy and sell. Our ESG obligations and interests can be impacted in both directions, even though we can recognize that we have more leverage with our suppliers than with our customers
		Within this workstream (which may in practice be simple and straightforward), we look candidly at pre-existing and emerging ESG requirements and opportunities, to establish (at high level) whether direct implications arise from our commercial relationships. Link this to S18 and S19
S18 External	Know your customer (sales)	Is our market "customer pull" or "supplier push"? Do we principally respond to customer demand (e.g., FMCG sector) or do we introduce innovative products and services that change customer behavior?
		In terms of ESG considerations, can we achieve some of our targeted outcomes by working with our customers? What conversations will be required, and what preparation do we need to undertake?
		Working with our customers, what ESG "benefits" might we target and how much effort will be required to achieve them? Will the effort be worth the practical outcome?
S19 External	Know your supplier (procurement)	In the field of "procurement," we need to understand with clarity:
		• Where are we exposed to direct or indirect "E," "S," or "G" risks (and opportunities)?
		• In the "S" arena specifically, do we see any opportunity for supplier community engagement? Are there supplier workforce health and safety issues? How well do we understand labor standards in supply markets? What are generic supplier working conditions—what do we know and what do we not know?
		• What is the geographic footprint of our suppliers? Are certain regions of the planet (or certain countries) known to represent high or low risk in terms of "E," "S," or "G"?
		• Do we have a good insight into our supplier base (e.g., Kraljic *supplier positioning* technique)?
		• What is our relative bargaining position with our suppliers (and especially our strategic suppliers; Kraljic definition)?

(Continued)

(Continued)

Stage	Description	Detailed Notes
S20 External	Risk reviews	As regards our supply base, we should undertake risk reviews within our "normal" business operations Various techniques are available to help assess risk. Among these will be Porter's Five Forces, and PESTLE analysis, at the "strategic" level. Beyond these, there will be varying elements to an overall risk appreciation: ***Operational*** Distributor logistics Suppliers and sub-subsuppliers Product or service quality Employee issues Fraud Projects Natural events IT Fire ***Strategic*** Markets Competitors Technology Economy Consumer needs Legal: contracts, litigation, and IPR Merger Acquisition ***Financial*** Exchange rates Interest rates Liquidity Profitability Credit Costs ***Compliance*** Stock exchange rules Taxation requirements Environmental legislation (ESG) Accounting standards Internal controls Ethics (ESG) From here, we move away from internal review and into external action (roadmap stage S33)

Stage	Description	Detailed Notes
S21 Procurement	Category management approached agreed	To add insight into the likely tasks that follow on from S19 and S20, above, many organizations use a procurement approach known as category management
		What type of procurement operation does your organization utilize?
		If your organization is relatively small, then your "procurement" activity may be purely tactical and offer few opportunities to achieve ESG advances. If you operate a strategic procurement strategy, then opportunities are likely to be greater
		Where organizations want to achieve a more "strategic" approach to procurement, then category management may be a part of this
		As regards ESG within a category management approach, we may be able to agree at S21 how we leverage the category strategy to specifically achieve ESG advantages
S22 Procurement	Category plan(s)	These may be updated specifically to achieve ESG advantages
S23 Procurement	Terms and conditions (review)	Terms of trading (for purchasing) may require amendment to better reflect ESG requirements being "down-flowed" to suppliers
S24 Procurement	Review progress at (periodicity)	Having set up the procurement response to ESG demands (never forgetting that procurement must broadly respond to a range of *other* demands to secure quality, value, and supply security), we can now diary-in progress reviews
		If we diary-in reviews, let's ensure we observe them!
S25 Procurement	Feedback	Within S24, there needs to be a process to feed back information and adjust plans accordingly
S26 Procurement	Remedial action	S24 to S25 lead directly to the opportunity to take corrective action where we may be failing to achieve expected benefits
S27 Procurement	Comms messages (with suppliers) (with stake-holders)	Communications are vital to the whole ESG task
		As regards specifically the ESG implications of procurement activity and 3PM subroutines, we need to be aware that communications can be a powerful element of "relationship management." If we are to secure mutual (win–win) outcomes with our supplier base, then "good stories" will need to be aired and shared

(*Continued*)

(*Continued*)

Stage	Description	Detailed Notes
		Beware "*greenwashing*" (perhaps in this context, *socialwashing*), however. Your good stories need to be true stories. Where specifically ESG implications are involved, there is a possibility of fines and reputational damage if it transpires that our "story" is misleading. This may include the legal concept of *negligent misrepresentation* Caveat emptor!
S28 Marketing	See step S18 plus ...	At this stage, we should be in a position to say that we recognize our sales market and the context in which we operate (step S0). We ought also to be in a position to say that: • "Customers X, Y, and Z represent the greatest potential for finding 'wins' in terms of ESG risks" • "Customers P, Q, and R represent the biggest risk in terms of social shortfall" • "Customers J, K, and L represent the clearest opportunity to help us meet our obligations under *Scope 3* emission requirements (and will probably be happy to work with us as this will present a win–win outcome)" We may need to undertake additional research to scope out opportunities, but we now know the "direction of travel" and where "wins" might be secured If we do not have strong *ongoing* customer relationships (e.g., FMCG or retail outlet), the idea of "working with" customers will be somewhat different. Here our narrative might be: • "We recognize that products A, B, and C can all be reengineered so as to reduce adverse social impact, and we can target "wins" within a given timeframe of ..." • "We recognize that product lines D, E, and F represent opportunities to reengineer via bought-in goods that in turn can secure positive social impacts" • "We recognize that product lines G, H, and J are undergirded by supplies from [N] country which is known to be a source of social conflict. Should we re-source from [N] country, we can secure a definite 'win' in terms of our social obligations" At this stage S28, we still have more work to do, but the picture is becoming clearer and the direction of travel more obvious

Stage	Description	Detailed Notes
S29 Marketing	Sales (customer) materiality review	"The customer is King!" … Except when he isn't!
		Not all customers are of equal value to your organization. Sophisticated selling departments have formalized "customer account management," which may include "key account managers"
		A simple customer account matrix will help to clarify with which customers you need to invest time, effort, and energy. Many call this a *customer materiality* approach, which recognizes that some customers are "material" to our success and our future
		In the same way, there will potentially be some customers that are material in the way we (your organization, specifically) address the "downstream" concerns raised via ESG
S30 Marketing	Sales (customer) risk review	There are inevitably a range of risk reviews undertaken relating to existing, and potential new, customers.
		Within this activity, we explore specific concerns raised via the "E," the "S," and the "G" arenas. It is recommended that your organization first "brainstorm" internally to "surface" any practical risks and what additional controls and information may be required. In addition, you can compare and contrast elements of this via your trade organization and/or equivalent companies operating in (or adjacent to) your particular business sector
		Where you are working with direct or indirect competitors, there may be antitrust implications. Take legal advice as necessary, but transparency may be a clear line of defense—try to keep discussions and decisions in the public sphere
S31 Marketing	Sales— determine whether to enter dialogue with potential customer to remedy or address identified risks	There may be opportunities to engage directly with potential customers (and existing customers) where there is opportunity to work collaboratively to reduce or eliminate ESG-type adverse impacts. You may find customers very willing to talk with you and to perceive these discussions as a potential mechanism to make advances in their own ESG journey
		Customer materiality (S29) may suggest the managerial level at which exploratory dialogue is first engaged in. Nevertheless, at some point, you will need to field the right technical or professional expertise in both organizations, which suggests support from middle managers and other technically qualified personnel

(Continued)

(Continued)

Stage	Description	Detailed Notes
S32 Marketing	Remedial action	Having entered discussions via steps S28 to S30, we can now address problem areas. There may be "quick wins" available that we shall want to secure. Nevertheless, at this point, we factor-in practical steps to "remedy" identified deficiencies
S33	**Action Phase**	In our high-level roadmap in five sub-"steps" we inserted a "flag" to move to "Action Phase." It is hugely important that we move beyond the theory and the "white-collar" activity of planning and research, and all the senior to middle management activity suggested in this book, *into doing things at a practical level that will directly and favorably impact our ESG requirements* An action plan, or project plan, is essential. This was suggested at step S12, but it is plain that there is so much work to do that any plan will be a "living document," continually updated to reflect experience, practical progress, and new learnings or challenges Such plans and all that arises from them will require to be securely evidenced in your corporate filing system (audit trail maintained) as suggested at step S14
S34 "3PM"	Determine link to corporate strategy and policy objectives (S5, S17, S21 to S27, S28 to S32)	This step ensures consistency and "joined-up thinking" as well as "joined-up action" relating to our ESG challenges It also ensures we do not embark upon strategic initiatives that do not contribute to achieving our corporate goals Allowing that most organizations have greater leverage with their suppliers than with their customers, a key plank in our earliest "wins" is likely to be achieved via our suppliers. This is true across "E," "S," and "G" subcomponents of the ESG challenge. Our contract management competencies will enable us to reflect ESG tasks into the contractual relationship and then to "manage" them throughout the life of the commercial contract. Our broad "3PM" methodology and competencies will assist here Even with our key customers, however, there is a contractual element to the relationship that must be proactively managed. Likewise, our broad "3PM" methodology and competencies will assist here. *Remember that your customers may "flowdown" ESG demands to you and specify the achievement of these as a contractual deliverable under the commercial relationship.* If so, you must manage and provide the supporting practical evidence, of successful "delivery"

Stage	Description	Detailed Notes
S35 "3PM"	Explore potential mutual interests and "wins" with 3P	As noted (S34), we can work with our commercial partners, be they suppliers or customers, to achieve wins. Beyond that, in a truly strategic relationship, we may be able to work collaboratively with both customers and suppliers to deliver benefits at various "layers" of the value chain
S36 "3PM"	Establish whether specific ESG targets are best achieved in combination with 3P	(*via contract*) As indicated at S35, there are opportunities at different layers of the value chain. The key question becomes: do we want to make this a contractual requirement, specified in the "terms of reference" or the "technical specification" or the "service-level agreement" or "key performance indicators"? This requires careful thought and may depend on the specific demands of any regulatory requirements to which your organization is subjected Incorporating ESG requirements as contract deliverables ensures that both parties are focused on outcomes and it is recognized that (in some way) this requirement is an essential feature of the commercial relationship. A failure to "deliver" outcomes will give rise to the potential to pursue the counterparty for financial damages under the terms of the agreement (*via noncontract commitments*) There may be a compelling argument that the requirements are not made subject to the contract that governs the relationship, but rather becomes a noncontractual commitment. Depending on the dynamics of the relationship, it may be quicker, easier, or less contentious to make progress in a noncontract deliverable. Progress here may be more dependent on mutual, coinciding, business interests rather than a straight master–servant-type contract relationship. Provided both parties are achieving valuable benefits, this ought to be enough. The "beauty" of the emerging ESG paradigm is that it impacts all sectors of the organizational world in the same way and almost demands a collaborative and collegiate approach throughout the value chain If we determine on a noncontract relationship, a memorandum of understanding (MoU) style of record may be suitable. This really is a case of "horses for courses" and readers must evaluate what will work best in their business context

(*Continued*)

(*Continued*)

Stage	Description	Detailed Notes
S37 "3PM"	Codify objectives	The point here is that irrespective of the decisions at S36, we need to record and monitor our decisions and ensure follow-up or remedial *action* where progress is below what we legitimately expect This will link to our audit trail (S14)
S38 "3PM"	Establish RAM measures	S38 overlaps with S37. The key difference is that we are seeking realistic, achievable, and measurable outcomes. Attainment of (or failure to achieve) such outcomes becomes a matter of specific interest between ourselves and our counterparty (whether customer or supplier) "What you cannot measure, you cannot manage." To demonstrate our contribution across the ESG task, we need hard evidence that will be meaningful to our varying stakeholder groups, especially regulators
S39 "3PM"	Establish "project" plan(s) (S6, S7)	Remember we are here speaking about establishing 3PM links. For procurement (focusing on the downstream activities of our value chain), *project plans* as regards "E," "**S**," or "G" can easily be wrapped into our category strategy—or whatever we style our approach to managing our supply chain The social dimension of the ESG challenge is likely to be focused around our direct impact upon, and interaction with, suppliers and communities from which we procure, and thence downstream from that, subsupplier and then sub-subsuppliers. The approach adopted by many buying organizations to the scourge of modern slavery (e.g., in the United Kingdom, under the *Modern Slavery Act* (MSA), 2015) is a good illustration. Indeed, the granularity of MSA responses suggests a 'model' for dealing with other elements of the "social" challenge before us For sales, the thought process is analogous. With which customers can we, should we, work? What are the issues around key customers and to what extent might adverse issues indirectly impact us as a supplier to this customer? We will then either (1) create a project plan to deal directly with the customer or (2) wrap such considerations into our broader marketing plan(s)

PART 5

"G"

CHAPTER 16

Governance—The Rationale

Why Governance Is Different

Earlier in this book, we noted that governance is probably the most difficult aspect of ESG to get to grips with. Today, boards and their directors are under increased scrutiny. In terms of ESG, there may be a temptation to resist the sort of scrutiny that ESG reportage implies; if the board resists, however, investors may—in any case—insist on greater transparency and accountability. It is a truism that incompetent boards and directors command reduced public sympathy, and corporate governance qualifications are increasingly required of directors[1], which is no bad thing! Good governance has a positive impact on society and the planet. Poor governance can lead to negative outcomes for organizations and the communities in which they operate.

We tend to think of governance as principally a *private sector* domain. Yet, public organizations must be held accountable to equally high standards, and poorly run public organizations are as much a menace as poorly run private ones.

"Governance" goes beyond the mechanics of running organizations. Sound corporate governance has long been considered a bedrock of an open free society and of the "market" method of economic distribution. So, in well-developed market economies, we already have powerful and institutionalized "high-level" governance, much of it underpinned by legislation, convention, and case law. Yet, beyond these mechanisms, we must "govern" our environmental ("E") and "social" ("S") outcomes.

---

[1] In the United Kingdom, think of "The Corporate Governance Institute"; internationally, think of "The International Institute for Management Development." The International Compliance Association today runs governance education—and many business schools major in this area.

Increasingly, these are part of the governance equation. And governance itself must be subject to a degree of external, as well as internal, scrutiny.

Is governance itself changing? In the private sector, *shareholder-based governance* predominates in the Anglosphere (the United States, the United Kingdom, New Zealand, Australia, and arguably India) as these are market-based economies with dispersed ownership (via shareholders). This is not, however, the global norm where a majority of firms are family owned and with centralized ownership. Socioeconomic factors, such as strong labor unions, business groups, government-owned banks, and even institutionalized corruption, significantly impact business strategies and decision making. In these societies, it is more correct to speak of *stakeholder-based governance*. The broad ESG agenda may push organizations toward greater convergence aligned to stakeholder-based governance, which raises many interesting questions that are beyond the scope of this book.

Governance is linked directly to "compliance," and the onward advance of standards in governance has led to a far more professionalized corporate compliance operation. Today, some organizations have a chief compliance officer (CCO). This emerging role is evolving into a key player within management teams subject to heavy external regulation,

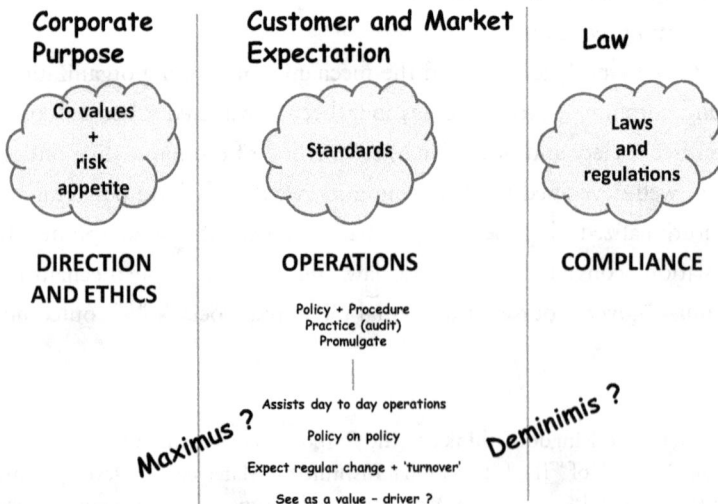

Figure 16.1 Governance ecosphere—drivers

being primarily responsible for overseeing and ensuring compliance with laws, regulatory requirements, policies, and procedures. In terms of ESG, the role will probably be the 'first port-of-call' for reporting and monitoring. We can think of overarching governance as a sort of business "ecosphere" with three key drivers:

The three "drivers" are *direction and ethics*, which will be set by the board; *operations* (which is everything that the organization does on a day-to-day basis); and *compliance* itself, which seeks to ensure that laws and regulations are properly observed and that internal policy is applied effectively. An ever-present question will be whether we apply a maximum or minimum (above, "maximus" or "deminimis") approach to all this. Do we enforce rigorously to the highest standard possible or do we apply only the minimum to "get by"? This will be answered in part by our ESG positioning (see Chapter 5) but, more generally, this is an ethos that will essentially be set by the board itself. In turn, our three "drivers" are powerfully influenced by our risk appetite and corporate values, our application of external "standards" (think ISO-type standards), and the legal regime within which we seek to operate.

Governance is potentially different, then, from the "E" and "S" dimensions of ESG, to the extent that governance itself must be applied to the "E" and "S" aspects, to meet levels of compliance that may be heavily driven by external considerations (e.g., stakeholder communities). Governance, by contrast, must also meet its own codes and could potentially find itself in a conflict of interest conundrum—do we "lower" standards of governance to achieve quick wins where higher standards might be "inconvenient?"

Governance standards internationally, at least in terms of financial management, were heavily influenced by the British *Cadbury Report* (issued in 1992), which would go on to influence codes of conduct for listed companies across the world. After being progressively updated, a consolidating revision was issued in 2018 as the U.K. *Corporate Governance Code*, now a part of U.K. company law. This establishes certain principles of good corporate governance aimed at companies listed on the London Stock Exchange. Overseen by the Financial Reporting Council (FRC), its importance derives from the Financial Conduct Authority's Listing Rules. These have statutory authority under the Financial Services and Markets Act 2000 and require that public listed companies disclose how they have complied with the code and explain where they have chosen not to apply it. This is what the code refers to as "comply or explain." Private companies are also encouraged to conform, but there is no requirement for disclosure of compliance in private company accounts. The code adopts a principles-based approach in the sense that it provides general guidelines of best practice.

What Matters, Matters!

As regards ESG reporting, it is likely that in the 10 years from 2024, there may develop "comply or explain"-type provisions as regards some ESG questions. Interestingly, this was the general approach to certain noncriminal elements of the British *Modern Slavery Act 2015*. There may develop some divergence in approach across the broadly western world[2] as regards how ESG-type rules are applied, but there is an expectation of a broad degree of alignment, if only because investors will demand it.

In Appendix 1, we provide a nonexhaustive listing of key ESG issues worthy of consideration by most organizations. Readers will want to consult the list to acquire a wider perspective, but as regards governance alone, the "bigger" issues are these:

- Accountability (code of conduct or clear business principles)
- Board diversity and structure
- Bribery and corruption or money laundering
- Cumulative voting (fair voting systems)
- Executive compensation (pay for performance and pay equity)
- Fraud defenses—internal
- Majority voting (fair voting systems)
- Say on pay
- Shareholder rights
- Stakeholder engagement or relations
- Transparency and disclosure

---

[2] For example, OECD nations.

We highlight these as, potentially, there could be scope for ethical conflict of interest, where the board may be tempted to apply a lower standard or less rigorous threshold simply because it directly impacts the way the board itself operates. The best advice your author can offer at the time of writing is to apply simple and basic "measures" as to what is important. Think in terms of reputational impact should there be any whiff of conflict of interest. Seek to be as transparent as possible within the confines of commercial confidentiality. Finally, apply the "what would I tell my mom" test? Would you feel comfortable explaining to your mother why you took a certain course of action (or inaction)?! If not, perhaps you need to apply a more rigorous and transparent measure. If it matters to your mom, it will probably matter to your stakeholders!

CHAPTER 17

ESG High-Level Roadmap—Governance

Using This Chapter

Please refer to Appendix 7—The 39-Step ESG Roadmap. The "steps" required to project-manage ESG activities are similar for "E," "S," and "G" subcategories. Cross refer each "step" with the associated "notes" in Chapters 12, 15, and 18, respectively.

Where in the "roadmap" in Appendix 7 you see, for example, *step 12*, the associated notes for each "E," "S," and "G" subcategory will be, respectively, E12, S12, and G12. Please navigate through the 39 steps in this way.

CHAPTER 18

ESG High-Level Roadmap— Governance—Explanatory Notes

Explanatory Note

This chapter adds detail and context to the high-level "governance" roadmap in Appendix 7.

In common with the other places in this book, stage G0 (not cited below, where we begin at G1) indicates that there has been—and continues to be—a thorough-going business context appreciation and ongoing review. In turn, these lead to effective *business strategy* development and associated detailed *business plans*. A soundly run organization and an effective senior manager will have a good grip on the overall business environment and how their own organization interacts within its business sector and how it relates to other business sectors. Bluntly, "we know our onions!" as previous generations might have put it. We know our business, and we know what we're doing!

With that an in-depth insight undergirding strategic direction, we confidently factor-in our broad ES**G** response and develop detailed plans to progress, deliberatively, in this area. The notes below add further insights into the tasks relating to Governance questions. Be clear, however, that we do not "slavishly" follow each and every step, and these are not necessarily assembled in a chronological order. Rather, it is likely that subsections of the roadmap will be undertaken in parallel, at the same time. There may also be a periodic revisiting of earlier steps to improve outcomes. Within these "39 steps," we should find the critical responses necessary to research, define, and, finally, execute our overall plan.

Step 33, *Action Phase*, may seem a little cryptic. What this step indicates is that after planning and research, we need eventually to move to carry out "concrete actions," upon which we can later report in accordance with regulatory demands and stakeholder requirements.

Stage	Description	Detailed Notes
G1	"G" objective(s) documented	Corporate governance is a set of rules, best practices, and processes that determine how an organization is managed. The purpose is to facilitate effective, entrepreneurial, and prudent management that can deliver the long-term success of the organization
		It may be that our business already has a clear "governance policy." At this early stage, we reconsider our present stance in the light of emerging requirements associated with the UN's 17 SDGs
		Beyond this, we need a clear insight into the emerging demands associated with governance generally and how practical day-to-day governance interacts with the "E" and the "S" dimensions of ESG
		We should carry out a simple *materiality assessment* in terms of our normal operations and geographic footprint. Do our "normal" business operations adversely impact the environment or natural ecosphere? Are there "social" dynamics to our operations that are not well understood and controlled? What "governance" implications may arise?
		In relation to "governance," in particular, are we satisfied that our policies and procedures adequately reflect our current needs and norms in, for example: <ul><li>Antibribery or money laundering</li><li>U.K. *Corporate Governance Code* (or local domicile equivalent)</li><li>ESG clauses in typical trading contracts</li><li>Stakeholder relations</li><li>Employee working conditions</li></ul>
		We may perceive quick win opportunities as well as longer term challenges associated with present or planned future business developments
G2	What does this mean in practical terms?	We may be able to see quick win opportunities as well as longer term challenges associated with present or planned future business developments
		Review the existing governance "policy" and brainstorm possible changes. This is only exploratory at this stage; yet we may be able to devise some fairly "obvious" changes that will be needed, even at this early stage

Stage	Description	Detailed Notes
G3	Board exec nominated	As we consider the wider "ESG" picture, we can determine to what extent board-level support and backing will be required *to really make things happen*.
		Will we appoint one board member to oversee "ESG" or will we subdivide this, possibly involving three directors? And in your context, are "E," "S," and "G" of equal materiality, or does one predominate given your business situation?
		While "E" and "S" may be competently managed by operational managers to a large extent, "G" may require closer scrutiny of the board as the questions concern the board directly and entail implications across the enterprise as well as its strategic direction
		The *materiality* question will be considered in the light of the UN's 17 SDGs and the EU's taxonomy which remains (at the time of writing) the most comprehensive appreciation of risk and materiality, sector by sector
		For governance, a board-level champion is required. But the board may decide to spread the workload among several directors
G4	Stakeholder engagement	We are considering here "governance," and today's heightened focus is in this complex area. Your organization may already have in place extensive and effective stakeholder management strategies. These may be fully adequate to give practical expression to the need to formally communicate and consult with relevant stakeholders
		There is, of course, a growing *body of knowledge* and associated *protocols* and *methods* around stakeholder management. Is this a hard skill, a soft skill, or an amalgam of both? How good are you presently at stakeholder management?
		Your purpose right now is to establish who are the right (legitimate) stakeholders and what is their required level of involvement?
		Dependent on your precise operational and business context, these are the types of stakeholder you may need to engage with:
		• Legal and compliance specialists • Accountants • Strategy consultants • Operational directors • Communities adjacent to operations • Investor groups

(Continued)

(*Continued*)

Stage	Description	Detailed Notes
		Having identified potential stakeholders, the next step is formally to "engage" with them. Prepare a stakeholder engagement plan with specific objectives including: • Informing and exploring • Seeking (clarifying) perceptions • Seeking buy-in • Seeking active cooperation, where appropriate • Agreeing future communications approach
H7 to H10	Data integrity	Please refer to the high-level "map" in Figure 7.2 The broad task is to establish what data is required to be sought or recorded, its accuracy, and relevance In terms of "governance," the data question may not be so much a reflection of raw data and many data sources; rather, it may be in policy development protocols, audit trails, and measurement of compliance to governance standards, as well as measurement of outcomes and improvements pursuant to governance revisions and overall improvements In common with the idea of "greenwashing," we should expect a measure of external interest in, and focus on, organizational governance. We need to avoid *negligent misrepresentation* of facts ("white-collar washing"?!)
G5	3-year horizon targeted (with metrics)	At this relatively early stage, we should be able to outline a rationale for our next steps in the "governance" arena of ESG. This will give us a "direction of travel" and some clear relevant targets. While such targets may be modified as time goes by, and especially in the light of practical experience, we should be able to assess approximate timeframes and tasks Within this, we shall want to put in some measures ("metrics") that we consider relevant, even if we have to modify those metrics at a later stage
G6	Project manager appointed	It is recommended that a project-management style is adopted to manage each of the "E," "S," and "G" subelements of our ESG task. In turn, this suggests appointment of a dedicated manager Considerations will be: • Can we have one project manager handling the entire "E," "S," and "G" question? • Is this a full-time task or is it a subelement of an FTE role?

Stage	Description	Detailed Notes
		• Is this a task for a general manager or a task for a specialist? Given the sensitivities around governance, the task may require active day-to-day involvement of one or more board members. • Will special training be required? • What external specialist advisory might be required?
G7	Project management protocols enabled	In adopting a project management style, associated protocols and methodologies will be required. Do they already exist? Is your organization, for example, already certified to ISO 21500? Do you use PRINCE2 or equivalent?
G8	"G" policy draft tabled	G8 to G10 may be considered as a single step In the light of emerging ESG challenges and reporting requirements (think regulation), does our existing policy(ies) require change? In practice, existing policy(ies) may be perfectly adequate and require no modification. Beware the temptation to devise policy statements that use today's faddish language or respond to lobbying of pressure groups (that may, or may not, be legitimate stakeholders)
G9	"G" policy draft socialized	Internal stakeholders certainly should be consulted. What about external stakeholders? Where do you "draw the line"? Socialization may result in an iterative document development process, with several drafts before securing agreement and senior manager buy-in
G10	"G" policy draft published	Following general internal agreement, the policy document must be presented to senior management and then formal "sign-off" achieved Diary-in policy review steps
G11	Communications (internal and external)	Communications will be an ongoing task. In a project management environment, communications will typically be a separate workstream. Link this to your communications policy, if you have one Beware making governance "promises" that have not been properly thought through and stress tested. Remember that communications will be both internal and external—possibly they are handled as two separate work streams? Irrespective of that, they need to be harmonized. Avoid the potential for internal and external communications containing conflicting messages What is to be communicated and in what format? Our year 1, 2, and 3 plans (see G12) may suggest the content of at least some communication messaging

(*Continued*)

Stage	Description	Detailed Notes
G12	Year 1 plan Year 2 plan Year 3 plan	This is likely to be a mixture of narrative and data information. Treat this as you would any formal business plan Remember that the added dimension (difficulty?) in the ESG arena is that today we live in an era where *greenwashing* is under active scrutiny and, in some situations, can constitute a tort (a civil wrong). In terms of governance, we might add the risk of malfeasance Your own house style will be observed in the presentation of the plan, but you may consider it useful to keep the format consistent across the years of the plan itself
G13 Internal	Communications messages (website) (marketing)	The realities here are likely to be similar to those for G11 and G12, and there may be direct linkage. The core difference is that website and marketing messages are essentially public domain, may be very widely distributed or accessible, and can be argued as being a key factor in potential customers making purchasing decisions (or otherwise to engage with us commercially) It is important, therefore, that we stay on-message and avoid accusation of "*greenwashing*" in the broad sense of that term. As always, our messages need to be proportionate and truthful
G14 Internal	Associated filing systems created (audit trail)	An area often forgotten. Too many organizations have ad hoc filing "systems" Given increasing regulatory intrusion in the ESG arena and the associated demand for data integrity and avoidance of *greenwashing* and also given that staff turnover is (at the time of writing) experiencing increased velocity, it is vital that we can both preserve and access records. We need to leave a sound audit trail and one that does not over depend on individuals being "good" at preserving information in their private "filing system" You require a companywide system that everyone understands and is suitably backed up. Generally, records are stored electronically but, where relevant, manual record keeping must be equally robust and dependable

Stage	Description	Detailed Notes
G15 Internal	Managerial and team targets devised and promulgated	These may have been articulated as step G12, but more likely, this will be linked directly to performance appraisal and job role or description. Plainly, staff members need to know what is expected of them Given the growing importance of ESG, individuals need to have a genuine sense of "ownership" of the task and clear targets to achieve
G16 Internal	Review loop embedded	Not only linked to G15 but also, more broadly, we need to review our plans and be able to actively manage progress as well as spot deviation from objectives From here, we move away from internal review and into external action (roadmap stage G33)
G17 External	3PM workstream	This is linked to the 3PM (or third-party risk and relationship management) aspect of this book In the governance arena, the question of 3PM is somewhat different to the more "obvious" interactions in the "E" and the "S" subdomains If our governance is poor and recognized as such, this will impact our risk profile in the eyes of potential investors, partners, and customers Perhaps, the key "3P" with an interest in governance are collectively our investors under, for example, the UN's Principles for Responsible Investment (PRI). There are also the ICGN and the CRD platforms to consider (see our glossary in Appendix 2) Within this workstream (which may in practice be simple and straightforward), we look candidly at pre-existing and emerging governance requirements and opportunities, to establish (at high level) whether direct implication arises from our financial relationships. This may be linked in some way to G18 and G19
G18 External	Know your customer (sales)	Is our market "customer pull" or "supplier push"? Do we principally respond to customer demand (e.g., FMCG sector) or do we introduce innovative products and services that change customer behavior? In terms of ESG considerations, can we achieve some of our targeted outcomes by working with our customers? What conversations will be required and what preparation do we need to undertake?

(Continued)

(Continued)

Stage	Description	Detailed Notes
		Working with our customers, what ESG "benefits" might we target and how much effort will be required to achieve them? Will the effort be worth the practical outcome?
		In terms of governance, our opportunity to work "with" customers may be very limited, but our ability to demonstrate excellent governance is part of the selling proposition, as well as setting a good example that others may want to emulate
G19 External	Know your supplier (procurement)	In the field of "procurement," we need to understand with clarity:
		Where are we exposed to direct or indirect "E," "S," or "G" risks (and opportunities)?
		In the "G" arena specifically, do we have adequate insight into the governance standards applied by our "key suppliers" (see the 3PM section of this book for more insight)
		What is the geographic footprint of our suppliers? Are certain regions of the planet (or specific countries) known to represent high or low risk in terms of governance standards?
		Do we have a good insight into our supplier base (e.g., Kraljic *supplier positioning* technique)?
		What is our relative bargaining position with our suppliers (and especially our strategic suppliers; Kraljic definition)?
G20 External	Risk reviews	As regards our supply base, we routinely undertake risk reviews within our "normal" business operations
		Various techniques are available to help assess risk. Among these will be Porter's Five Forces and PESTLE analysis at the "strategic" level. Beyond these, there will be varying elements to an overall risk appreciation:
		Operational Distribution or logistics Suppliers Product or service quality Employee issues Fraud Projects Natural events IT Fire

Stage	Description	Detailed Notes
		Strategic Markets Competitors Technology Economy Consumer needs Legal: contracts, litigation, and IPR Merger Acquisition **Financial** Exchange rates Interest rates Liquidity Profitability Credit Costs **Compliance or Governance** Governance standards Ethics Stock exchange rules Taxation requirements Environmental legislation Accounting standards Internal controls From here, we move away from internal review and into external action (roadmap stage G33)
G21 Procurement	Category management approached agreed	To add insight into the likely tasks that follow on from G19 and G20, above, many organizations use a procurement approach known as *category management* What type of procurement operation does your organization utilize? If your organization is relatively small, then your "procurement" activity may be purely tactical and offer few opportunities to achieve ESG advances. If you operate a strategic procurement strategy, then opportunities are likely to be greater Regarding governance, you may question the governance standards applied by key suppliers. We want to avoid "guilt by association!"

(Continued)

(*Continued*)

Stage	Description	Detailed Notes
G22 Procurement	Category plan(s)	These may be updated specifically to achieve ESG advantages
		Where heavy investment is required to meet higher ESG standards, your supplier base may demand greater commitment over time from yourselves as customer. This is always a difficult area for procurement, but may be a quid pro quo to achieve greater action and commitment in, for example, improving governance transparency
		With suppliers, governance represents a profound challenge. An "open line" from the CPO (chief procurement officer) to the board is important here
G23 Procurement	Terms and conditions (review)	Terms of trading (for purchasing) may require amendment to better reflect ESG requirements being "down-flowed" to suppliers
G24 Procurement	Review progress at (periodicity)	Having set up the procurement response to ESG demands (never forgetting that procurement must broadly respond to a range of *other* demands to secure quality, value, and supply security), we can now diary-in progress reviews
		If we diary-in reviews, let's ensure we observe them!
G25 Procurement	Feedback	Within G24, there needs to be a process to feed back information and adjust plans accordingly
G26 Procurement	Remedial action	G24 to G25 lead directly to the opportunity to take corrective action where we may be failing to achieve expected benefits
G27 Procurement	Comms messages (with suppliers) (with stake-holders)	Communications are vital to the whole ESG task
		Irrespective of step E27, governance questions rarely lend themselves to public communication. We may be seeking to avoid bad publicity rather than actively seeking good publicity!
		Caveat emptor!
G28 Marketing	See step G18 plus ...	At this stage, we should be in a position to say that we recognize our sales market and the context in which we operate (step G0). We ought also to be in a position to say that:
		• "Customers X, Y, and Z represent the greatest potential for finding 'wins' in terms of ESG risks"
		• "Customers P, Q, and R represent the biggest risk in terms of governance queries"

Stage	Description	Detailed Notes
		• "Customers J, K, and L represent the clearest opportunity to help us meet our obligation to demonstrate we take governance seriously" We may need to undertake additional research to scope out opportunities, but we do know the "direction of travel" and where "wins" might be encountered If we do not have strong *ongoing* customer relationships (e.g., FMCG or retail outlet), the idea of "working with" customers will be somewhat different. Here our narrative might be: • "We recognize that product lines A, B, and C are undergirded by supplies from [N] country which is known to hold low or suboptimal governance standards generally. It is actively under consideration that we should re-source from [M] country we can secure a definite 'win' in terms of our governance obligations" At this stage G28, we still have more work to do, but the picture is becoming clearer and the direction of travel more obvious Governance standards are plainly a more sensitive and complex area than even the "E" and "S" subcomponents of ESG. Tread carefully …
G29 Marketing	Sales (customer) materiality review	"The customer is King!" … Except when he isn't! Not all customers are of equal value to your organization. Sophisticated selling organizations have some sort of formalized "customer account management" which may include "key account managers" A simple customer account matrix will help to clarify with which customers you must invest time, effort, and energy. Many call this a *customer materiality* approach, which recognizes that some customers are "material" to our success and our future In the same way, there will potentially be some customers that are material in the way we (your organization, specifically) address the "downstream" concerns raised via governance questions

(Continued)

(Continued)

Stage	Description	Detailed Notes
G30 Marketing	Sales (customer) risk review	There are inevitably a range of risk reviews undertaken relating to existing, and potential new, customers
		Within this activity, we should explore specific concerns raised via the "E," the "S," and the "G" arenas. It is recommended that your organization first "brainstorm" internally to "surface" any practical risks and what additional controls and information may be required. In addition, you might compare and contrast elements of this via your trade organization and/or equivalent companies operating in (or adjacent to) your particular business sector.
		Where you are working with direct or indirect competitors, there may be antitrust implications. Take legal advice as necessary, but transparency may be a clear line of defense—try to keep discussions and decisions in the public sphere
G31 Marketing	Sales— determine whether to enter dialogue with potential customer to remedy or address identified risks	There may be opportunities to engage directly with existing (and potential) customers to work collaboratively in reducing or eliminating ESG-type adverse impacts. You may find customers very willing to talk with you and to perceive these discussions as a potential mechanism to make advances in their own ESG journey
		As regards governance standards in particular, some customers may welcome external pressure to "raise their game"
		Customer materiality (G29) may suggest the managerial level at which exploratory dialogue is first engaged in. Nevertheless, at some point, you will need to field the right technical or professional expertise in both organizations, which suggests support from middle managers and other technically qualified personnel
G32 Marketing	Remedial action	Having entered discussions via steps G28 to G30, we can now address problem areas. There may be "quick wins" available that we shall want to secure. Nevertheless, at this point, we factor-in practical steps to "remedy" identified deficiencies

Stage	Description	Detailed Notes
G33	Action Phase	In our high-level roadmap in five sub-"steps," we inserted a "flag" → to move to "Action Phase." It is hugely important that we move beyond the theory and the "white-collar" activity of planning and research, and all the senior to middle management activity suggested in this book, *into doing things at a practical level that will directly and favorably impact our ESG requirements*

An action plan, or project plan, is essential. This was suggested at step G12, but it is plain that there is so much work to do that any plan will be a "living document," continually updated to reflect experience, practical progress, and new learnings or new challenges

Such plans and all that arises from them will require to be securely evidenced in your corporate filing system (audit trail maintained) as suggested at step G14 |
| G34 "3PM" | Determine the link to corporate strategy and policy objectives (G5, G17, G21 to G27, G28 to G32) | This step ensures consistency and "joined-up thinking" as well as "joined-up action" relating to our ESG challenges

It also ensures we do not embark upon strategic initiatives that do not contribute to achieving our corporate goals

Allowing that most organizations have greater leverage with their suppliers than with their customers, a key plank in our earliest "wins" is likely to be achieved via our suppliers. This is true across "E," "S," and "G" subcomponents of the ESG challenge. Our contract management competencies will enable us to reflect ESG tasks into the contractual relationship and then to "manage" them throughout the life of the commercial contract. Our broad "3PM" methodology and competencies will assist here

Even with our key customers, however, there is a contractual element to the relationship that must be proactively managed. Likewise, our broad "3PM" methodology and competencies will assist here. *Remember that your customers may "flowdown" ESG demands to you and specify the achievement of these as a contractual deliverable under the commercial relationship.* If so, you must manage and provide the supporting practical evidence of successful "delivery" |

(*Continued*)

(Continued)

Stage	Description	Detailed Notes
		Governance questions are far less amenable to contractual requirements and to contract clauses than "E" and "S" questions. Where "G" improvements are identified as necessary, the discussions may well be informal and the pressure applied may be oblique rather than direct. The important point is that we should be in a position to say we have recognized the question(s) and have taken action
G35 "3PM"	Explore potential mutual interests and "wins" with 3P	As noted (G34), we can work with our commercial partners, be they suppliers or customers, to achieve wins. Beyond that, in a truly strategic relationship, we may be able to work collaboratively with both customers and suppliers to deliver benefits at various "layers" of the value chain
G36 "3PM"	Establish whether specific ESG targets are best achieved in combination with 3P	*(via contract)* As indicated at step G34, pressure to improve governance standards of third parties is unlikely to be applied via contract commitments *(via noncontract commitments)* There may be a compelling argument that the requirements are not made subject to the contract that governs the relationship, but rather becomes a noncontractual commitment. Depending on the dynamics of the relationship, it may be quicker, easier, or less contentious to make progress in a noncontract deliverable. Progress here may be more dependent on mutual, coinciding, business interests rather than a straight master–servant-type contract relationship. Provided both parties are achieving valuable benefits, this ought to be enough. The "beauty" of the emerging ESG paradigm is that it impacts all sectors of the organizational world in the same way and almost demands a collaborative and collegiate approach throughout the value chain. If we determine on a noncontract relationship, a memorandum of understanding (MoU) style of record may be suitable. This really is a case of "horses for courses" and readers must evaluate what will work best in their business context

Stage	Description	Detailed Notes
G37 "3PM"	Codify objectives	The point here is that irrespective of the decisions at G36, we need to record and monitor our decisions and ensure follow-up or remedial *action* where progress is below what we legitimately expect
		This will link to our audit trail (G14)
E38 "3PM"	Establish RAM measures RAM = *realistic, achievable, and measurable*	G38 overlaps with G37. The key difference is that we are seeking realistic, achievable, and measurable outcomes. Attainment of (or failure to achieve) such outcomes becomes a matter of specific interest between ourselves and our counterparty (whether customer or supplier)
		"What you cannot measure, you cannot manage." To demonstrate our contribution across the ESG task, we need hard evidence that will be meaningful to our varying stakeholder groups, especially regulators
G39 "3PM"	Establish "project" plan(s) (G6, G7)	Remember we are here speaking about establishing 3PM links. For procurement (focusing on the downstream activities of our value chain), *project plans* as regards "E," "S," or "G" can easily be wrapped into our category strategy—or whatever way we style our approach to managing our supply chain
		The governance dimension of the ESG challenge is likely to be focused around our direct impact upon, and interaction with, key suppliers and communities from which we procure, and thence downstream from that, subsupplier and then sub-subsuppliers. However, as noted at G34, governance is more difficult and nuanced than the "E" and "S" subcomponents of ESG
		For sales, the thought process is analogous. With which customers can we, should we, work? What are the issues around key customers and to what extent might adverse governance issues indirectly impact us as a supplier to this customer?
		We will then either (1) create a project plan to deal directly with the customer or (2) wrap such considerations into our broader marketing plan(s)

PART 6

3PM

CHAPTER 19

What Is Third-Party Management?

Outline Definition

Whether public or private sector, organizations today rely increasingly on third parties to deliver mission-critical goods or services. In the United States, "third-party management" tends to be considered as simply *tactical suppliers*, so the term is underutilized and underleveraged there. The management of tactical suppliers in United States is considered to be essentially a software question, with software products supporting *contract management* disciplines.

In Europe, the concept of third-party management is more nuanced, emerging from the schools of risk management and compliance. Here, third parties are considered to be *any organization with which our company has a contractual relationship*, including upstream and downstream in our value chain (downstream = "suppliers", upstream = "customers," loosely defined). Potentially, third-party management may be expanding toward the management of other noncontractual stakeholders, but your author considers this to stretch the concept beyond breaking point. Stakeholders may be considered as "fourth parties," as discussed below.

We repeat, *a third party is one with which your organization has direct contractual relationship*, where a failure of the relationship can impact our performance of our core mission and/or represent a risk to our reputation. In Britain especially, the Financial Conduct Authority (FCA) has long taken a deep interest in "outsourcing" operations, where a financial services firm outsources some aspect of its operations. The view is taken that an organization can "outsource" its activity(ies), but not the responsibility *or legal risk* for correct and professional performance. The FCA introduced the concept of *materiality* in this regard, where a financial services firm is required to assess, in some consistent and well-considered way, the materiality of an outsourced task to the operations of the company. In principle, if the relationship is *high materiality*, then internal management scrutiny is focused accordingly.

Before getting into deep contractual relationships and dependencies, financial services firms are required to exercise an appropriate level of "due diligence" in selecting contracting partners. Under the ESG imperative, this concept is being applied legislatively beyond financial services to any firm meeting certain threshold criteria (e.g., at the time of writing, the German Supply Chain Due Diligence Law). We must expect sophisticated third-party management to become more central to operational management in the 10 years from 2024.

The concept of third-party management has been titled in differing ways, but the most popular are:

- Third-party risk management ("TPRM")
- Third-party risk and relationship management ("TPRRM")
- Third-party management ("TPM" or increasingly "3PM")

Your author finds the last of these, "3PM," to be the optimum.

A Minor Technicality: 1P, 2P, 3P, and 4P

Strictly speaking and in legal terms, a "third party" is "one who is a stranger to a transaction or proceeding" (Osborn's *Concise Law Dictionary*). We speak routinely about third-party liability insurance with this idea. So, the traditional view is that two directly "contracted" parties are effectively party 1 and party 2, and everyone else is a third party. That understanding has stood the test of time and will undoubtedly persist.

In terms of modern organizational management, however, the need for more layered or nuanced understanding has emerged and has begun to change language. The "old" understanding does not quite "fit" with modern realities where there are a range of internal and external relationships that need to be understood and managed. The newer view as regards contractual relationships can best be styled as in Figure 19.1.

1P to 4P

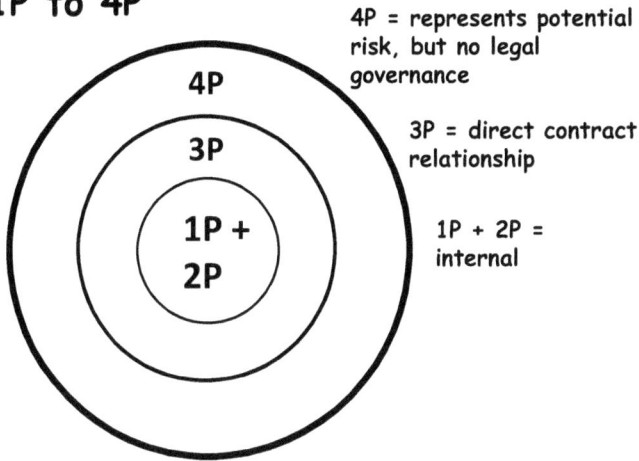

4P = represents potential risk, but no legal governance

3P = direct contract relationship

1P + 2P = internal

Figure 19.1 1P to 4P—contractual relationships

In Figure 19.1, we recognize our organization itself to be party # 1. Whether public or private sector, this is a "corporate legal personality" established under relevant legislation and, as such, can enter into contracts. In this regard, this corporate personality can sue, and be sued, under contract and/or for other civil wrongs (torts).

Within our organization we have employees. These are 2P, yet they work directly for 1P and are recognized as such. While they do have a contractual relationship with 1P (contract of employment), they also owe a *fiduciary duty* to 1P, which is a duty of trust and runs beyond a mere contract of employment. So it is legitimate to place 1P and 2P side by side *within* our inner circle above.

Our 3P relationships are those governed by a formal contract (usually of sale or of supply, but there are other types). It is these direct relationships that have to be managed and where "due diligence" must be exercised before we enter into contractual commitments. 4P are those with which we have an indirect and generally noncontractual relationship. Subcontractor to a prime contractor is one example. "Sub-sub-sub" contractors are another example. Stakeholders, by broad definition, may also be considered as 4P. We have no direct contractual relationship with stakeholders, but we do have a symbiotic relationship which may, or may not, require deliberative "'management."

Who Are Third Parties?

Typically, and in no particular order, third parties that require systematic and ongoing management are:

Key customers: These are customers that are "high materiality" to our firm and with whom we have direct contract relationship that needs to be managed. They will also include smaller customers but they may require a lower level of contractual oversight, depending on circumstances.

Agents: International intermediaries, domestic intermediaries, marketers, and advertisers, sales representatives, resellers, and so on. As *agents*, they may act on your behalf and be perceived as 1P. In Britain, the FCA, in the early 2000s, noted the potential for financial intermediaries (selling financial products on behalf of banks and insurance companies) to be a source of systemic risk and one on which there was insufficient contractual oversight or risk management. The FCA demanded better 3P controls.

Distributors: Dealers and resellers; foreign distributors and their local resellers. Similar implications to agents (above).

Consultants: Management consultants, auditors, lobbyists—generally knowledge-based and professional services.

Contractors: Often "key suppliers" and outsourcing firms. Also, temporary employees as "contractor staff."

Joint ventures: Partnerships and international joint ventures (dealers, factories, and "'badged" manufacturing).

Suppliers: All those organizations that "supply" directly to us. Some may consider these to be "contractors" by a broader definition. Typically, suppliers are those who supply goods or services, but have no ongoing or significant *on-site* work. While suppliers may seem financially and operationally to represent a lower risk, they can represent a heightened degree of reputation risk in ESG terms—think "sweat-shop labor."

Vendors: The distinction from "suppliers" is minor. We can say, however, that bespoke maintenance, on-demand *service* suppliers, offshore service suppliers, and outsourcing specialists are often thought of as "vendors."

Plainly, some of these terms overlap and there is no universally agreed definition, but the above are generally recognized as helpful and relevant. These third-party relationships require deliberative and often ongoing management ("3PM").

Why Does It Matter?

There are a number of reasons why 3PM is increasingly important. Of direct interest to this book, our *third parties* are undoubtedly an avenue toward closer ESG implementation, management, and progress. We explore this in the pages that follow. Besides this, we can cite three other compelling considerations:

1. *Increased globalization*: As markets expand and competition becomes fiercer, so engagement in overseas markets becomes potentially more attractive; yet, at the same time, this increases risk exposure. Foreign intermediaries can be a special risk in terms of bribery and corruption, for which we may be held liable.
2. *Growing reliance on third parties*: Organizational exposure is growing apace. Offshoring and engagement with intermediaries may have stalled (at the time of writing, and pursuant to the COVID-19 pandemic and Russia–Ukraine conflict), but seem set to resume at some point.
3. *Increasing enforcement*: The U.K. Bribery Act and equivalent legislation, outsourcing risk rules via the Financial Conduct Authority (FCA), antislavery moves, and the German Supply Chain Due Diligence Law (2023), which is likely to be emulated elsewhere. We can repeat: the direction of travel in 3PM is plain to see. Organizations need to "up their game" in managing this ever more effectively.

Benefits of "Getting It Right"

Navex Global, a U.S.-based *specialist* in integrated risk and compliance management software (and services), conducted a survey in 2016 which revealed that one-third of respondent organizations had experienced legal or regulatory issues involving third parties, and half of these involved direct costs of £8,000 or more. Reputational harm, however, is difficult to measure and may well dwarf direct monetary on-costs. Without going into detail, which others have well covered in the literature and media, we can summarize the benefits of effective and robust 3PM as:

- Avoid fines, regulatory enforcements, and legal costs.
- Promote our organizational values and culture.
- Create a more accurate and realistic appreciation ("map") of risk.
- Promote continuity (especially, in the supply chain).
- Protect our organization's reputation.

3PM and ESG

As we explore in the next few chapters, resolving many of the questions we face in ESG—and especially in its "E" and "S" subcomponents—does not lie fully within our control. It is only via third parties up and down our value chain that we can make real inroads and gain real traction on active mechanisms to make progress. ESG provisions need to be built in to 3P relationships, including sometimes into the commercial contracts we have with our third parties.

A factor sometimes ignored in the rush to achieve burnished environmental credentials or improved social outcomes is that "doing the right thing" as regards ESG can help to drive competitive advantage. This is suggested in Figure 19.2.

ESG pressures impact our third parties, often in much the same way that they impact our own organization. We will unquestionably take into account sales and supply markets (see Figures 20.4 and 20.5) and link these to our ESG targeting and responses. ISO[1] standards may provide

---

[1] International Standards Organization.

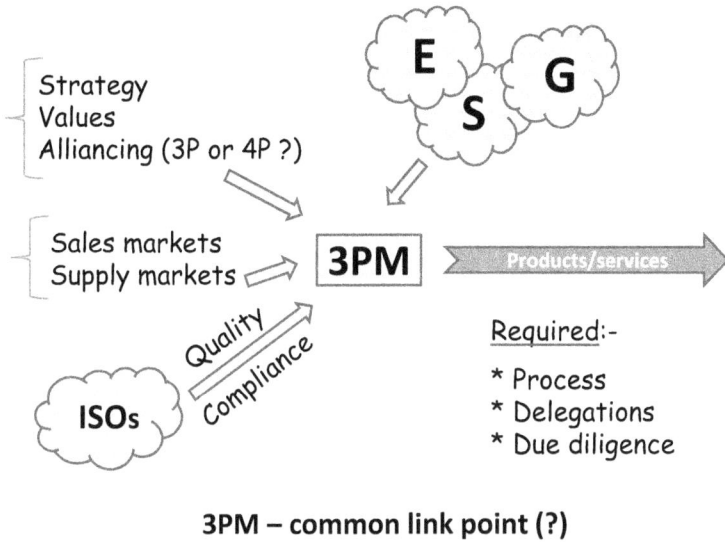

3PM – common link point (?)

Figure 19.2 3PM—competitive advantage via business relationships

an obvious mechanism to meet, or help move us toward meeting, certain *specific* technical needs and objectives. These ISO standards have the clear advantage of broad acceptance and acceptability. Our own strategy and values will be considered *in regard to* third-party relationships: To what extent are these shared or transferable? And within that there might be the opportunity for some form of joint venture, "partnership" (loose definition) or "alliancing" arrangement that may move us more quickly toward ESG "wins." To what extent does "third party risk and relationship management" (3PM) provide a common link-point in your business sector?

Third-party dynamics, especially measured in terms of "relationship," increasingly provide opportunities for mutual win–win outcomes. In Figure 19.3, we compare what "sits" under the heading of 3PM (left of the schematic) and under ESG (right side). There may be differences, but there are certainly fairly obvious "overlaps." Under 3PM, we find the overarching need for policies, procedures, and protocols for engaging with 3P organizations, risk assessment, relationship definition, and ongoing management. There may be a measure of technological support in *relationship management*, as well as training in optimum management techniques. Certainly, there will be requirements for collection and preservation of data on performance and external questions such as environmental GHG

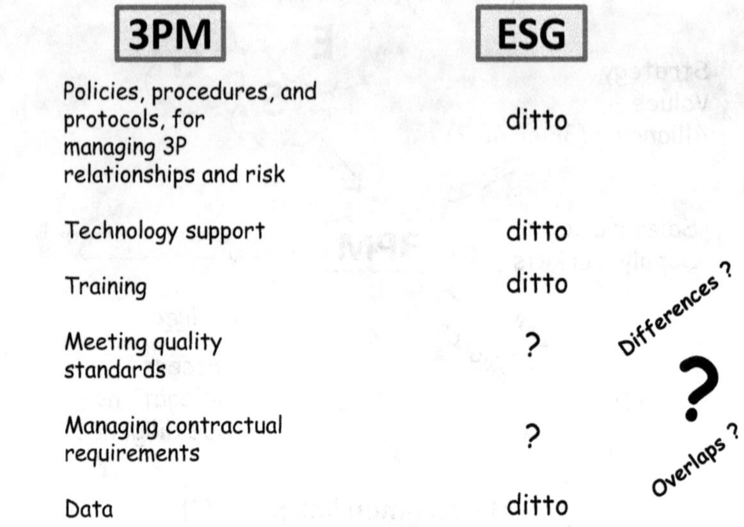

3PM	ESG	
Policies, procedures, and protocols, for managing 3P relationships and risk	ditto	
Technology support	ditto	
Training	ditto	Differences?
Meeting quality standards	?	**?**
Managing contractual requirements	?	Overlaps?
Data	ditto	

Figure 19.3 Link 3PM and "E," "S," and "G"

reporting. In each of these areas, there is likely to be a coinciding interest with the external 3P.

Where we have used query marks above (?), there will again be potential opportunity for *jointly* meeting quality standards and managing the contract(s) in an aligned manner. Certainly, there will be differences in pressures, practices, and perceptions, but there will likely be many "overlaps" and mutual interests to be exploited. In the field of professional procurement, in particular, for the past 20 years, there have been calls for greater and more expert SRM (supplier relationship management) measures, to align interests and secure better overall value. Will ESG provide further impetus to realize this ambition? Addressing Scope 1, 2, and 3 GHG emissions provides the most pressing common-interest area at the time of writing this book. We explore this in our next chapter.

CHAPTER 20

How Can Third Parties Help?

Scope 1, 2, and 3

Many organizations in the western world are required to actively report their GHG emissions as well as evidence progress in reducing them. Claiming that we buy our power from supposedly "renewable" sources is no longer adequate to meet the rising demand for accuracy, verity, and transparency. Furthermore, over time, we are all expected to be able to *demonstrate* progress in reducing GHG *actual* emissions. Please see Appendix 3 for more insight into Scope 1, 2, and 3.

It is well understood that Scope 3 emissions are those most amendable to joint action. Accordingly, if your organization is a large one with clear reduction commitments, then to work with customers and suppliers and align the strategy to GHG emission reductions can prove to be a valuable mutual "win." Downstream (supplier) emissions might be expected in:

- Employee commuting
- Business travel
- Waste generated in operations
- Transportation and distribution
- Fuel and energy use
- Capital goods
- Purchased goods
- Leased assets

Upstream (customer) emissions might be expected in:

- Transportation and distribution
- Processing of sold products

- Use of sold products
- End-of-life treatment of sold products
- Leased assets
- Franchises
- Investments

Both customers and suppliers as "third parties" may be very happy to talk with you about strategies to reduce GHG. Beyond this, your normal "third-party" arrangements may provide opportunities for improvements in the "S" dynamic of ESG. Think, for example, of *modern slavery* demands, supplier due diligence demands, and the continued existence of "sweat shops." While many businesses have sought to distance themselves from direct involvement with infringing third parties, especially suppliers, it is true to say that few businesses have visibility beyond their direct suppliers ("tier 1") and possibly direct subcontractors or subsuppliers to tier 1 ("tier 2"). Likewise, "tier 2" may have little sense of their own "downstream" world, so there is an emphatic *information gap* affecting not only ESG questions but also supply security questions.

Third-party management (3PM) is a mechanism that "bridges" a number of "gaps" in our visibility, and in our ability to achieve significant

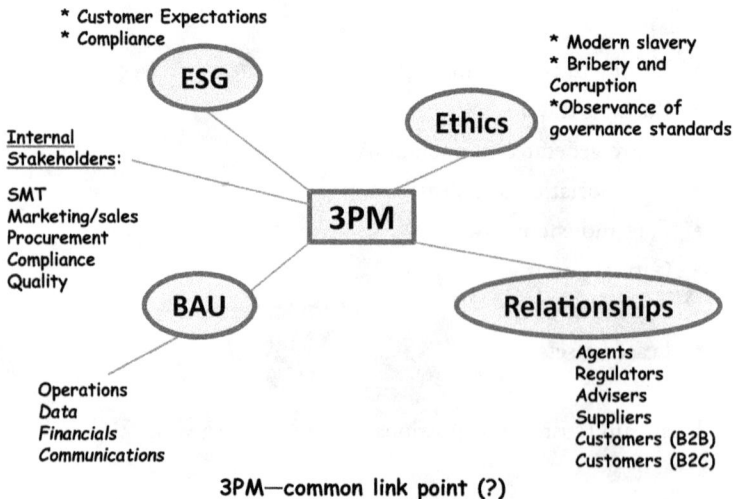

Figure 20.1 *3PM and ESG—bigger picture—common link point*

ESG "wins." Figure 20.1 considers the bigger picture of 3PM and ESG. 3PM is a common link-point in broad governance as well as in day-to-day operations. 3PM directly influences business as usual ("BAU") operations. And, within these operations, we generate considerable data and financial reports. These must be managed and understood—and acted upon. Where data emerges from our third-party relationships, remember that it may need to be protected under varying data protection rules.

ESG, as we see above, directly influences 3PM and "managing" our third parties—again "suppliers" are perhaps the most obvious example. On the *ethical* side of our business, there may be pressing questions that require better defined relationships with third-party organizations. "Modern slavery" has long been an ethical question, but today it is a regulatory reporting question as well. Anti bribery and corruption measures ("ABC measures") will also find actualization via our third-party relationships. In this fairly basic way, we can see that third-party management provides a common link point. For many organizations, the question is: *How good is our 3PM management?* Readers may want to pause here and do a quick "stock-take" on your 3PM capabilities.

Sustainability is, at the time of writing in 2024, a key agenda item for all management boards, whether private or public sector. As Sustainability sits "at the center," so 3PM can be seen as a potential delivery mechanism for worthwhile ESG or Sustainability advances. This is suggested in Figure 20.2. Here, we recognize that ESG or Sustainability responses can be focused both inwards and outwards. On the left of our illustration, we see that "S" and "E" focus will be broadly external, while "G" focus is principally directed inwards.

In terms of Sustainability, the EU taxonomy helps advance our discussions internally as we try to unravel what are, and where are, our main "emissions" areas. Of course, this will be a discussion we shall also have with our key suppliers (and perhaps key customers too), so the taxonomy approach also has an outward focus. In Figure 20.2, the reference to "S list," "E list," and "G list" directs our thoughts toward *practical* measures and these lists are found in relevant sections of this book (chapters 11, 14 and 17). Straddling both sides of our responses are our key motivators for making progress. There is plainly a self-interest dynamic to this: the profitability of, and "license to operate" for, our business demands that we do

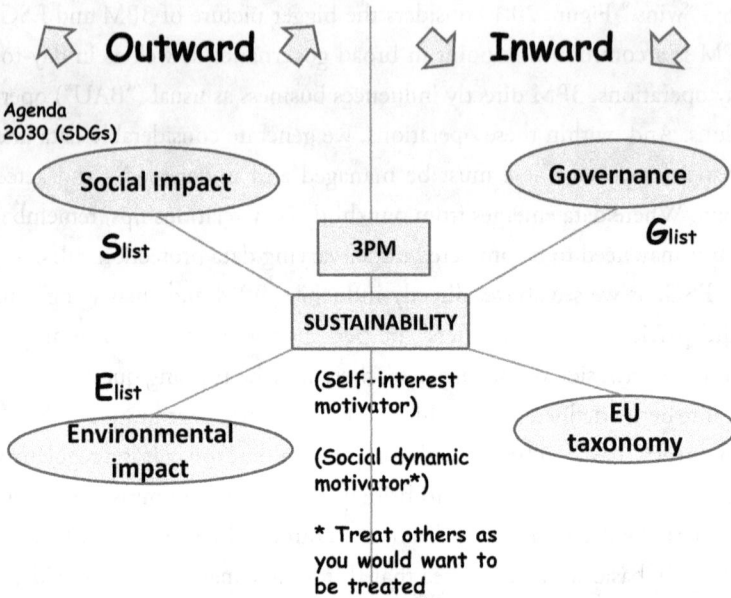

Outward | **Inward**

Agenda
2030 (SDGs)

Social impact | Governance

S~list~ | 3PM | G~list~

SUSTAINABILITY

E~list~ | (Self-interest motivator)

Environmental impact | EU taxonomy

(Social dynamic motivator*)

* Treat others as you would want to be treated

Figure 20.2 Sustainability at the core [the same schematic as in Figure 1.1]

the right thing and are seen to do the right thing. As we meet internal or external targets, our long-term interests as an organization are also served.

Another motivator is unquestionably the broadly social dynamic of the personal values and expectations of our staff. Our staff wish to know whether they are working for an organization that recognizes its place and its impact in the business ecosphere, and its broader social obligations, and is active in "doing its bit" to make the world a more equitable place. This motivation might be "measured" in the old idea of staff morale and staff commitment to their employer. Our main "takeaway" from Figure 20.2 should be the recognition that third-party risk and relationship management (3PM) is an increasingly valuable tool in burnishing our ESG credentials and meeting necessary practical targets.

Leverage: With Whom Can We Work?

There's an old saying: "the customer is king." Most organizations recognize the axiomatic importance of their customer base, or in public service terms, those stakeholders we are required to serve within our overarching mission task. The truth of the matter, however, especially in the private commercial sphere, is that not all customers are "equal." We can adapt a well-known phrase[1] from George Orwell's famous novel, *Animal Farm*, when we say "all customers are equal, but some customers are more equal than others!" This in turn implies there are some customers, and indeed some suppliers, with whom we have more "leverage" than others. We shall explore this shortly. We should reflect for a moment on the big components of the 3PM world. As suggested several times in this book, we need to have a thorough-going insight and understanding of our entire business context, that is, a *sine qua non* in strategy development and execution. Beyond this, there are several "components" to strategic management. These are suggested in Figure 20.3. The schematic reminds us that in our business ecosphere, there are four major components to be controlled and managed. Above the horizontal line is the broadly "external" picture. Porter's Five Forces help us to understand and characterize our entire business rationale. Within Five Forces analysis, ESG is today recognized as a distinct subcomponent, which impacts up and down our value chain. As a part of any Five Forces analysis, Sustainability considerations inevitably play their part. Kraljic *supplier positioning* is a technique that, today, commands almost universal acceptance as a method to "view" our entire supplier portfolio and is a valuable addition to Porter's Five Forces.

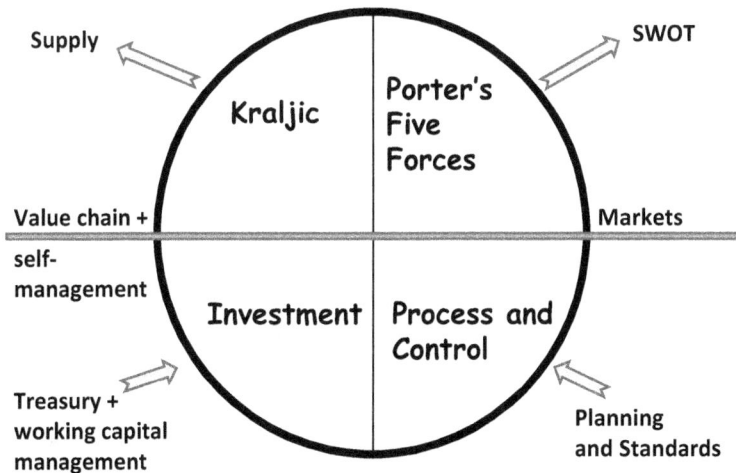

Figure 20.3 3P components—the big picture—external and internal

---

Without delving into detail, Kraljic helps us to establish which suppliers are "material" in terms of supply risk and economic importance. More on this in a moment ....

Below the horizontal line in Figure 20.3 are located the broadly internal considerations of financing ("investment") and internal process and controls. Whereas *above* the line, we focus on *external* markets and our value chain, *below* the line we focus on those *internal* matters that are essentially about self-management. Internal management, in ESG terms, is where we identify what we need to do to establish, characterize, and progress toward our ESG targets. The external world, *above* our horizontal line, provides the biggest opportunities to "make a difference" and to engage with our value chain to (mutually?) reengineer management processes, materials, mechanisms, production processes, energy mix, and social impact of operations and investment. Above the line, we are addressing mainly the "E" and "S" subcomponents of the ESG challenge. Below the line, we focus more on the "G" subcomponent.

In terms of leverage and who we can (or preferably should) work with, let us consider briefly *Kraljic supply market segmentation*. The idea, in brief, is that we broadly " segment" our suppliers into *four categories*, which are identified by reference to supply risk (from low to high) and financial expenditure (from low to high). This gives us a simple four-box matrix where high-spend and high-risk are "located" in the top right-hand box and low-spend and low-risk in the lower left-hand box. Pareto's 80–20 rule maps across this matrix quite naturally, with 80 percent of spend in the top right-hand box and the remaining three boxes (generally speaking) accounting for the remaining 20 percent. We do not need to investigate this further, here, as the technique is well-enough known and applied in the world of supply management—your organization may already routinely apply this methodology. The ESG facet to focus on, however, is this: your key or strategic suppliers are the ones with which you have most leverage and where there is likely to be greatest amenability to working *collaboratively* to achieve ESG targets.

In Figure 20.4, the left-hand side shows the Kraljic segmentation and typical "titles" applied to segmented suppliers (acquisition, leverage, bottleneck, and strategic). What is sometimes forgotten, especially by Procurement people (!), is that the supply market itself has an analogous

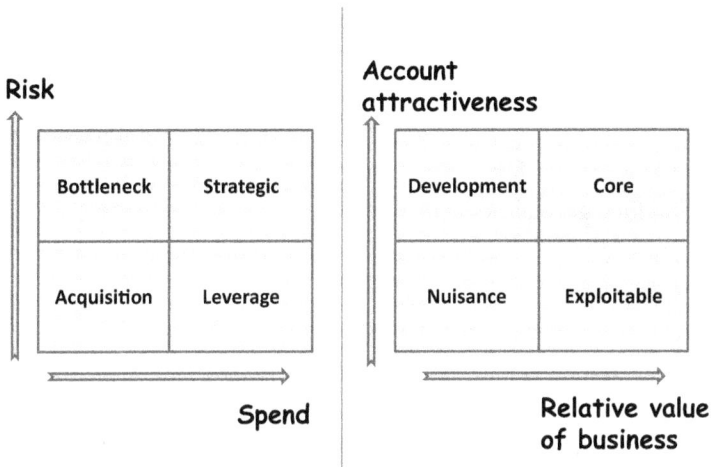

Figure 20.4 *How we see each other—supplier segmentation versus account attractiveness*

methodology to "view" potential customers, often dubbed the "account attractiveness matrix." As its name suggests, this helps to segment potential customers into how "attractive" they are in terms of revenue generation and the advancement of our marketing goals. In the salesman's world, the customer is not always "King!" The customer may, in fact, be a *nuisance*!

Again, we do not need to investigate this in detail. But, in outline, the four-box matrix, above, demonstrates that high-spend and high strategic attractiveness of a particular customer make that customer a "core" customer. Viewing the two matrixes side by side, we can draw this clear and simple conclusion: where *strategic suppliers* meet with *core customer* sentiments, it is within these overlapping commercial relationships that we are likely to secure most interest in ESG collaboration. The final point we make about leverage[2] here is that it is downstream in the value chain where your organization will be seen to have most influence or power. To

---

[2] Note that the Kraljic term "leverage" in the supplier positioning matrix refers to something rather different. In supply management (procurement) terms, a *leverage supplier* is one with whom we can expect to exploit our bargaining power to drive reduced prices and/or improved trading terms.

use another ancient cliché, "he who pays the piper, calls the tune," which we can translate as *the organization that is spending money, especially if they are viewed as a core customer, can leverage that relationship and can place Sustainability issues firmly on the agenda.* In these relationships, ESG considerations may well be on both parties' to-do list, in any case.

The final general point in this question of *how can third parties help* in terms of ESG is that "leverage" will have more "traction" downstream in the value chain.

In Figure 20.5, we reflect on "leverage" in the value chain context. Our organization sits in the center of our value chain. Within that, we have 3PM available as a management tool helping us govern relationships and get the most out of them, hopefully to achieve genuine "win–win" outcomes. It is likely that it is with our "suppliers" that we shall have most "traction" in terms of keeping ESG considerations "on the radar," but there may be increasing interest among organizations in different "tiers" of the value chain in collaborating to achieve favorable ESG outcomes. Certainly, a little thought and imagination must be invested to make this happen, but we are likely to discover a mutuality of interest. Figure 20.5 reminds us that with our suppliers we have a *contractual* relationship. The key question becomes: to what extent do we reflect ESG imperatives into

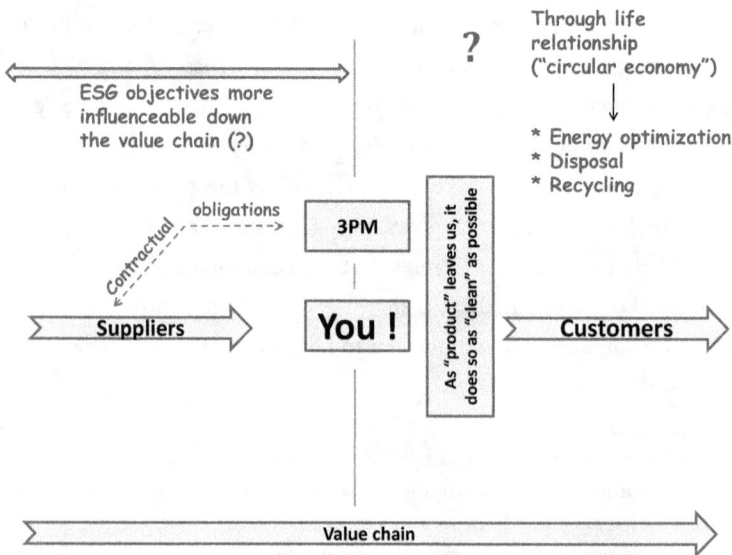

Figure 20.5 ESG—3P leverage

the contractual *terms*? Should these be a contractual requirement and, in some sense, material to the deliverables under the contract?

Imposing Obligations

To what extent should we seek to impose ESG obligations *as a contractual requirement?* This is a developing field and under active discussion, at the time of writing this book. Ideas are evolving slowly, and we do not presently (2024) have "case law" to guide us. Your author's view is that we should be cautious about imposing yet more contractual obligations on third parties. It may well be that we can (and should) expect third parties such as suppliers and contractors to work within the broad thrust of our ESG requirements. But as these can be nebulous and difficult to measure, in terms of "carrot and stick" incentives it is perhaps "the carrot" that will prove to be more effective, and sustainability benefits might be sought that can best be measured via KPIs[3] or SLAs[4] that do not have to be immediately contractual. In one policy document *guidance note* known to your author, this comment was made:

> Third parties such as contractors and suppliers are expected to work within the general spirit of [*Organization's*] personnel protection efforts but are not expected to directly apply our Policy. Clear and egregious cases of breach of this, or any other, Policy may be addressed under any contract between the parties.

While it is not unreasonable to expect third parties to work broadly aligned to our policy(ies) and to be aware of any specific *mission objectives* or *values statements* that we have, we do not want to attempt to pull third parties directly under our "policies." If we do, it is possible we might undermine the terms of any commercial contract(s) between ourselves and the corresponding third party. A commercial contract is certainly the place to specify requirements and/or "conditions," but only ones that are achievable and measurable.

---

[3] Key performance indicators.
[4] Service-level agreements.

If an ESG requirement is "measurable" and with a high degree of certainty and specificity, then to frame it as a contractual requirement is entirely reasonable. So, and for example, in terms of the social objective of any *modern slavery* requirements specified, a contractual demand might be framed in this way:

> Contractor undertakes in its supply chain to review and examine all contracted suppliers to their third tier [supplier > subsupplier > sub-subsupplier] in order to identify material risks in the sphere of modern slavery as specified in the U.K. Modern Slavery Act 2015. Contractor undertakes to make available such records of review(s) as required by [our organization] as may reasonably be required. Contractor undertakes to challenge subsupplier behavior that breaches the letter or the spirit of the Modern Slavery Act 2015 (or equivalent legislation, where relevant) and in the absence of material progress toward elimination of such behaviors, to deselect such suppliers from their supplier portfolio. Furthermore, the contractor undertakes to keep [our organization] fully informed of such questions in a proactive manner.

The immediately foregoing would be considered realistic, achievable, and measurable. However, were we to sue our supplier for breach of contract in the event that it egregiously failed to manage this objective of our contractual relationship, might we lay ourselves open to a counterclaim in the event that we were found to be "delinquent" in the management of *our own* direct modern slavery obligations? That is why, at the time of writing this book, there remains an argument for handling some (or all) ESG requirements off-contract, and instead via KPIs linked to an SLA, which might be deemed semi-contractual, and via which said *third parties* can be effectively managed in the ESG sphere, especially if there is a coinciding mutuality of interest.

Characterizing Third-Party Relationships

To round off our discussion on how and where third parties can help, we can reflect on the "type" of 3P and what sort of "agreement" we might typically reach with them. The first question is: Are we involved in consumer sales—are our customers "ordinary" consumers, such as found in the FMCG sector? The recognized term describing such relationships is "B2C" (business-to-consumer). If so, then our relationship with our customers may be fleeting and irregular. In terms of ESG requirements, the ability of the consumer to directly help may be very limited. If, conversely, the relationship is business-to-business (or "B2B"), then opportunities will be much broader. Figure 20.6 summarizes these ideas.

A follow-on comment we can make is that we have broad options in considering how to work with our third parties along the value chain. If our relationship is B2C, then it is principally via "the circular economy" that we find opportunities for consumers to play a role in the "E" and possibly "S" subcomponents of ESG. But, if our relationship is B2B, then the opportunities are considerable and varied. On the right-hand side of our schematic, we see defined contractual relationships, largely of the "master–servant" variety, where one party pays the other for goods or services rendered. In that sort of relationship, we may be able to define specific "deliverables" as regards ESG. If our requirements are considerable, or extensive, then the counterparty will want some form of commitment to a solid and ongoing relationship, especially if they are expected to invest financially ("at risk") to secure ESG wins. Where the relationship is less defined, then some form of "alliancing" structure

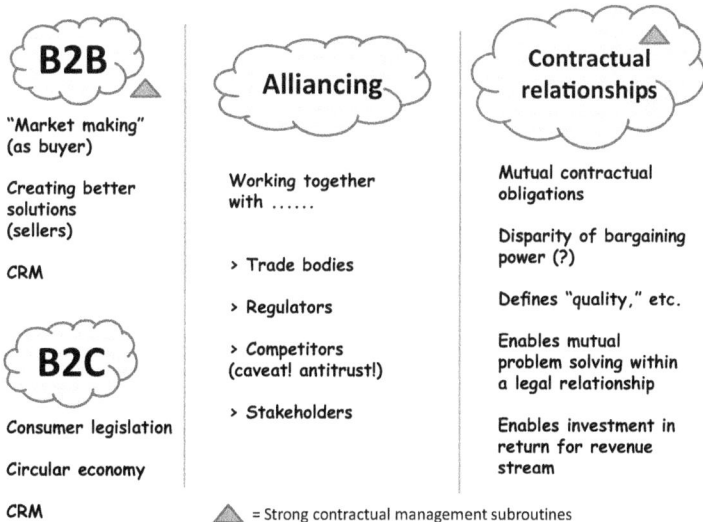

B2B

"Market making"
(as buyer)

Creating better
solutions
(sellers)

CRM

B2C

Consumer legislation

Circular economy

CRM

Alliancing

Working together
with ......

> Trade bodies

> Regulators

> Competitors
(caveat! antitrust!)

> Stakeholders

= Strong contractual management subroutines

**Contractual
relationships**

Mutual contractual
obligations

Disparity of bargaining
power (?)

Defines "quality," etc.

Enables mutual
problem solving within
a legal relationship

Enables investment in
return for revenue
stream

Figure 20.6 ESG—characterizing 3P relationships

might bridge the gap; we may be able to work mutually in alliance with others toward favorable ESG outcomes, seeking win–win opportunities. The range of "stakeholders" involved may be much broader in this sort of scenario. Where strong and systemized *contract management*[5] subroutines are likely to be required, this is indicated, above, in the triangular pyramid symbol. We repeat that where the relationship is defined by a clear "master–servant" or "buy–sell" dynamic, we need to be careful that we are "flowing down" to the counterparty targets that can legitimately be handled by them. There is an old truism that "contract risk should lie where it is best managed." If you are best able to manage a specific risk, then do in fact shoulder that risk; do not try to offload it to the counterparty.

---

[5] The author's book "Contract Management—Core Business Competence" may be useful if your organization is reconsidering its present approach to entering-into, and subsequently managing, commercial contracts.

CHAPTER 21

Opening the Conversation With Third Parties

It Is Good to Talk (1)

It is relatively straightforward to establish whether, and how, we might be able to work with third parties, at least in outline. If yours is a trading organization and you trade in products known to entail material ESG considerations, especially of the "E" and "S'" variety, and if you are heavily dependent on third-party suppliers or have a few, very major distributors, then any "due diligence" considerations applying to you will likely also apply to your major counterparties.

In this chapter, we open up suggestions for general avenues for discussion and encourage readers to "see" this question in terms of relationship management generally, which will also have a degree of formal and informal *negotiation* entailed. Be aware of this *negotiation dynamic* and ensure that all discussions are entered into with appropriate insight into your organization's broad relationship objectives; do not work in a silo! Where necessary, upgrade your corporate negotiations capability, if you think this may be under performing. Having warned about this underlying consideration, let us not overcomplicate things. Providing certain discussions are recognized and understood to be informal, and in a real sense *without prejudice*, then we should feel comfortable that we can be open and direct within the normal bounds of commercial confidentiality. Discussions can be purely exploratory, yet still valuable and advance our mutual agendas.

Before we consider generic areas for discussion, we focus briefly on German legislation effective 1 January 2023, which has broader implications beyond Germany. The expectations are that (1) this legislation will capture many organizations domiciled outside Germany and (2) the legislation may be emulated in other countries.

On 1 January 2023, the Lieferkettensorgfaltspflichtengesetz (Lieferkettengesetz or LkSG) came into effect in Germany. Known in English as the German *Supply Chain Due Diligence Act* (SCDDA), the law mandates companies with offices in Germany to conduct due diligence on their supply chains to protect human rights and the environment. With up to 800,000 Euros in fines, restricted market access, and potential for lawsuits, compliance for many organizations will be a major concern. Under SCDDA, German companies are obligated to establish processes to identify, assess, prevent, and remedy violations of human rights and the environment in their supply chain. Such violations could occur at all levels of the chain. The Act, therefore, impacts both direct and indirect suppliers.

SCDDA—Which Companies Are Affected?

As of 1 January 2023: Companies with at least 3,000 employees that have their head office, administrative seat, or statutory seat in Germany OR companies that have a branch in Germany and usually employ at least 3,000 employees in this branch

As of 1 January 2024: Companies with at least 1,000 employees that have their head office, administrative seat, or statutory seat in Germany OR companies that have a branch in Germany and usually employ at least 1,000 employees in this branch.

Group companies are included in calculations of the number of employees of the parent company. Temporary workers are included where duration of their assignment exceeds six months. Smaller companies are *indirectly* affected because directly affected organizations are obliged to enforce *compliance*, to the best of their ability, in their own supply chain. Measures implementing this have direct impact on subsuppliers, for example, through the implementation of a code of conduct. In addition, directly affected companies are often dependent on the active support of suppliers, so they will want to have this support contractually assured, for example, in the form of detailed reporting obligations and KPIs[1].

---

[1] KPIs = key performance indicators.

Companies impacted must make reasonable efforts to ensure that there are no violations of human rights in their own business operations or in their supply chain. *The SCDDA explicitly clarifies that a duty of effort is mandated, but not a duty to succeed.* Record keeping and audit will be increasingly important in order to demonstrate compliance.

SCDDA—Own Business Operations, Supply Chain, and Human Rights

"Own operations" covers any activity for production and exploitation of products and for provision of services, regardless of whether it is carried out at a domestic or foreign location. "Supply chain"-affected companies must conduct a formal risk analysis and implement remedial measures for *indirect* suppliers, where it gains substantiated knowledge of possible human rights violations or violations of environmental obligations.

Human rights violations are derived from internationally recognized agreements, in particular the International Labour Organization (ILO) *core labor standards*. The SCDDA defines human rights risks as child and forced labor as well as modern slavery, disregard of labor protection obligations including freedom of association, inequality or withholding of adequate wage, certain environmental pollution relevant to human rights, as well as land deprivation, torture and cruel, inhuman, or degrading treatment.

SCDDA references the environment to the extent that environmental damage leads to human rights violations and mandates corporate due diligence obligations including environment-related obligations arising from (1) the *Minamata Convention* (risks from involvement in the production and disposal of mercury-containing products), (2) the *PoPs Convention* (risks from the production or use of certain persistent organic pollutants), and (3) the *Basel Convention* (risks from the import and export of waste).

SCDDA—What Measures Must Be Taken?

What an organization must do depends on (i) the nature and scope of its business, (ii) the company's ability to influence the immediate violator, (iii) the expected severity of the violation, (iv) the reversibility of the violation, (v) the likelihood of the violation occurring, and (vi) the nature of the contribution to causation. Within this the following five actions are to be taken:

1. **Risk management and risk analysis**
   Organizations must adapt their existing risk management accordingly, determining whether there is a risk that their own business activities or business activities in the supply chain violate human rights.

2. **Policy statement**
   Organizations must publish a policy statement on their human rights strategy, including procedure for abiding by human rights and environmental due diligence obligations in their supply chain, specific risks identified, and the company's human rights and environmental expectations of its employees and suppliers.

3. **Preventive and remedial measures**
   Based on risk analysis, companies must take or review appropriate preventive and remedial measures. This applies, for example, to supplier selection and supplier monitoring, the creation of codes of conduct, implementation of training courses, and also sustainable contract drafting.

4. **Complaints procedure**
   Organizations must establish, implement, and publish a complaint mechanism in writing through which (potentially) affected persons and persons with knowledge of possible violations can highlight human rights risks and violations.

5. **Documentation and reporting obligations**
   Fulfillment of human rights-related due diligence obligations must be documented. In addition, a report must be prepared and published annually. The report must also be submitted to "the competent authority" in Germany.

SCDDA—Penalties for Violations

Fines for violations of due diligence and reporting obligations of up to EUR 8 million depending on the nature and gravity of the violation.

Note: Companies with an average annual turnover of more than EUR 400 million may be fined up to 2 percent of their average annual turnover for breaches of the obligation to take remedial action or to implement an appropriate remedial action plan at a direct supplier.

Exclusion from public tenders for up to three years. The SCDDA does not provide for any extension of civil liability.

Note: Even if it is unlikely that a German company will be liable for misconduct on the part of a supplier abroad, liability under general (tort) principles in German law (in particular, duties of care) is still possible. Thus, if the damage occurs in another country, the laws of that country—and thus not the SCDDA—will be generally applicable.

At European Union Level

Adjacent to the SCDDA (see immediately above), the European Union is seeking to harmonize legislation and standards across the bloc. At the time of writing this book, the EU had made a proposal on general corporate and supply chain due diligence, which was expected to be enacted in subordinate legislation. Aspects of the EU proposal may find their way into domestic legislation in advance of any wider directives. In essence, that is what Germany did with its SCDDA. We summarize this in Figure 21.1.

This schematic reminds us that the European Union's ambition is to impact large companies directly (implying smaller companies will be impacted indirectly). Group 1 companies are the earliest to be captured under expected legislation, with Group 2 following on at some unstated future point. Both groups are defined by financial turnover plus employee numbers and will have environmental and human rights monitoring obligations extending into supply chains. At the time of writing, this is a "proposal" at EU level, but it expected to be followed up by a formal directive (identified as "Z" in our schematic), which will, in turn, become national legislation. The EU's ambitions here are quite clear.

There are seven specific obligations set out in the proposal, which we summarize in Figure 21.2.

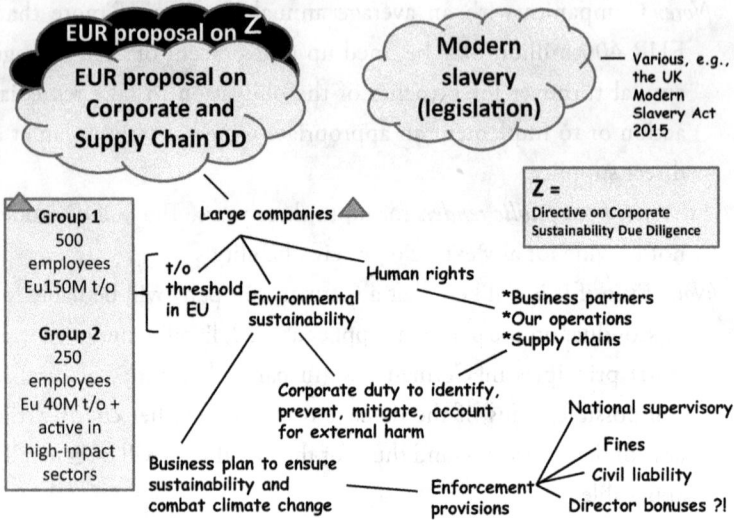

Figure 21.1 *Corporate and supply chain due diligence (1)*

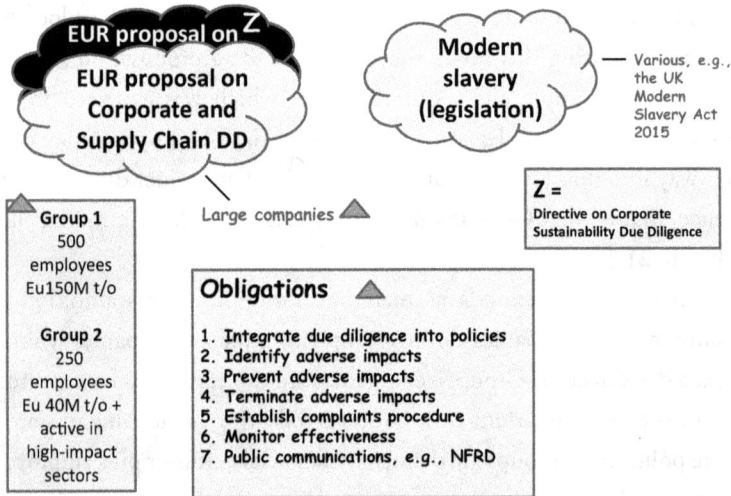

Figure 21.2 *Corporate and supply chain due diligence (2)*

We will not examine these seven obligations in detail; in fact, the summary points above are adequate for our purposes, reminding us of the scope and extent of the EU's ambitions. The *direction of travel* is clear and, one way or another, will demand specific 3PM subroutines to assist in monitoring progress. We repeat the general comment that organizations must work closely with their key suppliers to meet the demands being made upon them. While all this legislation will apply within the European Union bloc, it will undoubtedly become a benchmark for *supply chain due diligence* globally. There will be a ripple effect ....

It Is Good to Talk (2)

Within our value chain and our broad range of 3P (third-party) relationships, there will be synergies and coinciding interests in the ESG field, as in other fields. This will prompt many organizations toward what we might call a *360-degree global response* as they look thoroughly, and search in every direction, for tangible benefits from, and methods to comply with, new regulatory demands. At this point, some readers may feel disheartened that they face a mountain of regulatory and compliance work with potentially low "payback" in terms of increased efficiencies and reduced costs. Yet, a positive attitude applied to all of this will evince that within these heightened regulatory demands, lie new possibilities, *and the long-term payback may be reduced costs and even enhanced market presence.* Consumers, in particular, are willing to reward good corporate behavior (and are quick to punish bad). Corporate clients are looking for aligned outcomes, especially in the regulated sphere. It's not all bad news!

Opening up a dialogue with major clients or customers is likely to devolve around what products or services we currently sell and what is the market seeking in the future—and is there a mismatch? What "E," "S," and "G" benefits do we believe are achievable and what might the upfront costs be? If we make specific proposals to the market regarding improved products and services, how does the market view these benefits? Can we "sell" to the market not only the product (or service) but also the anticipated future "E," "S," and "G" benefits? What is this "worth" to the market? Does the seller work "at risk" or is the client willing to "partner" with key suppliers to secure benefits and potentially shoulder some of the investment required? Where might we work together? Where must we work apart?

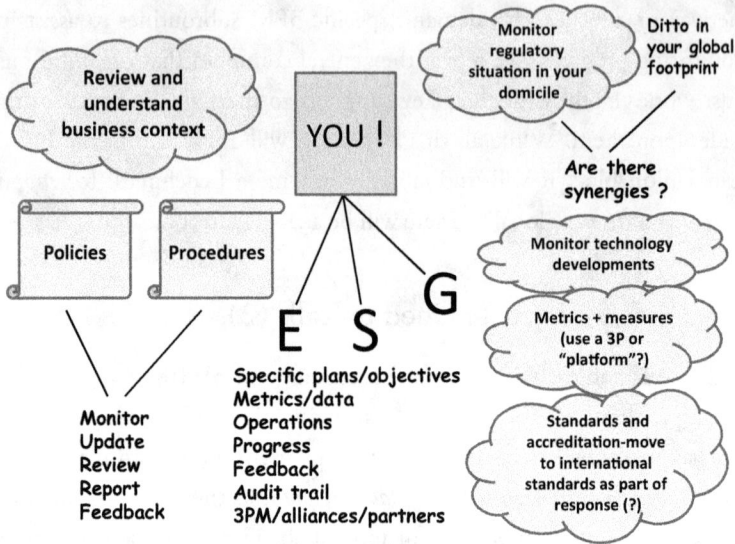

Figure 21.3 360-degree global response

A 360-degree response will entail many of the features summarized in Figure 21.3. In this schematic, our organization sits in the middle ("YOU!") with ESG concerns feeding-in. Our response to these concerns will have an outworking in planning, operations, third-party relationships, and audit trail. At some point, we are likely to have to formally amend policies and procedures. Beyond that, we must "stay on top" of the evolving regulatory landscape and proactively monitor technological developments. Some of these may offer significant opportunities to hasten progress toward achieving our ESG obligations.

Opening a dialogue with suppliers is generally more straightforward than with customers. In principle, the "buyer" has a certain degree of influence over the "supplier," within the limitations explored in Chapter 20. Our next chapter provides some perspectives on engaging with suppliers.

CHAPTER 22

Developing the Conversation With Third Parties

It Is Good to Talk (3)

It should be relatively straightforward to establish whether, and how, we might work with third parties—at least in outline. If yours is a commercial organization and you trade in products known to entail material ESG challenges, especially of the "E" and "S" variety, and if you are heavily dependent on third-party suppliers or have a few very major distributors, then any "ESG due diligence" considerations applying to you will likely also apply to your major counterparties.

As regards the "E" and the "S" aspects[1] of ESG, many organizations recognize that they can make little progress without the full participation of their suppliers. Absolutely essential to success is the accurate, current, and complete supplier data. Here, we are speaking about data on specific question relating to the Sustainability challenge, typically:

"E"

- Energy consumption or sources
- Land contamination or biodiversity impacts of operations
- GHG emissions (Scope 1 in particular, but also Scope 2 and 3)
- Sustainable procurement
- Water consumption

---

[1] For the remainder of this chapter we style both "E" and "S" as Sustainability.

"S"

- Health and safety
- Human rights + labor standards
- Modern slavery
- Social enterprise partnering

Readers can establish what is vital in their specific circumstances and devise their own listing. (See Appendix 1 for a more granular list of "E," "S," and "G" subsets.) From your "baseline" of information, you then measure progress. Those measurements are the "data" we speak of here. In order to collect, analyze, and report such data *as it relates to Sustainability*, large organizations run numerous data gathering exercises. Such organizations generally carry the large overhead that enables serious investment in data analysis. Yet, a common and persistent criticism is that *simply auditing suppliers on a regular basis does not necessarily lead to substantial improvements or target hitting*. Measurements can become a proverbial "box-ticking exercise."

To make the most of data surveys, it is vital we communicate with the optimal *supplier segments* for each specific data survey. In doing this, we need to consider what are our essential information goals and how can they best be achieved. What data[2] is required? Why and how often? Who is best placed to provide this material?

Best practice in data gathering involves investment of time and resource sufficient to properly plan the survey approach. This up-front work can lead to efficiencies, particularly as we repeat the exercise. For example, an organization may need to determine whether sustainable *waste management* regulations are being followed. In this case, the procurement department should group suppliers by category and country and set up a monitoring process via which data is received in a sequence, probably starting with suppliers from countries having stricter regulations.

---

[2] "Data" does not have to be rendered in numeric form. In some cases, "information" might be a better word. Our data ultimately will reside in both numerical measures and interpretive text analysis. But the key point is that whatever we devise must be "measurable" in a consistent manner.

Segmenting Suppliers for Data Gathering

Many buying organizations continue to issue bulky *survey forms* (often as part of a wider *supplier prequalification process*) to all suppliers, using a "scatter-gun" approach to obtaining information. This tends to rely on responding supplier firms to determine which questions are relevant and how to answer. By contrast, modern *best practice* is to distribute survey questionnaires to only those suppliers—and, ideally, to specific individual contracts—for whom the questions are intended. This is a key to receiving good quality information. If we think of our Kraljic supplier positioning technique (see Chapter 20), we can see quite readily which relationships are likely to be the more relevant.

In terms of getting quality data relevant to our "E" and "S" (and possibly "G") requirements, we may need to "bespoke" a survey form for specific segmented group(s) of suppliers or categories. Here is an illustrative example: if a sustainable packaging survey was to be sent to a wide group of suppliers, many recipients might struggle to know how, or even whether, to respond. A "creative agency" might translate "packaging" to mean certain promotional boxes they had recently designed, while a packaging manufacturer might consider the pallets and shrink-wrap they use for shipping. There would be little insight into and consistency to the "data" provided. This, in turn, would compromise the results.

If suppliers cannot decipher whether survey questions relate to them (and how), then they will not prioritize the task. Firms that ought not to have been invited may waste time determining this fact. Those that *should* respond, and to which our questions are genuinely relevant, may still underestimate the size of their task. As a result, suppliers in the first group waste time, effort, and energy in a generally nugatory way. Suppliers in the second group lose time working out how to respond, which may adversely impact the quality of their responses. Both groups are likely to feel their time is being wasted, and this is not good for relationship development.

Survey questionnaires do not have to be a one-direction communication—suppliers and contractors will represent a valuable untapped source of information; we repeat, it's good to talk! By properly and thoughtfully segmenting suppliers so as to elicit strong and targeted data responses, Procurement can work more effectively. Quality survey forms enable easier communication with suppliers, speed responses, and often assist with specific tasks such as certificate location. Furthermore, they help to create transparency, which is vital in this day and age, and tend to spotlight "E" and "S" areas for improvement, so leading actively toward positive change.

Opening the Conversation With Customers

Customers (clients) may be the prime mover in raising ESG concerns and objectives. Where clients are Fortune 500- or FTSE 250-type companies—or otherwise large or sector dominant—discussion initiation will likely come from the client side of the relationship. The simplest way to think of this is that the client side will seek to "flow-down" obligations imposed on them via various legislations under UN-SDG and COP-26 initiatives.

Generally, the client will set out what it seeks in terms of information, data, and hard practical Sustainability outcomes. Your most urgent involvement in these things will be via your client relationships. A clear advantage of this approach is that the client will have done some of the "heavy-lifting" in terms of establishing what is required, and your role will be to respond. Your client will hopefully have done the difficult thinking and associated in-depth research. A disadvantage may be that the client side has misunderstood or "overegged" their requirements. In this situation, remember you are not a disinterested observer of what goes on; rather you may have to probe, query, and challenge requirements if you believe these are pushing you in the wrong direction. (Your author considers this outcome is relatively unusual. Hopefully, your client(s) do have a good overall sense of what is needful and beneficial.)

The obverse of this is where ESG or Sustainability obligations directly impact your organization and, as a result, you seek to engage with your major clients to establish to what extent there may be mutual "wins" in working toward favorable Sustainability outcomes. How should these discussions be initiated? Opening the discussion will depend to a large extent on existing relationship dynamics. If there are good and long-lasting personal relationships, then to raise the question informally and in discussion at peer-group level will be sensible. Ideally, if there are pre-existing director-to-director relationships, then that is the right level to initiate action, but the task will quickly devolve down to technical questions and issues, and no doubt, this will be handled via junior managers and specialists. However way these discussions may be initiated, the underlying ethos should be that:

- We identify you as a key or valued customer.
- We believe you may have ESG or sustainability obligations and we think we may be able to help you.
- We also have sustainability obligations or targets and the upstream value chain appears a suitable place to make (substantial) progress.
- We would like to open an informal discussion.

Even where discussions appear to be at an informal level, never forget that, in a real sense, they are the opening of a negotiation and should be handled with that thought in mind.

Opening the Conversation With Suppliers

Relationship dynamics will be important, and even vital, to this. Kraljic supplier positioning (see Chapter 20) informs us as to which suppliers are "key" and using this technique we can "segment" with a degree of accuracy and dependability. Such segmentation may already have "flavored" the relationship and helped us perceive which suppliers have direct "materiality" in our day-to-day operations, especially in terms of supply failures. That analysis would have given us confidence as we seek to open up a discussion. In terms of Sustainability, however, Kraljic is of only limited assistance and we need more granular "E," "S," and "G" risk or opportunity parameters to take us forward.

Earlier in this book, in Chapters 11, 14, and 17, we highlight a "roadmap" to help us address the "E," "S," and "G" tasks. As we seek to open up discussions with suppliers, at the early stage and by reference to the roadmap, we shall make tentative decisions at stages 1 through 5.

Having established, in outline, where Sustainability opportunities (and risks) may lie, we can then assess where certain supply categories[3] are "material" in meeting ESG challenges and open up supplier discussions accordingly. The two primary categories as regards Sustainability management via suppliers are those with "high" ESG materiality and those that have low materiality. These are unlikely to "map" neatly into Kraljic's four supplier portfolios (strategic, bottleneck, leverage, acquisition), but there will be some overall resonance. It is a suitable starting point for consideration. In Figure 22.1, we suggest a nuance on this analysis.

What we suggest above is that, measured against the standard two Kraljic axes, *spend* and *risk*, it is likely that our high materiality ESG suppliers will be those at the "top" of our matrix (i.e., high risk and high spend) and lower ESG materiality suppliers will be those that also represent low supply risk. The map-across is certainly not foolproof and the illustration is a generalization. It will be recognized, however, that we are likely to enjoy greatest leverage with, and more developed commercial relationship among, our top right-hand ("strategic") suppliers. These

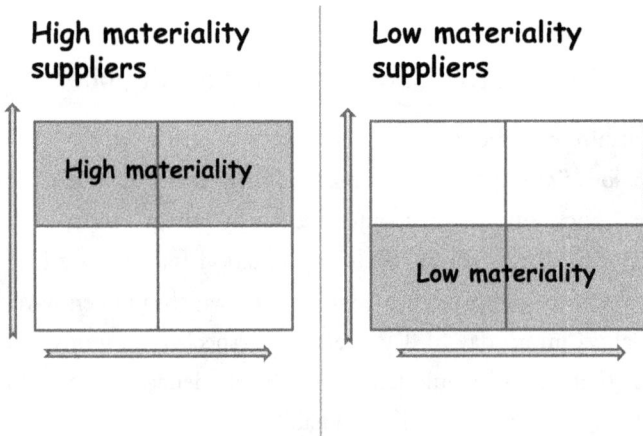

Figure 22.1 Supplier segmentation—ESG partnerships

---

[3] Procurement professionals use a technique known as category management to best address their varying supply categories and associated suppliers.

are the most likely to have a coinciding interest in ESG considerations, especially if they are "large"[4] organizations.

With *high materiality suppliers*, the conversation is likely to devolve around mutual Sustainability obligations and the opportunity for win–win outcomes. A "partnering" approach may be possible with these suppliers. The dialogue then may be similar to that with important client organizations:

- We identify you as a key and valued supplier.
- We have Sustainability obligations or targets and the *downstream* value chain appears a suitable place to make (substantial) progress.
- We believe you may have equivalent or coinciding ESG or Sustainability obligations and we think we may be able to help you.
- We would like to open an informal discussion.

ESG targets may best be expressed as KPIs[5] via an SLA[6] adjunct to the main contract. As suggested above, even where such initial discussions appear to be at an informal level, we should not forget that, in a real sense, they are the opening of a negotiation and should be handled with that thought in mind.

With our *low materiality suppliers*, the dynamic will be different; here, we are more likely to "specify" precisely what we require. The relationship may be more akin to the traditional "master–servant" dynamic where the supplier seeks to meet the client's requirements as demanded but with less "strategic" input to the solutions required. The client-side requirements will perhaps be more closely defined via a *technical specification* (goods) or a *terms of reference* (services) document. The measures of achievement may be direct ("meet target A, B, C," etc.) or indirect ("meet improvements within agreed parameters to be measured over time via KPIs").

---

[4] In U.K. terms, that could be characterized as FTSE 250 down to large SMEs.
[5] Key performance indicator.
[6] Service-level agreement.

Incentivization of these suppliers may come from two directions: (1) additional revenue earned from meeting ESG requirements or (2) assistance toward meeting the supplier's own ESG obligations. Or both!

Low materiality suppliers may be very happy to work with us, provided our requirements do not excessively push up their overhead costs. The basis of the discussion is likely to be:

- We have Sustainability targets.
- We identify your supply segment as holding out "promise" in finding Sustainability solutions and achieving RAM[7]-type improvements.
- We target you to achieve these specific outcomes ...*describe*.
- Please confirm you are able to comply.
- Please advise the impact on supply costs.
- The contracting process will be—the existing contract will be—amended in this way ...*describe*.

Throughout this chapter, we focus on *initiating* the dialogue. Plainly, there will be much thought, planning, and activity required to realize the potential, but we must begin somewhere and we have to begin deliberatively.

Leveraging Relationships

In the world of finance and business strategy, "leveraging" means *to use borrowed capital for an investment, expecting the profits made to be greater than the interest payable*. An example might be: "without clear legal title to their assets, they own property that cannot be leveraged as collateral for loans." So, there is something, here, about the idea of a "lever" enabling us to exert maximum force financially. In more common language, "leveraging" means *to use something to maximum advantage*. An example might be: "the organization needs to leverage its key resources." Both uses of the term have resonance in terms of our

---

[7] Realistic, achievable, measurable.

third-party relationships and utilizing or exploiting those relationships to achieve ESG "wins."

As we open up the conversation with third parties, it is certainly not ignoble to view various relationships in terms of their leveraging potential and how quickly we might achieve "wins" by working with customers and suppliers. Figure 22.2 sketches out how we should move these conversations, speedily, to transition from aspiration to achievement. In this book, we provide three high-level roadmaps (one for environmental, one for social, and one for governance). See Chapters 12, 15, and 18, respectively, which include checklists of tasks to cycle through to *deliberatively* develop our responses to the evolving ESG challenge.

Figure 22.2 reminds us, as always, that everything we do must be rooted in a thorough appreciation of our business context, which is the essential background to our challenge. On the left of the schematic, we are reminded that we must determine our overall "stance" in terms of ESG (and possibly develop a business case for investment, if this is necessary). We need to quickly establish "where we are today" in terms of emerging regulatory demands and then outline the targets what will help us meet these demands.

Then, we look toward our third party ("3P") relationships and to what extent these expose our organization directly to risk. From here, we

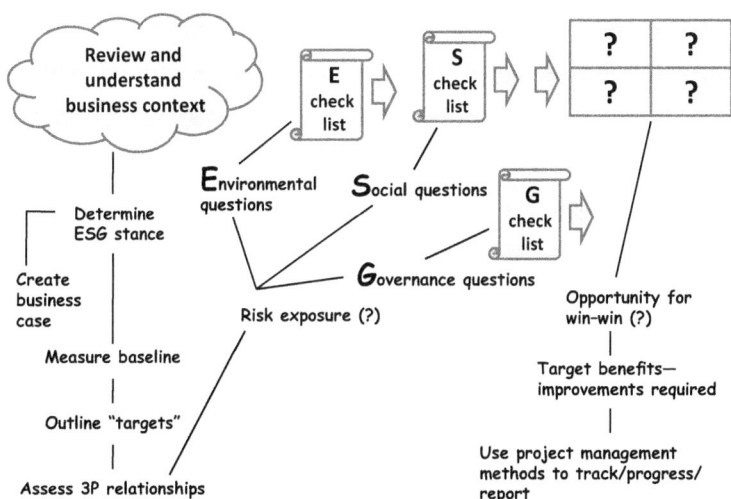

Figure 22.2 3PM + ESG—leveraging relationships

move into our "E," "S," and "G" roadmaps with their associated check-lists. The four-box matrix, above, reminds us that we are likely to iden-tify high materiality and low materiality relationships, especially in the "downstream" (supplier) part of our value chain. By mixing and matching these relationships and their potential, we are then in a good position to devise the optimum practical strategy to progress toward meeting ESG objectives, in concert with our key commercial partners.

PART 7

Data

CHAPTER 23

The Data Challenge

Data Pull

There is no universal definition of data, in terms of ESG. The word implies that an organization has sufficient and detailed information to demonstrate progress toward the achievement of ESG targets, no matter what those targets are. It implies *numerical* data, algorithms, software packages, and careful data harvesting and input. These ideas are not far from the practical reality, and it seems that regulatory authorities and other interested parties increasingly seek data provision in *accepted* ways and in a common and consistent *format*.

The practical challenge for any organization is to know what information is important or relevant, how to "measure" it in technical terms, what is today's baseline so we can measure and demonstrate tomorrow's progress against baseline, and how to achieve accuracy. Beyond that, there is the question of actually *reporting* facts and progress, while avoiding accusations of "greenwashing."

In this book, we make a simple observation about "data": It does not have to be numerical and other narrative information can be classified as "data," provided it is harvested and presented in a consistent manner—having said that, anything that can be reduced to numerical measures ideally should be.

The next general point to make is that there is a range of interested parties in this arena of ESG who wish to have sight of our data. We can call this "data pull" in the sense that varying stakeholders exercise a "pull" influence on what data we harvest and report. Historically, financial data has been the focus for management teams, but with *health and safety* legislation and other demands for more nuanced ethical management, there has come the need to report *other* qualitative information

3P (suppliers, value chain) require	Regulator(s) require
! YOU require	Stakeholder(s) require

Figure 23.1 Data pull

that demonstrates sound governance and ethics. ESG data is a natural development of this.

The first reason for collecting and collating *any* information is that it serves a purpose for the organization itself and helps us to manage effectively. All data harvesting costs money and adds to overhead. The modern preference is that we secure valuable data as part of our normal day-to-day operations and that the cost of the task becomes negligible[1]. Business professionals plan for ESG data as well. In Figure 23.1, the lower left "box" reminds us that it is YOU who require the data and this must be our starting point. We collect and analyze information such that our directors (board) can discharge their duties in their fiduciary relationship (legal meaning) to their organization. Rather than a data "pull," that lower left box might be considered a data "push" as there are definite legal demands pushing us to collect and harvest data (mainly financial). Today, the other three boxes *pull* our organization to provide *additional* information specifically related to "E," "S," and "G" subcomponents. Of the three, and at the time of writing this book, the "E" subcomponent is the most pressing for management teams. The *pull* factors now are our 3P relationships (think 3PM, and refer to Part 6 of this book), regulators, and *other* stakeholders. The challenge to, and the objective of, the management teams is to respond to these push–pull factors with a single, coherent response that does not add too significantly to overhead costs.

---

[1] Enterprise resource planning ("ERP") systems are designed to harvest information in an automated manner, eliminating much human interaction and minimizing overhead cost.

In preparing our data strategy, we first need to ask (1) who needs data and (2) why? This must be our starting point. Management teams must avoid any "rabbit in the headlights" response as regards data demands, taking a degree of corporate "ownership" and "remaining in the driving seat" on this:

- What is important to you?
- What is important to your investors?
- What is important to your stakeholders?
- What is important to your regulators?
- Does present data harvesting satisfy in terms of *our* objectives?
- Is present data harvesting meeting *our* business requirements?
- To what extent, and how, can we adapt what we are doing at present?
- What fresh data demands are on the horizon and how can we roll-in these new demands to what we presently do?

Proxy Data

What we design in terms of data harvesting needs to be as comprehensive as possible and we should not expect full maturity on "day one." Rather, we recognize that data requirements will develop and evolve over time.

The concept of "data proxy" is evolving as this book is being written. Generally speaking, *proxy data* is the practice of substituting a missing or inaccessible data source with a comparable or related *existing* data source. Another way of expressing this is to say that proxy data is data from a *similar* process or activity that is used as a stand-in for your given process or activity. At the time of writing this book, in recognizing that required data may be unavailable (or not as accurate as needed), there is a legitimate and accepted place for substituting "proxy" information, provided this is done in a transparent manner.

In the field of *climate change*, in particular, assessment calculations are undertaken using recorded *observation data* as well as prepared *proxy data*. Paleoclimatologists (climatologists who study past—or paleo—climates) use the term "proxy" to describe a way that climate change is recorded in nature, within geological materials such as ocean or lake sediments, tree-rings, coral growth-bands, ice-cores, and cave deposits. For organizations, the practical question will be: do we need to use proxy data in our own calculations and if so, from where do we source that data and what confidence do we (and/or our stakeholders) place in the proxy? This subject remains in its infancy as this book was being prepared. Our best advice to management teams is be aware of *proxy data* as an issue, and learn from what industry or sector peers are doing, as well as what your varying stakeholders find acceptable. It may be that proxy data is less of an issue for your organization, but more prominent for those tasked to interpret raw data and to draw from organizational reports much broader interpretations of Sustainability impacts. The investment community that seeks to promote *sustainable* investments may be the grouping most exercised about proxy data versus actual data.

Upping the Game

Not only do customers, employees, and NGO-type stakeholders demand insight into ESG performance, but increasingly national–international regulatory bodies as well. From 2019, disclosure of climate-related *financial* information became compulsory for many U.K.-registered businesses via the SECR[2]. From 2024, the EU requires an equivalent via its Corporate Sustainability Reporting Directive (CSRD), aiming to achieve more complete and transparent sustainability reporting across the bloc. The United States has signed up to net-zero targets but not yet finalized reporting regimes[3]. Organizational leaders have accepted that simply having "ESG initiatives" alone is inadequate. Instead, an ability to

---

[2] See Appendix 2.

[3] The U.S. Securities and Exchange Commission has indicated enhanced climate risk disclosure requirements to expand annual reporting for publicly traded companies. In 2023, the proposals are that the reports shall include (1) the company's climate risk management processes, (2) how identified risks might affect financial performance,(3) how risks are managed or mitigated, and (4) any scenario analysis, transition plans, publicly announced climate goals. Readers must "watch this space" as regards the United States. Final decisions are unlikely before 2025.

accurately and consistently report ESG data helps organizations identify gaps in, and drive forward with, improved ESG performance. To meet this evolving demand and to achieve progressively higher ESG standards, a vital factor is data.

Most large organizations have a *data infrastructure* in place, and business leaders are keen to derive better ESG insight and reporting through their *existing* infrastructure. They recognize, however, that this may not satisfy increasingly detailed and granular information demands that external agencies will make going forward. Where an organization's data lacks accuracy, consistency, and context, it will be impossible to report ESG realities as demanded by stakeholders. It could be said, at the time of writing this book, that *if organizations do not presently invest in the integrity of their data, then they are already "behind the curve," and upcoming ESG regulations will only widen that gap.* Four overlapping key tasks help enhance data integrity and ensure an organization's data infrastructure is focused on upcoming challenges:

Task 1: Data Integration

A professional data infrastructure must be able to integrate and make sense of data, regardless of how it is captured or delivered. This gives organizations a rounded and granular view of all data, ideally in one place, which helps identify trends that otherwise might remain hidden.

While this may sound relatively simple, in practice, it is quite complex. Large businesses generally have a range of internal functions that carry out business activities on multiple operating platforms. These organizations can have data "siloed" across the third parties with which they do business. Think, for example, of your supply chain where there may be hundreds (if not thousands) of suppliers.

Accessing siloed data and viewing it in one location is a difficult problem, but data integration can go a long way to ease the task. Understanding the profile, background ("provenance"), implicit and explicit assumptions, and calculations using such data is a very basic starting point for accurate ESG reporting.

Task 2: Data Quality and Manipulation

The time-honored mnemonic "GIGO" ("garbage in, garbage out") is a truism as relevant to ESG data as any other dataset. Organizations that work with suboptimal or poor data will glean unreliable information, which is why *a well-planned and rigorous data infrastructure is vital*. Not only does this help to assemble data into one location, but it can automatically cleanse it and so enhance its quality.

Most data infrastructures worthy of the name can manipulate data, but this can often be a largely manual process, and many data initiatives are led by the IT department, possibly not the right place for *leadership* to be located. By contrast, a board-level mandate on data is ideal, preferably backed by a good business case for suitable process-automation tools. Such software facilities can genuinely save time in data processing ("time is money!") but, in addition, can provide real-time analytics, giving assurance and speed of decision making. Timeliness (speed) of data acquisition becomes ever more important, and ESG concerns can only benefit from this.

Task 3: Location-Specific Data

Location-specific data can unlock particular information that can be weighed in the broader context of our organization and can serve as a common link between otherwise separate silos of data. Two superficially similar facilities, perhaps even colocated, might have radically different "E," "S," or "G" hazard exposures. Knowing this with precision is increasingly important for organizations and can furnish a broad "picture" of risks, including within supply chains. In turn, this can only assist the interpretation of high-materiality questions such as climate impacts of operations, a matter that will only grow in importance in the 10 years commencing 2024.

Location-specific intelligence can go a long way to improve organizational decision making in relation to personnel, hard assets including real-estate, as well as opportunity costs associated with differing investment opportunities or options. Data or information can usually be directly associated with a specific location in one way or another; the challenge is to render it in a consistent, accurate, and digestible form.

Task 4: Data Enrichment

This is the process of *adding approved and trusted third-party data to internal self-generated data* to reveal the broader context and enhance our insight. When approved third-party datasets (perhaps related to location, business-sector, climate-weather, or demographics) are incorporated into self-gleaned business information, there can be a valuable synergy that enhances confidence in decision making. The "trick" for management teams is to know what external data sources are trustworthy and how to manipulate third-party data. In this regard, we should add that *third-party* data (as broadly explored in Part 6 of this book) can be mutually helpful to ourselves *and* our third parties, but we have to overcome reluctance to share information that might be considered competitively valuable IPR (intellectual property rights) or otherwise sensitive. We revert to the idea of *relationship management* and developing mutually beneficial win–win type arrangements.

Heightened ESG regulatory demands, coupled to the requirement for tried-and-trusted disclosure frameworks, mean that organizations increasingly must report *competently* on potential "E," "S," and "G" impacts , both on their own business activities and across the broader "ecosphere." The addition of the so-called risk datasets related to floods, earthquakes, weather events, wildfires, and so on can help to highlight the history of, and likelihood for, hazard encounter in given locations. This genuinely empowers organizations to make quick business decisions with higher confidence that such decisions are prudent and have taken into account suitable risk-management measures.

Who Processes? Who Owns?

In practice, there are three key actors that can process data in order to secure dependable insights for reporting purposes: *ourselves* as data generators and analysts, *niche data aggregator* or analysts, and *third parties* within our value chain. We considered third parties in Part 6 of this book, and readers may want to reconsider that section as we focus on how data is manipulated and managed.

There are *specialist data aggregators* via which we may choose to "outsource" the task of data processing and analysis. Such aggregators must, of course, be recognized, properly appointed, and competent. While we may be able to outsource the *task* of data analysis, we cannot outsource the responsibility and associated legal *risk* where data proves to be incorrect (or, worse, massaged). It is to be expected that there will be greater scrutiny of data aggregators and analysts in the years ahead, and regulation of these types of business may be reinforced.

Elsewhere in this book, we have considered the "harvesting" of data and associated management tasks. And in Chapters 24 and 25, we shall discuss good practice solutions. Briefly, now, we consider questions around how we interact with others in our *value chain* as regards data analysis. Figure 23.2 highlights the idea of data flows and "ownership."

To meet ESG-type reporting demands, we create and harvest data from our own operations. Clearly, this is firmly in-house activity and the resulting information belongs to us—it is our own "IPR" (intellectual property right). Our obligation is to secure the relevant information and "record" it in an auditable and competent manner. In addition to this, and especially in regards to the pressing question of Scope 1, 2, and 3 emissions, we are highly likely to need information from "upstream" in our value chain (from suppliers and contractors) and also from "downstream," via

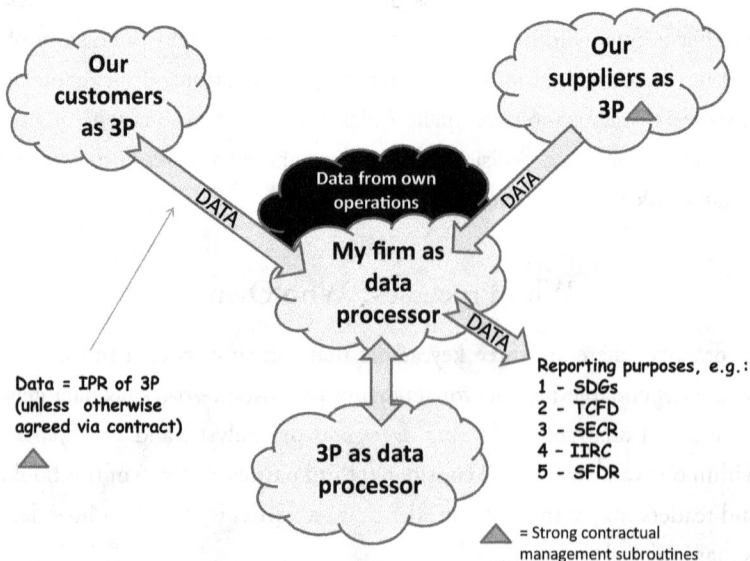

Figure 23.2 ESG—data considerations

customers and distributors, especially as regards Scope 3 (indirect) emissions. Yet, the principle of harvesting data and receiving reports is not a new one and does not only apply to "environmental" concerns. *Modern slavery* is another example.

Figure 23.2 reminds us that we may secure information from a number of sources. We considered in Chapter 20 the need for appropriate contractual terms to secure suitable "user rights" as regards data, and return to this in Chapter 24. One point to emphasize is that, in some third-party relationships, there is a firm and precise contractual relationship with associated strong contract management subroutines. Via these subroutines, we should secure the data we require. Data will eventually be "outputted" toward varying stakeholders and (probably) to report clearly and accurately under whatever regulated mandates have been imposed on us (in the schematic, we highlight them by their acronyms).

Throughout this book, we make the case for doing as much as we can "in-house," and this includes "data processing" leading to dependable insights and knowledge about our "E," "S," and "G" performances. Where we do choose to use an external data processor to assist or manage the task on an "outsource" basis, we must ensure that all activity is undertaken competently and that the relationship is underpinned by a suitable contract which secures appropriate user rights. This is all part of the *data challenge* ....

CHAPTER 24

Data Subcomponents

Where, in this chapter, we capitalize the term as "Data," this implies the subject is a business function or a defined task or a contractual deliverable. Where we use lower case as "data,'" then the meaning implied is the more generic sense of data as alphanumeric information which might also be an intellectual property asset. We trust readers appreciate the subtle distinction.

The Basics …

As noted in Chapter 23, there is no universal definition of data—in terms of ESG. The word implies that an organization has sufficient and detailed information to demonstrate progress toward the achievement of ESG targets, no matter what those targets may be. At a practical level, the subcomponents of data strategy are relatively simple:

- Assess "E," "S," and "G"-type risks
- Assess direct regulatory requirements
- Define what needs to be "collected"
- Define precise format (numerical and/or narrative)
- Distil to numerical where possible
- Define baseline and then measure progress against baseline
- Report, including upload to relevant database such as ESAP (see below)
- Archive

From all this activity, the "story" we create must be true, accurate, and a fair representation of the overall situation. There must be no deliberate misrepresentation and we should progressively try to reduce or eliminate any possibility of negligent misrepresentation. The standards we apply should be analogous to the rigorous standards applied to the collection of financial information.

In principle, much of this is intuitive and relatively simple—it is not "rocket science," to use an over worn cliché! Especially in the realm of energy management, many organizations already have a good "feel" for how to approach energy use reporting (and "savings") because most will have looked at energy supply as an overhead cost-driver and are used to speaking in terms of "metered" versus "unmetered" consumption, kWh, energy bills, consumption *reduction* targets, and so on. These approaches can also be used to more closely control any "utility" consumption (water, gas, phone, etc.).

There may be more challenge around the "S" and "G" data subcomponents of ESG, yet even here, the broad principles are the same. We must identify what the existing and emerging risks are; we must know precisely "where we are today" (baseline), and we need a mechanism to measure changes against self-imposed (or market-imposed) improvement targets.

What "happens" to our data? Essentially, it finds its way into specific reports (often linked to annual report and accounts) that demonstrate what we are achieving in a way intelligible to the intelligent non specialist observer (e.g., stakeholders and investors) and, in its "raw" form, is also securely archived for future analysis and audit. Data becomes a valuable asset ....

European Single Access Point

At the time of writing this book, the European Union was actively pursuing its European Single Access Point (ESAP) project, in turn linked to its political objective of achieving full Capital Markets Union (CMU). The aim was to create a *single point of access to public financial and sustainability-related information* about EU companies and EU investment products. ESAP was posited as providing *free, user-friendly, centralized, and digital access to financial and sustainability-related information* published by European companies, including small ones, to support decision-making process(es) for a broad range of investors, including retail investors. The first thing we note, then, is that ESAP aims to assist *investors* obtain better information about the performance of organizations (especially, private ones) in which they may choose to invest. The useful by-product should be better peer-to-peer access to information, across a range of metrics including ESG.

In 2022, the EU evinced that their plans would not impose any additional information reporting requirements on European companies, as ESAP would provide access to information *already* made public in response to relevant European directives and regulations. Sustainability information will be made available earlier via ESAP, to support the objectives of the European Green Deal. The EU was planning a phased introduction commencing 2024.

Why might this be important to you? In the years 2024 to 2026, we suggest proactive monitoring of the introduction of this facility, especially (of course) if your organization is domiciled in the European Union or has substantial operations there. Whatever methodologies are adopted by ESAP, these may become a useful model or "benchmark" for other open-access systems. Furthermore, whatever architecture is developed for ESAP, this may become a useful architecture *model* for equivalent systems. Given time, it is likely that a broad global alignment of such systems and the sorts of data they harvest will emerge. Who in your organization should carry responsibility for monitoring this? Can your trade association help you?

Initial Steps

In the "executive-level roadmap" (Figure 7.2 and steps H8 to H11), we suggest four data-related tasks with H8 = data baseline, H9 = data integrity assessment, H10 = data policy framework, and H11 = data quality improvement plan. These are unlikely to be one-time steps1 and will become iterative activities, developed over time. Remember, "Rome was not built in a day!"

As you prepare for these iterative tasks, there will be a number of subtasks:

---

[1] These are also reflected in each of the 39-step "high-level roadmaps" for "E," "S," and "G" as taking place between steps 4 and 5.

Data Sources

Internal data must be harvested, and this is perhaps your key asset. Internal data will be measured through manual input and via automated systems. It might also be harvested from internal documents. *External data* is gleaned from external parties (see our thinking on 3PM in Part 6 of this book) through questionnaires, suppliers, contracts, and even via invoices.

A more nuanced question for you is to what extent you buy data via third-party data suppliers and to what extent (and how) this may be used as proxy data. What is acceptable and are you getting any "steer" from regulators or industry trade associations? Your immediate task is to review and reflect upon data sources, in order to make early decisions.

Roles

Who will be responsible and who will be involved—and in what differing capacities? There seem to be two obvious categories: *producers and owners* (directly involved in collection and initial interpretation—they may also be subject-matter experts) and *reporters and coordinators*, responsible for collation, stakeholder inputs, professional interpretation, and manipulation. These personnel may be from the Sustainability team (if you have such) or perhaps the regulatory function. Again, some subject-matter expertise is assumed.

Processing Systems

Organizations export gleaned data into varying platforms. Almost inevitably there will be spreadsheet input, but possibly also bespoke database systems and even third-party (cloud-based) ESG reporting systems. Data visualization will be a powerful incentive—remember, a picture is worth a thousand words!

Once data has been harvested, it requires assessment for accuracy and validity. Mechanisms to assist will be typically:

- *Variance analysis*—comparisons with earlier reporting or data, with forecasts, and with "targets."
- *Sign-off process*—internal reviews, checklists, and eventually, formal sign-off.

- *Internal audit*—review of methodologies and use of methodologies and use of specific key performance indicators (KPIs).
- *External assurance*—usually, this will be most focused on the "E" part of the ESG, focusing on environmental data and its applicability. Such assurance may, in practice, be limited and with the assurer taking no "risk" for their assurance.

There may be particular difficulties associated with all this. It is possible that suppliers and contractors may fail to provide expected datasets and timeliness may also be an issue. If we rely on third-party Data, then who shall be responsible if the Data proves to be unreliable? There are obvious difficulties associated with manual input of data and subsequent data manipulation. Furthermore, there is potential for problems around local jurisdiction and even cultural mismatch (misunderstandings) where this is handled across differing jurisdictions, cultures, and nations.

Rather than repeat what others have done, your author recommends readers who need to delve more deeply into this whole subject to consult the United Kingdom's *Financial Reporting Council* (FRC) August 2022 Report issued by their "FRC Lab" called "Improving ESG Data Production." As noted throughout this book, the financial services industry is setting the pace and the ethos for much of this activity. While the FRC is a U.K. organization and aimed at a British business audience, the work it has done is extremely good and potentially applicable beyond Britain.

At the time of writing, the FRC Lab report is freely available via the FRC website.

Data Protection

We explored this subject briefly in Part 6 of this book as we considered how we can generate data in conjunction with (and through) our third-party relationships. Two things we did not discuss in that section were:

- Ownership and use of data
- Data protection

Let's take these in reverse order: first, "data protection." At one level, we can say this is relatively straightforward insofar that most organizations already have in place data protection provisions and associated policies. In principle, "data protection" relates to protecting *personal data* and preventing (or criminalizing) its incorrect use or dissemination. Businesses, particularly in the western world, have had to consider, at length, how they acquire, use, and protect information. ESG-type data (generally) is unlikely to impact *personal* data as harvesting "environmental," "social," or "governance" activities should rarely involve the harvesting of personal information. This potential remains, however, so we should be aware and cautious as we harvest information that could have personal implications. A *data protection* subroutine might be incorporated into ESG data planning where you sense a heightened risk, for whatever reason. Yet, this can be handled under your existing data protection policies; so, in principle, you should not need to devise new policies and processes.

Ownership and use of ESG data is not quite so straightforward. Your author has spent nearly a third of his career in the field of contracting for scientific research and development services, where ownership and use of information (intellectual property rights [IPRs] and other data) was an active, live, and ever-present issue and central to commercial contracts. Interestingly, there is a direct analogy with ownership and use of ESG-type data, and we can learn from the world of scientific research ("R&D"). At the time of writing this book, contractual provisions relating to ownership and use seem to be relatively immature in the ESG space and are likely to evolve and improve markedly in the years up to 2034.

Before examining some general principles, let's review an actual "rights in results" clause from an R&D contract. In the below text, the * symbol reminds the contract drafter that this particular sub-provision is optional:

11. RIGHTS IN RESULTS

11.1 Subject to any IPR which is vested in the Contractor and has been notified to the Client in accordance with the terms of the Contract Letter or any IPR which is vested in any third party, all IPR, reports, data, information, software, specifications, designs and drawings and any other results arising from the Service shall vest in and be the absolute property of the Client and the Client shall have the right to make such use as it deems appropriate of such results without further payment to the Contractor. No licence for use by the Contractor of such IPR or other information as aforesaid is hereby given to the Contractor [*except as may specifically be provided elsewhere in this Contract].

11.2 The Contractor shall as soon as practicable after becoming aware (and in any event in his final report or concurrently with any final contract deliverable) notify the Client of any IPR vested in or controlled by any third party which the Contractor has used, is using or may or shall use in connection with carrying out the Service or using the results, or which may be infringed as a result of carrying out the Service or using the results, and shall inform the Client of the steps that the Client may have to take in order to ensure use or non-infringement thereof by the Contractor and/or by the Client.

Hopefully, the analogy is intelligible to the reader. Where data is generated at the cost of the client, then the client owns the data. This implies free use of the data for all and any purposes. It does not preclude the contractor from use of the data, but this would be by separate agreement. In the contractual clause above, if certain data is owned by a *third party*, then the contractor is obliged to inform the client. In terms of ESG data, our thinking might be along similar lines. Below, we consider the question of "confidentiality":

*12. CONFIDENTIALITY

12.1 All details of the Contract including all IPR, results, data or information arising from it (the "Confidential Information") shall be treated as private and confidential and the Contractor shall not publish, advertise or otherwise make known any such Confidential Information to any other person in any way without the prior written permission of the Client.

12.2 All information given by the Client to the Contractor in connection with this Contract shall be treated as confidential and shall not be disclosed to any other person or used for any purpose other than this Contract. The Contractor shall ensure that all its employees who have access to such information are aware of these restrictions and are subject to them.

12.3 The Contractor shall disclose to the Client all information arising from the Service.

* 12.4 All information disclosed to the Contractor by the Client or the Supervising Officer (or his authorized representative) for the purpose of carrying out the Contract shall be returned to the Supervising Officer (or his authorized representative) (or if not capable of return, shall be destroyed or expunged) on completion or termination of the Contract.

12.5 This obligation of confidentiality shall not apply to any Confidential Information which the Contractor can prove by written evidence was known to it at the time of disclosure.

12.6 The Confidential Information shall not be deemed to be public knowledge or known to the Contractor solely on the grounds that:

(a) the general principle is public knowledge or known to the Contractor if the particular practice disclosed by the Client is not itself public knowledge or so known, or

(b) it constitutes a combination (not in itself public knowledge or known to the Contractor) of information that is public knowledge or so known.

12.7 The obligations of the parties under this Clause shall survive the expiry or termination of the Contracts for a period of [*five] years.

It is hoped, again, that the analogy to ESG data is reasonably obvious. Where ESG data is produced and provided as a consequence of a contractual relationship (buyer–seller relationship, in this example) then it must be treated as confidential and not passed on or otherwise abused. Yet, in relation to ESG, it is clear that there may be a mutual desire–need to use the information or data to respond to ESG reporting requirements, in which case, a "joint use" and "joint confidentiality" provision may need to be specially designed.

Your author is bound to comment that in researching this particular aspect for this book, the so-called ESG contract conditions he found freely available on the Internet were some of the worst he has seen in terms of poor drafting, wishful thinking, and sheer "other worldliness" in their scope and ambition. While we would all agree that sustainability is vital and ESG aspects important, some contract drafters seek to use contract terms as campaigning tools and are making available "template" materials that are unlikely to stand the test of time, or the chill wind of a commercial dispute! So, let the reader beware! Carefully consider what it is that you need to achieve and then design terms of contract that accurately reflect that requirement. Avoid use of material found on the Internet and avoid seeing your contractual relationships as vehicles to impose unrealistic or unrealizable standards on your counterparty—and resist these pressures if your counterparty seeks to impose such standards on your own organization.

General Principles in Contract Clauses

There are seven key issues that are fundamental to any contract—everything else is secondary:

- Jurisdiction
- Contracting party due diligence—normally reflected in company registration number (do you *really* know who you are dealing with?)
- Termination
- Indemnification
- Payment terms—how and when
- Warranties
- Intellectual property

NB: This is a lawyer's view. A lawyer looks only at *legal* risk as opposed to, for example, operational risk. *Contract design*[2] is a broader subject, and commercial people might "value" other matters rather more highly,

---

[2] *Contract design* is the precise manner in which a contract is articulated. Is it long or short? Simple or complex? Boilerplate or bespoke? And what is the balance of liabilities? Good contract design is a shared task between operational experts or business people and their legal advisers. See Peter Sammons, "Contract Management – Core Business Competence" (Kogan Page, 2017) for more insight.

such as liquidated damages for non performance or the right to assign the contract to another contracting party. As regards Data, we can say this would normally be considered a subset of intellectual property, our final bullet above.

For any contractual arrangement, your contract terms should reflect what you require and be written in words that your mother would understand! (A CEO at a bank—it should be added a consistently profitable bank—once stated he would not seek to market any financial product if he could not straightforwardly explain the product, and the associated contractual terms, to his mother. Anything more complex would entail "complexity risk" and this was something he would not countenance. His bank weathered the 2008 banking crisis better than most ….)

A well-designed contract would typically be simple, or at least as simple as possible. It will cover

The what	Definition and specification
The where	Destination
The when	Timescales or timing of performance
The how	Method of delivery
The how much	Price and payment
The what else	Dependencies or incidentals

Data considerations will be in the "incidentals" part of the contract, albeit defined in some detail. We can "sketch" the typical commercial contract (sometimes called "the shape of the contract") across eight distinct dimensions, outlined here:

1. *Privity and recitals*
   Expresses quite simply, who is party to the contract, and whom, accordingly, can be held accountable and sue (or be sued) under the terms of the agreement.
2. *Outputs and deliverables*
   Linked to the terms of reference (or specification) and any associated service-level measures, this expresses, at a technical level, what actually must be achieved.

3. *Intellectual property rights*

   Increasingly important in today's knowledge-based economy, this underlines and makes a term the protection and nondisclosure of *information* that often has its own discrete commercial value and, almost certainly, an identifiable "owner."

4. *Liabilities and indemnities*

   In the event of certain exigencies occurring, who is nominated to manage the situation and put things right? Insurance provisions will generally be incorporated under this heading.

5. *Ownership—passing of title*

   At some point, what is owned by one party will become the property of another. The precise point at which this transfer takes place should be well expressed and well understood.

6. *Money*

   Under English contract law (and with analogies in other legal jurisdictions), money is an essential element in any contract. It is generally referred to as "consideration" in the U.K. legal sphere. Money ultimately is what the contract is all about! Accordingly, when and how remittances become due, and payment is actually effected, need to be expressed in a contract with great precision. Note that a failure to pay on time is technically a *breach of contract* and, in many jurisdictions, gives automatic rights to financial compensation.

7. *Program or Time*

   Time is an important element of any contract. Time delinquency on the part of one or other contracting party will often be a cause of friction, if not actual dispute. Time, again, should be clearly expressed in the contract documentation.

8. *Incidentals*

   Many modern contract documents are nothing, if not voluminous! They often try cleverly to anticipate every conceivable situation and every conceivable exigency and provide specific contractual obligations and remedies to deal with such. Anything that is not an element of the preceding seven dimensions is, generally speaking, an *incidental* to the main purpose and the main metrics of any commercial contract. They can therefore be "lumped together" under this dimension as an incidental.

Coming back to the Data aspect of any contract, and especially in terms of ESG data gleaned for a specific purpose (reporting of sustainability outcomes), we can say that Data aspects may be dealt with in three places within a commercial contract. First is as an "output" or a "deliverable" under the agreement. If Data is vital to your agreement (and even is one of the specific reasons you have chosen to work with the counterparty), then it should be specified in detail in the "Terms of Reference" (or "Statement of Work" or "Specification," etc.). Second is in the *intellectual property* provisions of the agreement—because someone must ultimately own the Data and someone else (probably) has the right to use the Data. Third and last is in the incidentals part of the contract, where there may be other nuances spelled-out in terms of varying ways in which Data might be used, and associated liabilities for misuse.

Before Getting Into Contract …

Contracts are not to be entered into lightly. In principle, the approach adopted will be cautious and sequenced. An agreement may be the end point in a series of formal or informal negotiations aimed at closing the gap in interests and liabilities of the potential contracting parties. Before negotiating a potential contract, first make a list of points you wish to be included in the contract. Keep that checklist in mind at any negotiation meeting(s) and review again before signature to ensure the negotiated contract addresses everything that you need it to address. A few further points to note:

- When drafting, ideally use short simple sentences and short simple clauses.
- Never use phrases that are deliberately ambiguous (under the *contra proferentem* rule, a court will interpret any ambiguity against the draftsman).
- Where necessary, explain to the other party the need for particular wording which you wish to include in the contract.
- Ensure that the specification or scope of work addresses everything you wish it to address and ensure that it is what each party expects to be provided for the price.

- Never sign any contract or legal document which you do not understand.
- Never sign any contract which represents a poor deal for your organization and, if your company is a supplier or contractor, where the balance of risk outweighs the reward.

The above are basic good "housekeeping" on preparing to enter into a contractual commitment. As regards Data (and especially ESG data), you should know how the intended Data shall be used, how published, and necessary restrictions that must be applied. The types of "E," "S," and "G" datasets to be harvested from contractual operations might, for example, focus around:

- Reduction of GHG emissions ("E")
- Monitoring of modern slavery risks ("S")
- No sourcing from proscribed (blacklisted) nations or companies ("S")
- Appliance of good governance standards ("G")

The purpose of the contract document itself is to clarify measurable requirements as well as provide specificity to know with assurance (a) that a contract deliverable has been achieved or (b) that a contract deliverable has *not* been achieved. We want certainty; we need to avoid ambiguity. While it may be straightforward and simple to incorporate specific contractual provisions ("terms") that specify all this with great precision, there may also be a place for using a separate Service Level Agreement ("SLA") and/or key performance indicators ("KPIs") that move us powerfully toward achieving the improvements that we require, without trying to engineer *precision targets* that could easily be missed by our contracting counterparty. This may be especially true in the whole area of Data. The broad commercial experience of business process outsourcing provides a useful exemplar of how to handle ESG-type requirements via SLA and KPIs, where the satisfactory performance is measured not so much against hitting particular "targets" with 100 percent accuracy, but rather meeting a broad range of measures within acceptable *variable* limits.

In Chapter 6, Figures 6.1 and 6.2, we reflected on the sheer range of international standards documents now available. In flowing down ESG-type requirements to our contracting counterparties, or responding to demands made on our own organization, it is entirely possible that calling up (i.e., specifying adherence to) particular and relevant ISO standards may go a long way to meeting ESG-type obligations. If so, we would normally be looking toward implementation, certification (where relevant), maintenance and renewal, and transparent renewal scheduling. These might become basic *sine qua non* for the contractual relationship and essentially a specific contract deliverable. The contract then would specify that a particular standard (e.g., an ISO standard) must be attained and maintained throughout the life of the contract. Evidence of maintenance and adherence thereto would be required, scheduled, and measurable. Readers may wish to research whether ISO (or equivalent) standards can play a part in your response to ESG challenges.

We repeat the point made earlier. At the time of writing this book, ESG metrics (data) and associated contract terms are in relative infancy. Reader, watch this space. First, consider what is needed. Second, define what you want. Then (and only then!) speak to legal advisers!

CHAPTER 25

Good Practice Solutions

Materiality Assessment

ESG materiality assessment is a tool used to identify and prioritize the ESG questions most critical to our organization and bears similarities to other materiality assessment processes. We can also think of this as an exercise in stakeholder engagement. A materiality assessment helps us characterize and understand the relative importance of specific ESG and sustainability topics to our organization. Current good practice seeks to look at varying factors through two particular lenses: potential impact on our organization and importance to stakeholders.

Note that "impact" refers to both positive and negative impacts. We should not focus solely on risks, potential losses, and other potential negative outcomes associated with implementing a particular strategy. We should also factor in whatever positive opportunities are uncovered via the process, for example, attracting the best talent because our organization takes its social obligations seriously, including employee health and well-being.

Ideally, we identify a broad range of stakeholders, typically including customers, key suppliers, employees, board members, and investors. Beyond those perhaps "obvious" ones, we might also consider local (and even broader) communities or perhaps NGOs or other social advocacy groupings, industry trade groups, and so on. A part of this will involve *interviewing* stakeholders. While we might make educated guesses as to what is important, "results" will be better the more information we have. Conducting interviews gives immediacy and reality to materiality assessments. The more stakeholders we engage during our "research and strategy" phase, the broader the scope of our assessment. Each group of stakeholders is likely to provide diverse viewpoints and insights concerning factors we may not independently have identified.

As we consider what is important to our own organization, our starting point will be the "review and understand business context" task cited throughout this book. In turn, this will be linked to our mission and values and to our stated commercial strategy. That's on the positive side. On the negative side is our assessment of risks, which may begin with a SWOT analysis or a "Porter's Five Forces" type analysis.

Currently, at the time of writing this book, most pundits proffer a simple two-axis model to "plot" these considerations, as suggested in Figure 25.1.

Using this approach, we subcategorize ESG factors as being "moderate," "high," or "very high" materiality. We can also think along similar lines and envisage them in the consultant's favored "four-box matrix," equivalent in many ways to the Kraljic supplier positioning technique we encountered in Part 6 of this book. The equivalent ESG materiality matrix can thus be summarized as in Figure 25.2.

Beware, however, that this process does not become a search for external approval. While some stakeholders are legitimate, others frankly are not. But many "outsiders" will want to "muscle-in" on our business and impact its operations. Select your stakeholders wisely and prudently. Be prepared to politely resist attempts by non legitimate stakeholders to sway your strategy. At the time of writing, some big organizations have been

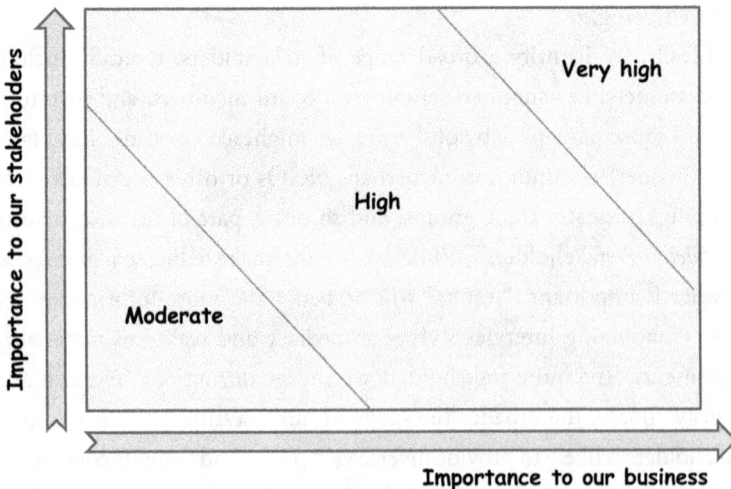

Figure 25.1 ESG materiality assessment—two-axis model

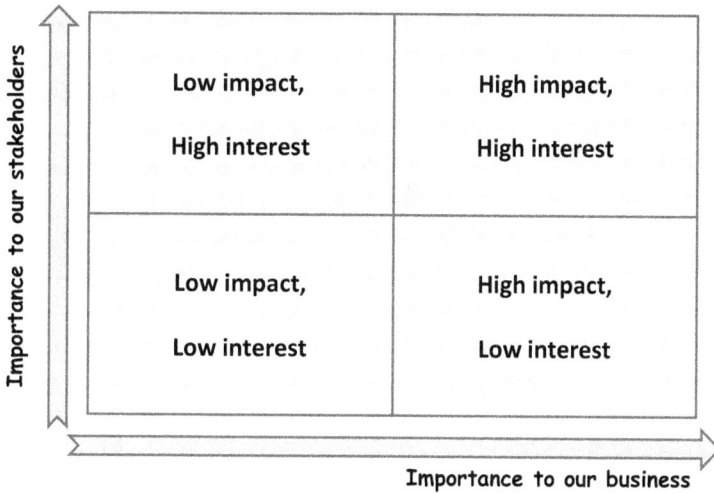

Figure 25.2 Materiality assessment—impact versus interest

suckered into "supporting" various lobby groups that can be considered as the vanguard of what is increasingly styled as "the culture wars." Select what's right for your business and do not try to "please all the people all of the time" because if you do, you will fail and you may actually antagonize your core customers.

Double Materiality

Not to be confused with the 1944 film noire, *Double Indemnity.*[1] In the film, a crooked insurance salesman and a femme fatale conspire to murder, and then clean up on insurance payments!

As we have already seen, the concept of materiality recognizes that some questions are more significant than others in terms of their potential impact on an organization and so a proper understanding of what is *material* (and thereby, what is not material) helps us to characterize risk and also what needs to be formally reported, especially for financial investment purposes. The word *material* was first introduced

---

[1] In insurance, a *double indemnity* makes possible payment of double the face amount of an insurance policy under certain conditions, for example, when a death occurs as a result of an accident.

in the U.S. Securities Act of 1933. Since the 1940s, the SEC has defined *material information* in financial statements as "those matters as to which an average prudent investor ought reasonably to be informed before purchasing the security registered." Former U.S. Supreme Court Justice Thurgood Marshall, in 1976, stated that an item is material if there is "a substantial likelihood that a reasonable investor would consider the information important in deciding how to vote or make an investment decision."

With the growing interest and pressure in the ESG arena, and especially the "E" part of that arena, matters that were once of no concern have suddenly emerged as potentially *material* in terms of understanding the viability of a business or organization going forward. The concept of "double materiality" refers to how information disclosed by a company can be material in terms of its *implications for the company's financial value* and *the company's impact on the world at large*. Plainly, the second aspect is by far the more difficult to agree upon and even to define. Double materiality recognizes that a company's impact on "the world beyond" purely financial considerations can be sizeable and therefore should be disclosed, for reasons other than any effect on a company's bottom line. At the time of preparing this book, it is the "E" aspect of ESG that is the most pressing, but there is an assumption that "S" and even "G" elements may, in the future, be considered potentially material in terms of what stakeholders (especially, investors) need to be aware of.

Looking at the environmental dynamic alone, determining what information is "material" depends on a person's view as to whether environmental impacts could translate into financial risks, for example, through legal liabilities or harms to a company's reputation; or a reasonable person might consider the information material for reasons other than direct financial impact. Always important (in common law systems, especially), we need to consider who this "reasonable person" is and what their legitimate interests are. This, in turn, helps define what counts as material and therefore what is important to them. Social issues, such as human and labor rights, are also important in this context, given that a company's approach to such issues might result in financial risks for the organization and are accordingly considered material to investors.

At the time of preparing this book, there is pushback in the U.S. investment and regulatory worlds as some ESG-type pressures are considered to drive anticompetitive behaviors and to introduce costs and overheads that risk making industries uncompetitive. They are even perceived as being part of the broader culture wars that so infect current western discourse and politics. So, the United States is still defining its approach in this area in 2024, but has one eye on developments in Europe and especially the EU political bloc. The concept of double materiality has been incorporated into the EU Regulatory Framework relating to sustainability reporting, which applies to financial institutions and companies operating across the European economies.

European regulators in the early 2020s moved further than their U.S. counterparts in formulating disclosure requirements on climate change and devised approaches aimed at reconciling the need for investors to have greater information on ESG issues and the question of whether such factors are considered financially material. In Europe, *double materiality* suggests how corporate information can be important for implications relating to financial value and also about a firm's impact on the world at large. Double materiality recognizes that a company's impact on "the world beyond" finance can be significant. At the time of writing, some experts argue that the meaning of double materiality requires further analysis. How do we know with certainty what a material impact is? Pundits say the answer fundamentally depends on a person's view of *why* information on environmental impacts should be material in the first place and suggest two likely reasons:

- Environmental impacts could translate into financial risks through legal liability or harms to a company's reputation.
- A *reasonable person* might consider the information material for reasons beyond direct financial repercussions.

What double materiality means then devolves down to who that hypothetical "reasonable person" is and what their interests are. These in turn go a long way to determine what is perceived as material, that is, what is important to them. To summarize, materiality is always an issue, but double materiality seeks to create a distinction between purely financial impacts and other important outcomes that may need to be reported. To the reader, the advices are (1) be aware of your own sector and how matters are developing in a sector-specific way and (2) try to define the most rational measures of the impacts on nonfinancial impacts, ideally becoming "master" of the theory so you are best able to defend your organization's stance to a sometimes skeptical and even hostile world of purported "stakeholders."

Market Data

In the world of finance, *market data* is price and other related data for a financial instrument reported by a trading venue such as a stock exchange. Market data allows traders and investors to know the latest price and see historical trends for instruments such as equities, fixed-income products, derivatives, and currencies. (The clear analogy for ESG data is that investors and other stakeholders have added granularity in information about key risks affecting potential investments arising from various ESG concerns).

At a technical level, market data for a particular instrument will include the identifier of the instrument (including where it was traded) such as the ticker symbol and exchange code plus the latest bid and ask price, and the time of the last trade. It may also include other information such as volume traded, bid, and offer sizes and static data about the financial instrument, which might have come from a variety of sources. A number of financial data vendors specialize in collecting, cleaning, collating, and distributing market data and this is today the most common way that traders and investors get access to market data.

Delivery of price data from exchanges to users, such as traders, is very time sensitive and involves specialized technologies designed to handle collection and throughput of massive data streams. These are used to distribute the information to traders and investors. Market price data is used not only in real time to make on-the-spot decisions about buying or selling, but also as historical market data, to project forward pricing trends and calculate market risk on portfolios of investments.

Alternative Data

Alternative data refers to non traditional data used in the portfolio investment process. Unlike traditional types of data, alternative data tends to
be unstructured, hard to find, and/or large in volume, and so requires
significant computational power to analyze. When properly used, alternative data can provide firms with an information edge. However it can lose
its potential for generating pecuniary advantage if it becomes too widely
available. At the time of writing this book, ESG data is considered to be
in this class. Alternative data can be bought and sold just as can market
data. In the early 2020s, a new "industry" achieved relative maturity in
servicing "alternative" data requirements. Alternative data might be specific intelligence gleaned from satellite images or by scouring websites.
Many Alt-data firms have been founded by entrepreneurs.

A key problem in the late "noughties," as Alt-data firms were first established, was the reality that some of the new firms were pushing the boundaries of legality. Some were noted as being careless about privacy (think
GDPR). There were anecdotal stories of former employees of big firms
starting their own Alt-data consultancies to "predict" the statistics released
by their former employer. Finance companies became uncomfortably aware
of the danger of *suspect data* and the potential for what might be described
as "insider dealing." The biggest risk, here, was deemed to be reputational.
It is true to say that only the most egregious transgressions are likely to lead
to penalties. In the United States, a conviction for insider dealing requires
not only proof that the information is *material* and non public, but also
proof of a "breach of duty" (generally that the information was obtained
without the owner's consent). These "proofs" are hard to obtain, but "mud
sticks" and any accusation that you are dealing with data providers that
"sail too close to the wind" might have reputational implications.

To deal with the risk of transgressing data privacy rules, some firms
use "differential privacy" techniques, such as adding "noise" to the data,
thus obscuring *personal identifiable information* but without destroying
the dataset's useful features. This seems to work in practice and some
household-name firms are utilizing such techniques. In addition, there is
now an Investment Data Standards Organization (a nonprofit set up in

2018; readers can "Google" if they need more insight), which is helping to raise standards and achieve respectability. What does all this mean for ESG data?

ESG data, almost by its very nature, is "Alt-data." So firms that buy datasets from such service providers need to be aware of the potential implications and (possibly) to move in concert with their industry peers. Trade organizations may be able to assist, here, and this will be a (permanent?) agenda item relating to proxy data going forward (see Chapter 23 on proxy data). Once more, the best advice we can give on buying data is *caveat emptor* and "watch this space." The *alternative data* market will develop significantly in the period 2024 to 2028.

In-House or External?

At this point, our discussion moves briefly to the more generic question of data analytics. Data analytics is a long-established tool aimed at unlocking the highest value extracted from data across our *own* organization. *Analytics* is the systematic computational analysis of data or statistics. It is used for discovery, interpretation, and communication of meaningful patterns within data. It also enables the application of data patterns toward effective decision making and can be highly valuable in areas rich with *recorded* information. Analytics relies on the simultaneous application of statistics computer programming, and operations research to quantify performance. It requires sophisticated computing power to do it well.

Organizations may apply analytics to business data to describe, predict, and improve business performance. There are certain subsets of data analytics including descriptive analytics, diagnostic analytics, *predictive* analytics, *prescriptive* analytics, and cognitive analytics. Analytics may be applied typically across marketing, management, finance, supply chain, information security, and software services. Since analytics can require extensive computation (think "big data"), the algorithms and software used for analytics harness the most modern methods in computer science, statistics, and mathematics. At the time of writing this book, global spending on big data and business analytics (BDA) was estimated at $200 billion plus per annum.

Analytics can be undertaken in-house or externally and can be bought in as a service. A key decision for senior managers is how to handle the sheer potential for such analytics and *how* to secure the relevant services if we buy them[2]. Given the sensitivities around ESG-type questions, we need to ensure we have a robust business case for whatever solution we adopt.

3PM and Data

The foregoing discussions lead inevitably to the question of dealing with data and our relationship with our key commercial partners (3PM). We noted in Part 6 of this book that there may be a coinciding interest in acquisition of relevant data across the "E," "S," and "G" areas of concern. As suggested in Chapter 24, thought must be given to the contractual arrangements covering generation and use of data.

While discussion of contractual provisions may give rise to the idea of commercial rivalry and associated win–lose dynamics, in reality, we may encounter a collegiate relationship in this area as we seek win–win outcomes across various "E," "S," and "G" areas of interest. The best advice your author can give is that despite any synergies in working toward ESG outcomes and whatever the goodwill evinced in co-working toward favorable outcomes, *do not forget this remains a commercial arrangement and it needs to have suitable contractual coverage and clear demarcation lines.*

Using the principles suggested in Chapter 24, is there anything to add in terms of "designing" and drafting suitable contract documentation as required to cover the data aspect of the relationship?

Rather than repeat what others have done, your author recommends readers who need to delve more deeply into this specific question to consult the materials freely provided by *World Commerce & Contracting*. This is a not-for-profit association that promotes standards and aims to raise capabilities in commercial practice. It undertakes research and is doing some very good work in the whole realm of *contract design*.

In February 2020, *World Commerce & Contracting* published a 46-page set of principles for contract design. At the time of writing

---

[2] For example, competitively or noncompetitively? Single source or multi source?

this book, the document (PDF format) is freely available; Google *World Commerce & Contracting—principles* and you should find this useful document. On pages 17 to 19, there are some helpful principles around use of data. Your author suggests this is a useful starting point in any search for controls on generating, sharing and use-of ESG-type data.

Using Data to Best Effect

The purpose of data collection is twofold: *to improve our own performance in business management* and ESG outcomes and to *report progress to interested stakeholder groups*. We suggest that it is the former that should truly drive business strategy, although at the time of writing and via so many public pronouncements, one might think it is the latter that is determining most outcomes! Throughout this book, we make the simple case that organizations should devise policies and processes that work best for themselves and keep as much activity in-house as possible. So, besides external reporting, be it your annual report, sustainability report, or other platforms, data can be used internally for a variety of useful purposes, but, in particular, scenario analysis and performance review.

Forecasting, Scenario Analysis, and Risk Management

ESG data, especially environmental data, is increasingly used in scenario analysis and risk modelling. For some firms, this may have been initiated as a response to comply with Task Force on Climate-related Financial Disclosures (TCFD) and its equivalents. Some organizations now build scenario models for sustainability questions beyond the overriding climate change issue. This can help them with risk assessments, and some ESG data points can serve usefully as risk indicators. Data can help an organization form a picture of future possibilities. The majority of data measures, however, tend to be *lagging or historical indicators* relating to frequency of incidents over a period of time. These can be used to build trend analysis, but are rarely sufficient on their own. Organizations increasingly seek to present *leading indicators* demonstrating their success in taking preventive and proactive action to influence future performance. Examples of this might be investigating and challenging supply chains to avoid modern slavery or conflict minerals abuses or hazards. At the time of writing, an increasing number of organizations are working on identifying and developing a wider range of meaningful leading indicators.

Performance Review and Progress Against Targets

Organizations can use ESG-specific data to assess performance both from an operational viewpoint (e.g., water preservation or energy efficiency) and from a *sustainability* perspective (e.g., environmental impact or pollution reduction). The same data may serve dual purposes and might be reviewed by senior managers in differing formats. It should be emphasized that organizationally there needs to be "one source of truth" and data needs to be consistent in providing a coherent message. Organizations that increasingly perceive *sustainable practice* as core to their business strategy try to devise KPIs that are reviewed regularly to assure the achievement of agreed targets. This helps with planning and, at the time of writing this book, is especially pertinent to net-zero targets and to set out organizational *transition plans*.

APPENDIX 1

Key ESG Issues to Consider—A Listing

Key ESG areas of concern for shareholders and other direct stakeholders: these and other issues present risks and potential opportunities to investors.

Analysts seeking a thorough understanding of an industry or a particular company will consider the relevance of these issues to that company and will evaluate each issue for its potential for financial impact.

This list is not exhaustive. Note that there is overlap in some areas of concern. Readers will keep an open mind as to the applicability in their particular circumstances.

Some descriptions below may seem a little cryptic; however, a simple Internet search on these generic titles will speedily provide useful information.

Environmental

Animal welfare

Biodiversity and habitat

Carbon emissions, greenhouse gas emissions, and disclosure or measurement and reporting

Climate change; effect on company, risk exposure, and opportunities

Ecosystem change—potential impacts

Ecosystem usage—impact and dependence

Energy consumption

Facilities (or sub-businesses) citing environmental risks

Hazardous waste disposal and cleanup

Indoor environmental quality

Innovation—enviro-friendly products and services

Land contamination

License to operate in communities

Location and transportation

Materials

Pollution—general

Renewable energy

Resilience to catastrophe or disaster

Resource depletion

Sustainable procurement

Toxic chemical use and disposal

Waste management—water, solids, and hazardous

Water use

Social

Child labor

Community relations and development

Controversial tenant (tenant vulnerability)

Customer health and safety

Customer privacy

Discrimination

Diversity (employee or board diversity)

Equal opportunity

Facilities, citing social risks

Genetically modified organisms

Human rights

Labor standards and working conditions

Living wage disputes

Modern slavery (coerced workers)

Occupier amenities (showers, changing rooms)

Predatory lending

Political contributions

Political risk of involvement in troubled markets and countries

Poverty and community input

Sexual harassment

Shareowner advisory vote on executive compensation

Social enterprise partnering ("social performance")

Stakeholder engagement (and ongoing management)

Supply chain management (plus "3PM")

Workplace health and safety

Governance

Accountability (code of conduct or clear business principles)

Board diversity and structure

Bribery and corruption or money laundering

Codes of conduct and business principles

Cumulative voting (fair voting systems)

Cybersecurity

Data protection

Dual-class share structure (differential voting rights)

ESG clauses—downflow

Executive compensation (pay for performance, pay equity)

Fraud defenses—internal

Majority voting (fair voting systems)

Poison pills

Say on pay

Separation of chairman and CEO position

Shareholder rights

Staggered boards

Stakeholder engagement or relations

Takeover defenses and market for control

Third-party risk and relationship management ("3PM")

Transparency and disclosure

APPENDIX 2

ESG-Related Acronyms

The ESG industry has produced a veritable alphabet-soup of acronyms to describe its various initiatives. It is no exaggeration to say that every week a new acronym is invented somewhere. The task for business people (and administrators) is to appreciate which are relatively important and which should feature clearly in their business planning.

Most acronyms provided below are mentioned in this book. They are in alphabetic order.

Acronym	Description
3PM	Third-party management
	Sometimes called "third-party risk and relationship management." 3PM is an acronym to depict the *proactive* management of all "third-party" relationships, up and down the value chain. Third parties are ones with which an organization has direct contractual relationships. In terms of ESG, and especially the "E" and "S" aspects, it is via third parties that many firms will encounter real ESG risks and opportunities and in collaboration with such third parties that they will best achieve broad Sustainability goals
APIs	Application programming interfaces
	An API is a way for two (or more) computer programs to communicate. It is a type of software interface, offering a service to other pieces of software. A document or standard that describes how to build or use such a connection or interface is called an *API specification*. An API may be custom-built for a particular pair of systems or it may be a common standard allowing interoperability among many systems. The term is often used to refer to web APIs, which allow communication between computers that are joined via the Internet. There are typically APIs for programming languages, software libraries, computer operating systems, and computer hardware
	An API comprises different "parts," which act as tools that are available to the programmer. A program that uses one of these "parts" is said to *call* on that portion of the API. The calls that make up the API are also known as "subroutines," "requests," or "endpoints." An API specification *defines* these calls, meaning that it explains how to use or implement them

(Continued)

(*Continued*)

Acronym	Description
BVCM	Beyond value chain mitigation
	Mitigation action or investments that fall outside a company's value chain, especially activities outside of a company's value chain that avoid or reduce greenhouse gas emissions, or remove
	greenhouse gases from the atmosphere and permanently store them
	Definition emerged from SBTI (see below)
CDP	Carbon Disclosure Project
	An international disclosure system for investors, companies, cities, states, and regions to help manage their environmental impacts, with specific focus on forests, climate, and water use
	CDP is a nonprofit organization based across the United Kingdom, Japan, India, China, Germany, and the United States that helps companies and cities report on their environmental impact. It aims to make *environmental* reporting and risk management a business norm, driving disclosure, insight, and action toward a sustainable economy. In 2021, over 14,000 organizations disclosed their environmental information through CDP
CDSD	Climate Data Steering Committee
	A self-appointed pressure group established in 2022 with the aim to bring greater transparency into the progress organizations make toward decarbonization goals. CDSD's first achievement was to publish a detailed proposal for the structure and aims of its global climate database. This is the putative NZDPU = Net-Zero Data Public Utility
	See NZDPU
CDSP (the United Kingdom)	Climate Disclosure Standards Board
	CDSB is a nonprofit organization working to provide material information for investors and financial markets through the integration of climate change-related information into mainstream financial reporting. In 2021, it became a part of the IFRS Foundation to help provide technical expertise for the ISSB (International Sustainability Standards Board)
CEAP (EU)	Circular Economy Action Plan
	The *Circular Economy Action Plan for a cleaner and more competitive Europe* is central to the "European Green Deal." It seeks to ensure that the EU economy can realize a green future, strengthen competitiveness, and protect the environment. CEAP introduces legislative and nonlegislative measures and target areas where action at EU level brings added value. CEAP details measures to make sustainable products the norm in the EU, for example, restriction of single-use products and ensuring that products on the EU market are designed to last longer, are easier to reuse, repair, and recycle, and incorporate recycled material as much as possible

Acronym	Description
CO_2e	Carbon dioxide equivalent or CO_2e
	CO_2 equivalent is a metric measure used to compare emissions from various greenhouse gases on the basis of their global-warming potential (GWP), by converting amounts of *other* gases to the equivalent amount of carbon dioxide. CO_2 equivalent is commonly expressed as *million metric tonnes of carbon dioxide equivalents*, abbreviated as MMTCDE.
	Carbon dioxide equivalent for a gas is derived by multiplying the tonnes of the gas by the associated GWP: $MMTCDE = (million\ metric\ tonnes\ of\ a\ gas) \times (GWP\ of\ the\ gas)$
	Example: The GWP for methane is 25 and for nitrous oxide 298. This means that emissions of 1 million metric tonnes of methane and nitrous oxide, respectively, are equivalent to emissions of 25 and 298 million metric tonnes of carbon dioxide
COP	Conference of the Parties
	COP is the name given to the United Nations Climate Change Conferences. The goal of these conferences is to review progress made by members of the United Nations Framework Convention on Climate Change (UNFCCC) to limit climate change. COP is the main decision-making body of the UNFCCC
	COP may be considered as a process with annual meetings that set the broad agenda on climate change
CRD	Corporate reporting dialogue
	CRD is an initiative, convened by the IIRC, designed to respond to market calls for greater coherence, consistency, and comparability between corporate reporting frameworks, standards, and related requirements. It aims to communicate the direction, content, and ongoing development of reporting frameworks, standards, and related requirements; also to identify practical ways by which respective frameworks, standards, and related requirements can be aligned and rationalized and to share information and express a common voice on areas of mutual interest. Wherever possible, CRD seeks to engage key regulators
CSRD (EU)	Corporate Sustainability Reporting Directive
	Enforced from January 2023, CSRD establishes common European reporting rules, requiring more than 50,000 companies to report sustainability information according to mandatory EU sustainability reporting standards and to conduct a double materiality assessment (financial versus impact)
	Despite the name, **a double materiality assessment does not require two separate assessments or draw two separate matrices.** It requires gathering evidence, assessing, and explaining why issues are material from the "impact" (stakeholders') perspective and/or from the "financial" perspective. See also ESRS

(*Continued*)

(*Continued*)

Acronym	Description
CTVaR	Climate transition value at risk
	An innovative (and proprietary) measure designed by *Willis Towers Watson* and certain partner firms. The measure seeks to grasp how companies are susceptible to losses and gains in revenue and asset values as the global economy moves to net zero. While distinctive at the time of writing this book, the measure may be emulated by others
	Decarbonization metrics are only partially useful in relation to real-world outcomes (e.g., they could prevent investment in carbon-intensive climate solutions). Historically, in terms of financial instruments, there has been little correlation between "carbon footprint" and financial risk
	CTVaR measures the value lost (or gained) during the transition to a low-carbon economy and is the methodology used behind the Climate Transition Index (CTI)
DNSH (EU)	Do no significant harm
	The EU's taxonomy regulation is designed to support the transformation of the EU economy to meet its *European Green Deal* objectives, including the 2050 climate-neutrality target. As a classification tool, it seeks to provide clarity for companies, capital markets, and policy makers on which economic activities are sustainable. As a screening tool, it seeks to support investment flows into those activities
	Demonstrating that investments "do no significant harm" is a cornerstone of the EU's sustainable finance framework. In practice, determining how to apply this principle can be complex for investors. Regulations such as SFDR, the taxonomy for sustainable activities, and the Benchmark Regulation all refer to DNSH with different nuances. How can investors demonstrate that their investments are doing no harm, notably for non-EU companies? What do they need to measure, and with what type of data? These are practical questions with constantly evolving answers
ESAP (EU)	European Single Access Point
	ESAP will be a EU-wide platform aimed at providing investors with seamless access to financial and sustainability-related information disclosed to the public by companies, including financial firms
	ESAP will be operational by 2024. It aims to make companies visible for cross-border investors and strengthen capital market integration. Company information, including financial, ESG, sustainability reports, product-related information in prospectuses, key information documents and other information, will together build the company's profile. Company data collected by national company registries and other authorities are expected to be shared via *APIs.
	* APIs (application programming interfaces) are *communication tools for software applications*. APIs are leading to key advances within the banking industry as financial institutions continue to collaborate with third parties

Acronym	Description
ESOS (the United Kingdom)	Energy Savings Opportunity Scheme
	ESOS is a mandatory energy assessment scheme, introduced by the U.K. government (2014—phase 2, 2019) to make sure large enterprises in the United Kingdom are energy efficient. Under the scheme, large organizations are required to assess their energy use every four years and to find new ways to save energy
ESRS (EU)	European Sustainability Reporting Standards
	Adopted in July 2023, ESRS provides basis for implementation of sustainability disclosures under CSRD. The first reports are expected to be submitted via ESRS in 2025. Bigger EU companies will be impacted first with further roll-out to a timetable yet to be defined
	ESRS comprises 12 standards for sustainable reporting as follows:
	two "cross-cutting" standards on general requirements and disclosures required, five environmental standards, four social standards, and one governance standard
ETF	Enhanced Transparency Framework
	Under the terms of the 2015 Paris Agreement, all countries will transition their climate reporting to the ETF by 2024. This represents a major stepping up of climate transparency, which will require significant capacity building
	While it is nation states that have to do the reporting, they will flow-down transparency requirements across their economies
E&C	Ethics & Compliance
	An organization's stance on both *ethical questions* and *compliance* is often called its "E&C stance." Many organizations link these two themes, even putting them under one head. At best, an E&C program provides an independent voice in the organization, helps train business leaders in E&C, serves as a resource across the organization to support E&C efforts, and is a visible contributor to high-level discussions of strategy, crisis management, and the day-to-day operations of an organization
	With *compliance*, the boundary is defined by a law, rule, regulation, or policy and adherence is *mandatory*. Ethics, by contrast, involves judgment and making choices about conduct that reflect values: right versus wrong or good versus bad. Words like "integrity," "transparency," and "honorable behavior" are relevant
	E&C professionals are expected to have knowledge and understanding of global and domestic regulatory guidelines and standards, as well as of the broader regulatory landscape for their specific sector. They are expected to understand the business, its goals, and its strategy. Ideally, they contribute toward the development of corporate strategy

(Continued)

(*Continued*)

Acronym	Description
FMP (EU)	Financial market participant EU regulation applies to a defined concept of "financial market participant" including MiFID firms, AIFMs, and UCTIS managers. This is under the EU's SFDR
GHG	Greenhouse gas A greenhouse gas (GHG or GhG) is a gas that absorbs and emits radiant energy within the thermal infrared range, causing the greenhouse effect. The primary greenhouse gases in Earth's atmosphere are water vapor (H_2O), carbon dioxide (CO_2), methane (CH_4), nitrous oxide (N_2O), and ozone (O_3)
Greenhush	"Greenhushing" Companies decide to remain quiet or reticent about their climate strategies. Concern about "greenwashing" (immediately below) and the strong possibility of litigation from special interest groups based on either purported "greenwashing" generally or a failure to meet policy targets in particular means that it can be a rational response to avoid drawing attention to otherwise laudable environmental (or social of governance) goals Two main reasons for "greenhushing": (1) organizations do not want to be challenged if they fall short of their stated targets and (2) organizations do not want to be accused of "greenwashing."
Greenwash (or "green sheen")	"Greenwashing" Greenwashing, also called "green sheen," is a form of advertising or marketing spin in which "green PR" and "green marketing" are used deceptively to persuade the public/investors that an organization's products, aims, and policies are environmentally friendly. While greenwashing applies obviously to the "E" element of ESG, the same avoidance strategies may be observed for the "S" and "G" subcomponents. All are under increasing external scrutiny
GRI	Global Reporting Initiative GRI is an international independent standards organization that helps businesses, governments, and other organizations understand and communicate their impacts on issues such as climate change, human rights, and corruption Under increasing pressure from different stakeholder groups, such as governments, consumers, and investors, to be more transparent about environmental, economic, and social impacts, many companies publish a sustainability report (sometimes called a CSR or *environmental, social, and governance* (ESG) *report*)

Acronym	Description
	The GRI framework for sustainability reporting helps companies identify, gather, and report this information in a clear and comparable manner. First launched in 2000, GRI's sustainability reporting framework is now the most widely used by multinational organizations, governments, small and medium enterprises (SMEs), NGOs, and industry groups in more than 90 countries. In 2017, 63 percent of the largest 100 companies (N100) and 75 percent of the Global Fortune 250 (G250) reported using the GRI framework
ICGN	International Corporate Governance Network
	Founded in 1995 at the instigation of major institutional investors, ICGN represents investors, companies, financial intermediaries, academics, and other parties interested in the development of global corporate governance practices
	Its objective is to facilitate international dialogue on issues of common concern. Through this process, the ICGN claims, companies can compete more effectively and economies can best prosper. The organization's charter empowers it to adopt guidelines when it feels they can contribute to achieving this objective
	Led by investors responsible for assets worth around $U.S. 70 trillion, ICGN advances the highest standards of corporate governance and investor stewardship worldwide in pursuit of long-term value creation, contributing to sustainable economies, societies, and the environment. This is achieved through a comprehensive international work program based around the ICGN Global Governance Principles and the ICGN Global Stewardship Principles
IIRC	International Integrated Reporting Council
	A coalition of leaders from corporate, investment, accounting, securities, regulatory, academic, and standard-setting sectors, as well as civil society. Founded in 2010 by *The Prince of Wales' Accounting for Sustainability Project*, the Global Reporting Initiative, and the International Federation of Accountants. Integrated reporting enhances or consolidates reporting practices to move toward a reporting framework that provides the information needed to develop the global economic model to meet the challenges of the 21st century
	Integrated reporting highlights links between an organization's strategy, governance, and financial performance—and the social, environmental, and economic context within which it operates. This helps business to make sustainable decisions and enable investors (and other stakeholders) to understand how an organization is really performing
IISD	International Institute for Sustainable Development
	IISD is an independent think tank (founded in 1990) working to shape and inform international policy on sustainable development governance. The institute has three offices in Canada and one in Switzerland

(*Continued*)

(*Continued*)

Acronym	Description
ISSB	International Sustainability Standards Board
	The ISSB is a standard-setting body established in 2022 under the IFRS Foundation, with the mandate to create and develop sustainability-related financial reporting standards to meet investors' needs for sustainability reporting
	The ISSB is a sort of *International Standards Organization* (ISO) specifically for the "sustainability" sector
LTAFR	Lost time accident frequency rate
	LTAFR refers to the number of lost time injuries occurring in a workplace per 1 million hours worked. An LTAFR of 7, for example, shows that 7 lost time injuries occur on a jobsite every 1 million hours worked. The formula gives a picture of how safe a workplace is for its workers. In terms of ESG, this is a "social" measure
MEI	Material ESG issues
	Material ESG issues are those governance, sustainability, or societal factors likely to *materially* affect the financial condition or operating performance of businesses within a specific sector. Under varying reporting mechanisms, *material ESG* factors are taking on greater importance in reporting regimes
	ESG questions or issues are not "equal!" Within any business, industry, or geography, relative importance varies. Organizations must focus on those elements of ESG that are financially material to the way they do business. Reduction of fuel consumption, for example, will have a more direct impact on a transport company's financial position than on that of an accounting firm. Paper recycling is a large-scale undertaking for a print media organization, while pesticide use is high on the list of environmental issues for farmers. Sustainability accounting should have ESG materiality at its core
NACE	Nomenclature of economic activities
	NACE codes are *the standard European nomenclature of productive economic activities*. They break down the universe of economic activities in such a way that a NACE code can be associated with a statistical unit carrying out the activity it designates
	From an ESG perspective, and in keeping with the taxonomy, NACE codes help reporting entities to accurately specify where in the ecosphere they encounter E, or S, or G questions and to report progress in these areas. Use of these codes encourages granularity in reporting

Acronym	Description
NDC	Nationally determined contribution
	The Paris Agreement is a legally binding international treaty on climate change. Adopted by 196 Parties at COP21 in Paris, on December 12, 2015, it became effective on November 4, 2016. Its goal is to limit global warming to well below 2°C, preferably to 1.5°C, compared to preindustrial levels. To achieve this long-term temperature goal, countries aim to reach global peaking of greenhouse gas emissions as soon as possible to achieve a climate-neutral world by mid-century
	NDCs are at the heart of the Paris Agreement and achievement of its long-term goals. NDCs reflect efforts by each country to reduce national emissions and adapt to the impacts of climate change. The Paris Agreement (Article 4, paragraph 2) requires each party to prepare, communicate, and maintain successive NDCs that it intends to achieve. Parties shall pursue domestic mitigation measures, with the aim of achieving the objectives of such contributions
	The Paris Agreement requests each country to outline and communicate their post-2020 climate actions, known as their NDCs. Together, these climate actions will determine whether the world achieves the long-term goals of the Paris Agreement and reach global peaking of greenhouse gas (GHG) emissions as soon as possible.
	The Paris Agreement recognizes that long-term goals will be achieved over time and, therefore, depends on a progressive ratcheting-up of aggregate and individual ambition. NDCs are submitted every five years to the UNFCCC secretariat. In order to enhance the ambition over time, the Paris Agreement provides that successive NDCs will represent a progression compared to the previous NDC and reflect its highest possible ambition. Parties are requested to submit their NDCs (new or updated) by 2025 and every five years thereafter (e.g., by 2030), regardless of their respective implementation timeframes
NFRD (EU)	Non-Financial Reporting Directive
	Directive 2014/95/EU established rules on disclosure of nonfinancial and diversity information relating to the ESG areas (environmental protection, social responsibility and treatment of employees, respect for human rights, anticorruption and bribery, and diversity on company boards) by certain large EU public-interest companies in their annual reports
	Large public-interest corporations (approximately 11,700 EU companies) are companies with more than 500 employees, including listed entities, insurance companies, and banks
	NFRD had two main purposes: make available nonfinancial information to stakeholders and investors to determine the companies' value creation and risks and encourage society to take responsibility for social and environmental concerns
	NFRD is being replaced by CSRD

(Continued)

(Continued)

Acronym	Description
NZDPU	Net-Zero Data Public Utility
	Envisaged in 2022 as a common data portal that financial institutions can use to inform their investment and risk-mitigation decisions. The NZDPU is the first major piece of work by the CDSD, which was inaugurated by French President Emmanuel Macron and financier Michael Bloomberg
	The utility would make climate transition-related data openly available in a single place and provide accurate, trusted, and verifiable data. At the time of writing, the idea was floated on the back of the COP27 process, but it remains to be seen whether such an idea will command widespread international support
PACTA	Paris Agreement Capital Transition Assessment
	PACTA is a free, open-source methodology or tool, which measures financial alignment of portfolios with various climate scenarios consistent with the Paris Agreement
	In 2018, the 2° Investing Initiative ("2DII")—an international, nonprofit think tank—launched the PACTA tool. Recognizing that participants had historically assessed climate risk and impact using "backward-looking carbon foot-printing," 2DII created the PACTA tool to help investors assess "the extent to which corporate capital expenditures and industrial assets behind a given equity, bond, or lending portfolio are aligned with various climate scenarios" and to enable investors to stress test their portfolios by analyzing the effects of different physical, legal, and transition risks related to climate change
	The tool enables financial institutions, major regulators, and central and international banks to understand how their portfolios, or those held by regulated entities, align with the goals of the COP Paris Agreement
PAII (EU)	Principle adverse impact indicator
	PAIs—negative, material, or potentially material effects on Sustainability factors that result from, worsen, or are directly related to investment choices or advice performed by a legal entity. Examples include GHG emissions and carbon footprint
	The PAI regime is one of the most challenging elements of the EU's SFDR. It will require relevant firms to provide extensive disclosures on various ESG-related matters, including GHG emissions and other indicators, in a (controversial) template format
PCAF	Partnership for Carbon Accounting Financials
	PCAF is an initiative led by the financial industry to develop a harmonized global standard to measure and disclose the GHG emissions of loans and investments. Measuring financed emissions is an important step that enables financial institutions to set science-based targets and align their portfolios with the Paris Agreement

Acronym	Description
PPN (the United Kingdom)	Procurement Policy Notice Guidance on best practice for public sector procurement. These are issued online by the Cabinet Office Infrastructure and Projects Authority. The guidance is issued for public sector organizations to help them procure in accordance with government policy and deemed present best practice
PPN 06/20 (the United Kingdom)	Taking Account of Social Value in the Award of Central Government Contracts A procurement model (effective January 2021) to deliver social value through government commercial activities. Central government organizations should use the model to take account of the *additional social benefits* that can be achieved in the delivery of its contracts, using policy outcomes aligned with the government's priorities Social value should be explicitly evaluated in all central government procurement, where the requirements are related, and proportionate to, the subject matter of the contract, rather than just "considered" as required under the Public Services (Social Value) Act 2012. Unnecessary burdens should not be placed on commercial teams or suppliers via PPN 06/20
PPN 06/21 (the United Kingdom)	Taking Account of Carbon Reduction Plans in the Procurement of Major Government Contracts In 2019, the U.K. government amended the Climate Change Act 2008 by introducing a target of at least a 100 percent reduction in the net U.K. carbon account (i.e., reduction of GHG emissions, compared to 1990 levels) by 2050. This is otherwise known as the "net-zero" target PPN 06/21 sets out how to take account of suppliers' net-zero carbon reduction plans in the procurement of major government contracts. PPN 06/21 applies to all central government departments, their executive agencies, and non departmental public bodies
PRI (UN)	Principles for Responsible Investment The UN PRI is an international organization that works to promote the incorporation of environmental, social, and corporate governance factors (ESG) into investment decision making Launched in April 2006 with support from the UN, the PRI has over 4,900 participating financial institutions, as of March 31, 2021. These institutions participate by becoming signatories to the PRI's six key principles and then filing regular reports on their progress The core philosophy behind the organization is that environmental and social considerations are relevant factors in investment decision making and should therefore be considered by responsible investors

(Continued)

(Continued)

Acronym	Description
	PRI put forward six core principles, to which signatory companies must agree to commit themselves. The six signatory principles are as follows. We will: • Principle 1: incorporate ESG issues into investment analysis and decision-making processes • Principle 2: be active owners and incorporate ESG issues into our ownership policies and practices • Principle 3: seek appropriate disclosure on ESG issues by the entities in which we invest • Principle 4: promote acceptance and implementation of the Principles within the investment industry • Principle 5: work together to enhance our effectiveness in implementing the principles • Principle 6: report on our activities and progress toward implementing the principles
Proxy data	See Chapter 23 for further insight. Proxy data is the substitution of missing, or inaccessible, data with a comparable or related data source Climate change assessments and evaluation should be undertaken using (1) recorded observation data, as well as, where necessary, (2) prepared proxy data. Paleoclimatologists (climatologists who study past—or paleo—climates) use the term "proxy" to describe the way that climate change is recorded in nature, within geological materials such as lake sediments, tree-rings, coral growth-bands, and ice-cores. This "data" is then prepared, analyzed, and used to inform us today of past events Proxy data, especially for past events, is then substituted for, or added to, modern observed data measures
REGO	Renewable Energy Guarantees of Origin The Renewable Energy Guarantees of Origin (REGO) scheme provides transparency to consumers about the proportion of electricity that suppliers source from renewable generation. All EU member states are required to have such a scheme. The United Kingdom adopted the scheme prior to Brexit, and in Britain, it is administered by OFGEM. OFGEM issues one REGO certificate per megawatt hour (MWh) of eligible renewable output to generators of renewable electricity. The purpose of the certificate is to "prove" to the final customer that a given share of energy was produced from renewable sources

Acronym	Description
	In June 2022, REGO was controversially cited as overstating "green" credentials for energy supply, with the suggestion that REGO certificates act to "greenwash" renewable claims. The criticism essentially was that—whether a business has on-site renewable assets or receives all its electricity through a standard supplier contract—the chances are that they receive a proportion of electricity through the same grid as everybody else. This entails the same continually varying mix of "dirty" and "clean" energy sources. Labeling such energy as "zero emissions" has serious implications for the robustness of corporate climate strategies
	For all organizations, this is a case of "watch this space" as the debate was only emerging as this book went to press, but it seems as though REGOs will need considerable overhaul to make them truly accurate. Incidentally, this is not a U.K. problem; this is a pan-European problem and potentially undermines any claim that we are avoiding *greenwashing*. The good news is that more sophisticated measures of energy mix are emerging at the time of writing (2023) so improvements to restore trust in REGOs may be on the way. Watch this space!
SASB	Sustainability Accounting Standards Board
	The SASB is an independent nonprofit, whose mission is to develop and disseminate sustainability accounting standards that help public corporations disclose material, decision-useful information to investors
	The IFRS Foundation's International Sustainability Standards Board (ISSB) encourages companies to persist in using SASB standards. SASB standards identify the subset of environmental, social, and governance issues most relevant to financial performance in each of 77 industries. They are designed to help companies disclose financially material sustainability information to their investors
	At the time of writing, the standards can be easily downloaded from
	www.sasb.org/standards/download/ and are free of charge
SBTi	Science Based Targets initiative
	A partnership between CDP, the United Nations Global Compact, World Resources Institute (WRI), and the World Wide Fund for Nature (WWF). The SBTi call to action is one of the *We Mean Business Coalition* commitments.
	SBTi:
	• Defines and promotes best practice in emissions reductions and net-zero targets in line with climate science • Provides technical assistance and expert resources to companies who set science-based targets in line with the latest climate science

(*Continued*)

(Continued)

Acronym	Description
	• Brings together a team of experts to provide companies with independent assessment and validation of targets • A lead partner of the *Business Ambition for 1.5°C campaign*—an urgent call to action from a global coalition of UN agencies and business and industry leaders, which mobilized companies to set net-zero science-based targets in line with a 1.5°C future 2023: 2,000 + organizations worldwide are leading the transition to a net-zero economy by setting emissions reduction targets grounded in climate science through the SBTi https://sciencebasedtargets.org/about-us
SCDDA	Supply Chain Due Diligence Act On January 1, 2023, the Lieferkettensorgfaltspflichtengesetz (Lieferkettengesetz or LkSG) came into effect in Germany. Known in English as the German *Supply Chain Due Diligence Act* (SCDDA), the law mandates companies with offices in Germany to conduct due diligence on their supply chains to protect human rights and the environment. With significant fines for noncompliance, the SCDDA is likely to become a model for similar legislation elsewhere
SCM	Supply chain management A subset of the procurement function at many organizations. At the most fundamental level, SCM is the management of the flow of goods, data, and finances related to a product or service, from the procurement of raw materials to the delivery of the product at its final destination In the ESG sphere, it is the 3PM mechanisms that often govern how suppliers and clients work together
SDGs (UN)	Sustainable Development Goals The SDGs, also known as the "Global Goals," were adopted by the United Nations in 2015 as a universal call to action to end poverty, protect the planet, and ensure that by 2030 all people enjoy peace and prosperity The 17 SDGs are integrated: they recognize that action in one area affects outcomes in others and that development must balance social, economic, and environmental sustainability. Countries have committed to prioritize progress for those furthest behind. Broadly, the SDGs are designed to end poverty, hunger, AIDS, and discrimination against women and girls. The 17 goals are summarized: (1) End poverty in all its forms everywhere (2) End hunger, achieve food security and improved nutrition, and promote sustainable agriculture (3) Ensure healthy lives and promote well-being for all at all ages

Acronym	Description
	(4) Ensure inclusive and equitable quality education and promote lifelong learning opportunities for all
	(5) Achieve gender equality and empower all women and girls
	(6) Ensure availability and sustainable management of water and sanitation for all
	(7) Ensure access to affordable, reliable, sustainable, and modern energy for all
	(8) Promote sustained, inclusive, and sustainable economic growth, full and productive employment, and decent work for all
	(9) Build resilient infrastructure, promote inclusive and sustainable industrialization, and foster innovation
	(10) Reduce inequality within and among countries
	(11) Make cities and human settlements inclusive, safe, resilient, and sustainable
	(12) Ensure sustainable consumption and production patterns
	(13) Take urgent action to combat climate change and its impacts (taking note of agreements made by the UNFCCC forum)
	(14) Conserve and sustainably use the oceans, seas, and marine resources for sustainable development
	(15) Protect, restore, and promote sustainable use of terrestrial ecosystems, sustainably manage forests, combat desertification, and halt and reverse land degradation, and halt biodiversity loss
	(16) Promote peaceful and inclusive societies for sustainable development, provide access to justice for all and build effective, accountable, and inclusive institutions at all levels
	(17) Strengthen the means of implementation and revitalize the global partnership for sustainable development
SECR (the United Kingdom)	Streamlined Energy and Carbon Reporting SECR was introduced in 2019 as a legislation to replace the Carbon Reduction Commitment (CRC) Scheme. SECR requires obligated companies to report on their energy consumption and associated greenhouse gas emissions within their financial reporting for Companies House. Organizations will also need to report on any energy efficiency measures and state emissions with reference to an intensity metric. The requirements are similar to the requirements of Mandatory Greenhouse Gas (GHG) Reporting previously in place for quoted companies. However, there are changes to the reported information for quoted companies too

(Continued)

(Continued)

Acronym	Description
	SECR applies to all quoted companies, large limited liability partnerships, and large U.K.-incorporated unquoted companies. Limited liability partnerships and U.K.-incorporated quoted companies are considered to be large and must comply with the legislation if they meet two or more of the qualification criteria: • 250 or more employees • Turnover in excess of £36 million • Balance sheet in excess of £18 million *What needs to be reported?* U.K. (and U.K. offshore) energy use and related Scope 1 and 2 GHG emissions
SFDR (EU)	Sustainable Finance Disclosure Regulation SFDR is an EU regulation introduced to improve transparency in the market for sustainable investment products, to prevent "greenwashing" and to increase transparency around sustainability claims made by financial market participants. It imposes mandatory ESG disclosure obligations for asset managers and other financial market participants, effective from March 10, 2021 SFDR was introduced alongside the EU taxonomy regulation and the Low Carbon Benchmarks Regulation as part of a package of legislative measures arising from the European Commission's Action Plan on Sustainable Finance SFDR aims to bring a level-playing field for financial market participants ("FMP") and financial advisers on transparency in relation to sustainability risks, the consideration of adverse sustainability impacts in their investment processes, and the provision of sustainability-related information relating to financial products SFDR requires asset managers such as AIFMs and UCITS managers to provide prescript and standardized disclosures on how ESG factors are integrated at both entity and product levels. A significant portion of the SFDR applies to all asset managers, whether or not they have an express ESG or sustainability focus. The SFDR manifests in additional disclosures for financial market participants *What must firms disclose?* **1. The adverse impacts of investment decisions on sustainability factors:** Obligated firms must disclose the potentially negative consequences an investment decision may have on sustainability factors and how they are mitigating the impacts. These sustainability factors include environmental aspects, such as energy performance and water usage, as well as social aspects like employee matters and respect for human rights

Acronym	Description
	One example of an environmental aspect that firms need to disclose is biodiversity. Firms need to demonstrate that the economic activity is not negatively affecting biodiversity-sensitive areas (through demonstrative evidence of ecological assessments, due diligence, and continual monitoring of any impacts—positive or negative)
	2. Considering sustainability (ESG) risk in investment processes
	Firms disclose where an ESG event could negatively impact material investment and align their remuneration policies with sustainability risk management
	3. Provision of sustainability information with respect to financial products
	Where a product is categorized as an Article 8 or Article 9 product, additional disclosures must be made
TCFD (the United Kingdom)	Task Force on Climate-related Financial Disclosures
	The TCFD was created in 2015 by the Financial Stability Board (FSB) to develop consistent climate-related financial risk disclosures for use by companies, banks, and investors in providing information to stakeholders. Increasing the amount of reliable information on financial institutions' exposure to climate-related risks and opportunities will strengthen the stability of the financial system, contribute to greater understanding of climate risks, and facilitate financing the transition to a more stable and sustainable economy
VUCA	Volatility, uncertainty, complexity, ambiguity
	VUCA describes the situation of constant, unpredictable change that is now the norm in most industries and areas of the business world
	The term VUCA originated in the American military to describe extreme conditions during warfare. It has more recently been adopted by an increasing number of business commentators and business strategists as a framework to approach different types of challenging situation, brought about via external factors (politics, economics, social change, advancing technology, and environment degradation)
	ESG challenges might be considered an aspect of VUCA, as the whole area of ESG is rapidly developing, and may entail considerable on-costs for organizations

Further material: The *Chartered Governance Institute* provides, freely, an extensive online list of ESG acronyms here:

www.cgi.org.uk/knowledge/subject-resource-hub/abc-of-esg#C

APPENDIX 3

Scope 1, 2, and 3 Emissions

Categories and Rationale

Scope 1, 2, and 3 is the preferred mechanism to categorize different kinds of carbon emissions an organization creates in its own operations and in its wider value chain (suppliers and customers). The term first appeared in the *Greenhouse Gas Protocol* of 2001, which is the world's most widely used greenhouse gas accounting standard. Today, scopes are the basis for mandatory GHG reporting globally. In order to take action to reduce emissions, it is necessary to understand and measure where they arise in the first place. "Scopes" help us see this more accurately.

It is unclear why they are styled "scopes" rather than "groups" or "types," but as the name used in the *Greenhouse Gas Protocol*, it is now the recognized term. As the *Greenhouse Gas Protocol* itself puts it: "Developing a full [greenhouse gas] emissions inventory—incorporating Scope 1, Scope 2, and Scope 3 emissions—enables companies to understand their full value chain emissions and focus efforts on the greatest reduction opportunities."

Scope 1, 2, and 3 Emissions—In General

Essentially, Scope 1 and 2 are those emissions that are owned or controlled by an organization, whereas Scope 3 emissions are a consequence of the activities of the company yet occur via sources not owned or controlled by it.

Scope 1 Emissions

Emissions from sources that an organization owns or controls directly, for example, from burning fuel in our fleet of vehicles (assuming they are not electrically powered).

Examples of Scope 1 Emissions

- From combustion of fuel in a furnace or boiler
- From combustion of fuel in company vehicles

Scope 2 Emissions

Emissions that a company causes indirectly when the energy it purchases and uses is produced. For example, for electric fleet vehicles, the emissions from the generation of the electricity they are powered by fall into this category.

Examples of Scope 2 Emissions

- From the power plant to supply electricity to a building
- From the power plant to supply electricity used to charge electric vehicles

Scope 3 Emissions

Emissions not produced by the company itself and not the result of activities from assets owned or controlled by them, but by those that it is indirectly responsible for, up and down its value chain. An example of this is when we buy, use, and dispose of products from suppliers. Scope 3 emissions include all sources not within the Scope 1 and 2 boundaries.

Examples of Scope 3 Emissions

- From the extraction of raw materials used in manufacturing
- From the manufacturing of products used by the organization
- From the downstream usage of products or services
- From waste disposal
- from business travel

Some Practical Considerations

- Scope 1 and 2 are most within an organization's control. Companies normally have sufficient source data needed to convert direct purchases of gas and electricity into a value in tonnes of GHGs. This information may sit with procurement, finance, or estates management or in a sustainability function.

- In some cases, solutions exist to deliver net zero for Scope 1 and 2 emissions.
  For example, an organization can source renewable electricity, renewable gas, or electrify its heat demand, or transition to electric vehicles.

- Scope 3 is often where most impact can be achieved.
  For many businesses, Scope 3 emissions account for more than 70 percent of their carbon footprint. For example, for an organization that manufactures products, there will often be significant carbon emissions from extraction, manufacture, and processing of the raw materials.

- Businesses generally have much less control on how Scope 3 emissions are dealt with.
  We can offer to collaborate on solutions to reduce emissions with current suppliers, or implement changes to our supply chain. In most areas, however, suppliers will have considerable influence on how emissions are reduced through their own purchasing decisions and product design.

- Reaching net zero inevitably involves addressing Scope 3 emissions.
  Defining what constitutes our own "net-zero" ambition can be difficult. Organizations that commit to adopting best practices will address Scope 3 emissions as part of their strategy. Mapping emissions footprint by scale, and how much control we have over the source, is the optimum way to begin this journey. In addition, we will seek low-hanging fruit (or easy wins) in terms of identified "hotspots" on our map. These will be our first "port of call" to make real progress.

Possible "Early Moves"

Assess and properly understand our carbon footprint. Know where our emission hotspots are across our value chain, including where emissions of our suppliers or products are critical parts of your business ecosystem. It may be possible to "map" these in a diagram fashion to bring the issues "alive."

Determine where we can make an impact. Develop a decarbonization strategy and make a clear commitment to cutting our organization's absolute emissions. While we may not have all the necessary information right now, defining a vision is vital. Ideally, this should be shared with key stakeholders; it helps to focus on our accountability as well as contributing to a change in industry norms.

Pursue "low-hanging fruit". Quick and/or easy wins; our competitors may take advantage of potential cost savings associated with lower emissions systems, fleets, or facilities. We do not want to be left behind! Transition in this direction as soon as possible.

Map-out emissions at a "systems level" and build partnerships to drive change across that system. Individual corporate action on climate change is great—but real change requires systemic action. Work with partners to accelerate emission reductions throughout our value chain. See Part 6 of this book.

Consider our operating model. Review culture, incentives, and (critically) acquiring adequate management information. This will be used to drive change internally and will be central to our external disclosures, as set out in various mandatory reporting regimes.

Avoid procrastination. Inaction could be a significant threat. The cost of doing nothing will almost certainly outweigh the on-costs associated with long-term business decarbonization. Beyond direct impacts to our business, a failure to get to grips with climate change will bring its own social, ecosystem, and economic costs.

In the United Kingdom, at the Time of Writing This Book

As part of the British government's strategy to simplify complexities within the "business energy policy" framework, measures were implemented to make it easier for companies to report their energy and carbon obligations more efficiently and effectively.

The introduction of the *Streamlined Energy and Carbon Reporting Regulations* aimed to encourage more businesses to quantify their emissions in a consistent and comparable manner. In 2022, U.K. organizations that satisfy two of the following criteria were required to disclose their business emissions *alongside the actions taken to reduce energy consumption* and subsequent GHG output:

- Turnover—£36 million or more
- Balance sheet total—£18 million or more
- Number of employees—250 or more

Equivalent regulations were being introduced in other jurisdictions.

Is There a Case for Scope 4 Emissions?

This is not an official category within the *Greenhouse Gas Protocol* and it is not mandated by any existing frameworks. Scope 4 has, however, been the focus of increased attention as organizations seek to quantify the positive impact of their products or services that avoid GHG emissions.

Unlike the first three Scopes, which refer to emissions *produced* as a result of an organization's actions, Scope 4 seeks to highlight *avoided* emissions. The most common example is emissions avoided by offering remote work (thereby reducing emissions from commuting and business travel). This is not to imply that other emissions associated with working from home would be ignored entirely—organizations would still measure such emissions to gain an accurate overview of their footprint. Remember, Scope 4 is not on any official agenda at the time of writing this book.

APPENDIX 4

Taxonomy 1—Why?

Key Point Summary

- The EU describes its *taxonomy* as "a tool to help investors, companies, issuers and project promoters navigate the transition to a low-carbon, resilient and resource-efficient economy."
- The EU taxonomy is a classification system of "environmentally sustainable economic activities."
- It was created to help investors make "green" investments.
- Six environmental objectives were identified:
  1. Climate change mitigation
  2. Climate change adaptation
  3. Protection of water and marine resources
  4. Transition to a circular economy
  5. Pollution control
  6. Protection of ecosystems
- It specifies how each activity can contribute to each objective.
- To be taxonomy aligned, an activity must contribute to at least one objective, do no significant harm (DNSH) to any of the others, and meet minimum social safeguards.
- From 2022, certain companies report the percentage of their overall turnover, CapEx, and OpEx that is taxonomy eligible.

What Is the EU Taxonomy?

In biology, taxonomy is the science of naming, describing, and classifying all living things. The European Commission applied this approach to Sustainable business, creating a classification system of environmentally sustainable economic activities. At the most basic, it is a dictionary-style tool detailing specific business activities considered by the EU to be Sustainable. It fills two important needs: (1) provides a common language for talking about sustainability and (2) uses objective and quantifiable criteria for assessing businesses. This is not to suggest it has met with universal acceptance and will not further develop, but it is a powerful starting point.

The EU taxonomy has been described as *the leading science-based classification system for green investment* and is expected to become the global standard for determining whether an economic activity can be considered environmentally Sustainable.

Taxonomy regulation establishes a list of environmentally sustainable economic activities that produce low-CO_2 emissions. An "activity" is defined as Sustainable when it produces under 100g of CO_2/kwh. Direct use of coal automatically disqualifies an activity from being considered "taxonomy-friendly."

The EU is developing, on an ongoing basis, regulatory reporting requirements with which all EU funds *with a Sustainability objective* must comply. Beyond these reporting demands, investors globally look to the framework to support their approach to Sustainable investing and to report on their funds' impact, regardless of where those funds may be situated.

Background

The EU set itself ambitious goals on climate policy, including a 55 percent reduction in greenhouse gas emissions by 2030 and to become climate-neutral by 2050. To achieve these goals, the European Commission released a *sustainable finance plan* in 2018, aimed at bringing together economic and environmental policies to encourage "green investment." Supporting this, they needed to establish clear definitions of what "green" actually means. Accordingly, the EU taxonomy was established in June 2020. While previous guidelines left considerable room for interpretation, the taxonomy adopts a more deliberative approach, looking at individual business activities in granular detail, using a science-backed methodology.

How the Taxonomy Is Structured

The taxonomy looks at a number of major sectors including agriculture, manufacturing, transportation, energy, construction, and communications. For each sector, it provides a list of industry-relevant activities that could be considered Sustainable. It then reviews each activity in the context of six environmental objectives by providing a list of "substantial contribution" criteria and "DNSH" criteria for each objective.

For an activity to be considered *taxonomy eligible*, it needs only to meet the substantial contribution criteria for *one* of the six objectives. For it to be *taxonomy aligned*, it must meet the substantial contribution criteria for at least one of the six, comply with the DNSH criteria for all six, and meet minimum social and governance safeguards (in accordance with OECD, UN, and ILO guidelines).

Who Is Directly Impacted by the EU Taxonomy?

The EU taxonomy establishes three key groups of taxonomy users:

- *Financial market participants*, offering financial products and services within the EU, including occupational pension providers
- *Large companies* that are required to provide a nonfinancial statement, according to the NFRD (Non-Financial Reporting Directive)
- The EU and *member states*, when establishing public measures, standards, or descriptions for *green financial products* or *green bonds*

The EU taxonomy focuses on Sustainable finance, but its scope is larger and stretches, potentially, far beyond banking or financial services.

What Needs to Be Reported and When?

Taxonomy rules apply to all large European companies considered as *public interest entities*, defined as organizations with more than 500 employees and financial market participants ("FMPs") offering products within the EU that promote environmental objectives. Where subject to taxonomy rules, you need to disclose in your annual report *how much of your overall business follows the activities outlined in the taxonomy.*

The taxonomy was rolled out in two phases. Beginning 2022, *phase 1*, companies report proportion of turnover, capital expenditure (CapEx), and operational expenditure (OpEx) that is taxonomy eligible. In *phase 2*, large companies and financial institutions report on the proportion of their turnover, CapEx, and OpEx that is taxonomy aligned beginning 2024.[1]

Notes

There is a difference between activities "aligned" with the European Green Deal and those "eligible" under the rules. An activity is "taxonomy eligible" if it is listed in the EU taxonomy, irrespective of whether it meets any of the specific conditions. If an activity is not described in the regulation, it will be considered non-eligible.

The taxonomy is subject to continuous review, allowing for new industries and activities to be added. As the first "green list" of its kind, scientists and business leaders are keen to ensure that it is as accurate and fair as possible.

Looking to the future, there is ambition to devising equivalent legislation, such as a "social taxonomy." This would broaden the challenge significantly, applying the same level of scrutiny to the "S" part of ESG. The taxonomy, its contents, and how it is used will certainly expand and develop over time.

What Does This Mean for Businesses?

The taxonomy provides an opportunity for organizations to *demonstrate* their performance and progress toward Sustainable business models and financial markets to make more informed investment decisions. Remember, EU companies with more than 500 employees are required to disclose:

1. The proportion of their turnover derived from products or services associated with economic activities that qualify as environmentally sustainable

---

[1] Plans at the time of writing this book.

2. The proportion of their CapEx and OpEx related to assets or processes associated with economic activities that qualify as environmentally sustainable

For organizations new to this, a good starting point is to assess business models and how much of their underlying activities qualify as "green." This information will be required by investors and insurers and will feed, in turn, into *their* disclosures and investment decisions.

A second step is to consider your company's compliance with minimum social safeguards, achieved when economic activities are aligned with the *OECD's Guidelines for Multinational Enterprises* and the UN's *Guiding Principles on Business and Human Rights*.

Depending on your assessment's result, internal controls may need to be developed or updated to meet emerging requirements. In addition, your business model or corporate strategy may need to be reconsidered, to secure your company's future.

A proposal to amend the NFRD was underway as this book was being written. This is expected to expand the remit of the EU taxonomy. If approved, a new Corporate Sustainability Reporting Directive (CSRD) will require all large companies to disclose their sustainability impact from January 2026.

Next Steps for Novices!

To comply with the EU taxonomy and its performance thresholds, organizations must establish what *data* they need, how to *analyze* it, and - most importantly - how to *report* on it. The EU taxonomy in practice will require enhanced reporting processes which necessitate companies providing crystal clarity in terms of their reporting. Companies need to think, in addition, what effect emerging reporting demands will have on their marketing, procurement, and broader investment strategies. Furthermore, organizations must consider needs such as people resources, training, data, systems, revenue overhead (budget), and subject matter expertise, in order to meet emerging reporting requirements.

EU taxonomy measures have considerable practical impact, not only within the EU, but potentially far beyond. It will influence the broader financial regulatory arena, shape the flow of investments, and reconfigure the practice of a range of financial professions.

Final Thoughts ...

At the time of writing this book, several commentators made similar suggestions on how organizations should optimally respond, summarized as follows:

Start early: As with any new regulatory requirement, the best way to keep on top of things is to get ahead of the game! Understanding and reporting on the taxonomy will take time, so it is prudent to initiate as early as possible.

Do not assume the taxonomy won't affect you: Be alert. Do not ignore the taxonomy simply because you are a small- or medium-sized organization. Alignment is emerging as a key consideration for investors, and therefore this represents a vital factor in securing capital. The scope of "who needs to report" will expand in the future. If you are not impacted today, you probably will be later on!

Be agile: Bear in mind that the taxonomy is still developing and this is likely to become an ongoing, iterative process. Adopting an agile mindset that copes with new requirements as they emerge, rather than needing to re-evaluate annually, is central to agility.

Think outside the box: There is a broader picture on ESG. The EU taxonomy is pointing the way forward but we should anticipate expanding regulation or legislation, heightened expectations, and new requirements in the next ten years. To meet this ever-developing situation, we must ensure we lay a sound foundation and responsive corporate culture. Most important, we must ensure that all collected data is fit for purpose and verifiable. To achieve this, we must institute a robust, cohesive process across the entire organization.

APPENDIX 5

Taxonomy 2—How?

Explanatory Note

It is important to understand that this is an ever-developing listing, and organizations should attempt to remain abreast of developments, especially in activities adjacent to their own business sector.

The EU taxonomy characterizes differing "industries" in terms of their Sustainability impacts and credentials. At the time of writing, the basic breakdown for industries in which significant contribution to Sustainability objectives may be anticipated was as follows:

PRIMARY	SECONDARY
Agriculture and forestry	Afforestation
Agriculture and forestry	Rehabilitation and reforestation
Agriculture and forestry	Reforestation
Agriculture and forestry	Existing forest management
Agriculture and forestry	Conservation forest
Agriculture and forestry	Growing of perennial crops
Agriculture and forestry	Growing of nonperennial crops
Agriculture and forestry	Livestock production
Manufacturing	Manufacture of low-carbon technologies
Manufacturing	Manufacture of cement
Manufacturing	Manufacture of aluminum
Manufacturing	Manufacture of iron and steel
Manufacturing	Manufacture of hydrogen
Manufacturing	Manufacture of other inorganic basic chemicals—manufacture of carbon black
Manufacturing	Manufacture of other inorganic basic chemicals—manufacture of disodium carbonate (soda ash)
Manufacturing	Manufacture of other inorganic basic chemicals—manufacture of chlorine

(Continued)

(Continued)

PRIMARY	SECONDARY
Manufacturing	Manufacture of other organic basic chemicals
Manufacturing	Manufacture of fertilizers and nitrogen compounds
Manufacturing	Manufacture of plastics in primary form
Electricity, gas, steam, and air conditioning supply	Production of electricity from solar PV
Electricity, gas, steam, and air conditioning supply	Production of electricity from concentrated solar power
Electricity, gas, steam, and air conditioning supply	Production of electricity from wind power
Electricity, gas, steam, and air conditioning supply	Production of electricity from ocean energy
Electricity, gas, steam, and air conditioning supply	Production of electricity from hydropower
Electricity, gas, steam, and air conditioning supply	Production of electricity from geothermal
Electricity, gas, steam, and air conditioning supply	Production of electricity from gas (not exclusive to natural gas)
Electricity, gas, steam, and air conditioning supply	Production of electricity from bioenergy (biomass, biogas, and biofuels)
Electricity, gas, steam, and air conditioning supply	Transmission and distribution of electricity
Electricity, gas, steam, and air conditioning supply	Storage of electricity
Electricity, gas, steam, and air conditioning supply	Storage of thermal energy
Electricity, gas, steam, and air conditioning supply	Storage of hydrogen
Electricity, gas, steam, and air conditioning supply	Manufacture of biogas or biofuels
Electricity, gas, steam, and air conditioning supply	Retrofit of gas transmission and distribution networks
Electricity, gas, steam, and air conditioning supply	District heating/cooling distribution
Electricity, gas, steam, and air conditioning supply	Installation and operation of electric heat pumps
Electricity, gas, steam, and air conditioning supply	Cogeneration of heat/cool and power from concentrated solar power
Electricity, gas, steam, and air conditioning supply	Cogeneration of heat/cool and power from geothermal energy

PRIMARY	SECONDARY
Electricity, gas, steam, and air conditioning supply	Cogeneration of heat/cool and power from gas (not exclusive to natural gas)
Electricity, gas, steam, and air conditioning supply	Cogeneration of heat/cool and power from bioenergy (biomass, biogas, and biofuels)
Electricity, gas, steam, and air conditioning supply	Production of heat/cool from concentrated solar power
Electricity, gas, steam, and air conditioning supply	Production of heat/cool from geothermal
Electricity, gas, steam, and air conditioning supply	Production of heat/cool from gas (not exclusive to natural gas)
Electricity, gas, steam, and air conditioning supply	Production of heat/cool from bioenergy (biomass, biogas, and biofuels)
Electricity, gas, steam, and air conditioning supply	Production of heat/cool using waste heat
Water, sewerage, waste, and remediation	Water collection, treatment, and supply
Water, sewerage, waste, and remediation	Centralized wastewater treatment
Water, sewerage, waste, and remediation	Anaerobic digestion of sewage sludge
Water, sewerage, waste, and remediation	Separate collection and transport of nonhazardous waste in source-segregated fractions
Water, sewerage, waste, and remediation	Anaerobic digestion of bio-waste
Water, sewerage, waste, and remediation	Composting of bio-waste
Water, sewerage, waste, and remediation	Material recovery from nonhazardous waste
Water, sewerage, waste, and remediation	Landfill gas capture and utilization
Water, sewerage, waste, and remediation	Direct air capture of CO_2
Water, sewerage, waste, and remediation	Capture of anthropogenic emissions
Water, sewerage, waste, and remediation	Transport of CO_2
Water, sewerage, waste, and remediation	Permanent sequestration of captured CO_2
Transportation and storage	Passenger rail transport (interurban)
Transportation and storage	Freight rail transport

(Continued)

(*Continued*)

PRIMARY	SECONDARY
Transportation and storage	Public transport
Transportation and storage	Infrastructure for low-carbon transport (land transport)
Transportation and storage	Passenger cars and commercial vehicles
Transportation and storage	Freight transport services by road
Transportation and storage	Interurban scheduled road transport
Transportation and storage	Inland passenger water transport
Transportation and storage	Inland freight water transport
Transportation and storage	Infrastructure for low-carbon transport (water transport)
Buildings	Construction of new buildings
Buildings	Building renovation
Buildings	Individual renovation measures, installation of renewables on-site, and professional, scientific, and technical activities
Buildings	Acquisition and ownership of buildings
ICT	Data processing, hosting, and related activities
ICT	Data-driven climate change monitoring solutions

Organizations should seek to locate their own industry or commercial sector with reference to this listing and/or that of their key Interlocutors, especially suppliers, but possibly also customers if there is a strong and ongoing close interaction.

The developers of the EU taxonomy sought first to target and describe those sectors where there is most direct Sustainability (environmental) impact. It is expected that this listing will develop and expand over time and that a similar listing for social impacts may be developed in the mid-2020s.

Within the listing, *adaptation* and *mitigation* strategies are cited, which means—at a practical level—that users can identify the riskiest industries and activities from a Sustainability viewpoint, as well as information about how to consider impacts, report them, and move toward mitigation (and eventual elimination?)

Technical screening criteria for "substantial contribution" to climate change *adaptation* are characterized below. Organizations in reporting their impacts can also use preconfigured classification for mitigation strategies. These seek to differentiate between "adapted activities" and "activities enabling adaptation."

Screening Criteria

Screening criteria for adapted activities	
Criterion	**Description**
A1: Reducing material physical climate risks	The economic activity must reduce all material physical climate risks to that activity to the extent possible and on a best effort basis
A1.1	The economic activity integrates physical and nonphysical measures aimed at reducing, to the extent possible and on a best effort basis, all material physical climate risks to that activity, which have been identified through a risk assessment
A1.2	The above-mentioned assessment has the following characteristics:
	• Considers both current weather variability and future climate change, including uncertainty
	• Is based on robust analysis of available climate data and projections across a range of future scenarios
	• Is consistent with the expected lifetime of the activity
A2: Supporting system adaptation	The economic activity and its adaptation measures do not adversely affect the adaptation efforts of other people, nature, and assets
A2.1	The economic activity and its adaptation measures do not increase the risks of an adverse climate impact on other people, nature, and assets or hamper adaptation elsewhere. Consideration should be given to the viability of "green" or "nature-based solutions" over "gray" measures to address adaptation
A2.2	The economic activity and its adaptation measures are consistent with sectoral, regional, and/or national adaptation efforts
A3: Monitoring adaptation results	The reduction of physical climate risks can be measured
A3.1	Adaptation results can be monitored and measured against defined indicators. Recognizing that risk evolves over time, updated assessments of physical climate risks should be undertaken at the appropriate frequency where possible

(Continued)

(*Continued*)

Screening criteria for an activity enabling adaptation	
Criterion	Description
B1. Supporting adaptation of other economic activities	The economic activity reduces material physical climate risk in other economic activities and/or addresses systemic barriers to adaptation. Activities enabling adaptation include, but are not limited to, activities that:
	• Promote a technology, product, practice, governance process, or innovative uses of existing technologies, products, or practices (including those related to natural infrastructure)
	• Remove information, financial, technological, and capacity barriers to adaptation by others
B1.1	The economic activity reduces or facilitates adaptation to physical climate risks beyond the boundaries of the activity itself. The activity will need to demonstrate how it supports adaption of others through:
	• An assessment of the risks resulting from both current weather variability and future climate change, including uncertainty, that the economic activity will contribute to address based on robust climate data
	• An assessment of the effectiveness of the contribution of the economic activity to reducing those risks, taking into account the scale of exposure and the vulnerability to them
B1.2	In the case of infrastructure linked to an activity enabling adaptation, that infrastructure must also meet the screening criteria A1, A2, and A3

The above devolves down to a quite granular technical understanding that we need to acquire *to the extent we are exposed to risks*. If we work in an economic sector that entails significant Sustainability "harms," then, of course, we invest in greater expertise to stay abreast of the relevant issues, as well as developing effective mitigating strategies.

The taxonomy describes individual sectors of industry or commerce as having the potential for "substantial contribution" toward environmental or Sustainability objectives and subdivides this into contribution toward:

- The circular economy
- Climate change adaptation

- Water usage
- Pollution
- Eco-systems

Mitigation and Adaptation

We repeat, this material reaches into fairly "technical" areas of Sustainability theory and practice, and we must acquire expertise to the extent we can accelerate moves either toward mitigation or toward economic or societal adaptation. These are described in the EU notes below.

Mitigation summary	Overview of economic activities that can make a substantial contribution to climate change mitigation. Columns indicate: 1. Whether the contribution is based on own performance or enabling improvements in other sectors 2. Whether the activity is considered to be transitional 3. Which environmental objectives also have "do no significant harm" objectives?
Mitigation full data	Full technical screening criteria and rationale for activities that can make a substantial contribution to climate change mitigation. Columns indicate: 1. The activity, description, and NACE* code 2. The principles, metrics, thresholds, and rationale for substantial contribution to climate change mitigation 3. The criteria for avoiding significant harm to environmental objectives 2 to 6, including whether the criteria are based on EU regulation and the relevant EU regulation(s)
Adaptation summary	Overview of economic activities that can make a substantial contribution to climate change adaptation. Columns indicate which environmental objectives also have "do no significant harm" objectives
Adaptation full data	Full technical screening criteria and rationale for activities that can make a substantial contribution to climate change adaptation. Columns indicate: 1. The activity, description, and NACE code 2. Description of how to use the technical screening criteria for substantial contribution to climate change adaptation (the full criteria are generic across all activities and can be found in tab "Adaptation screening criteria") 3. The criteria for avoiding significant harm to environmental objectives 2 to 6, including whether the criteria are based on EU regulation and the relevant EU regulation(s)

(Continued)

(Continued)

Adaptation principles	The technical screening criteria for substantial contribution to climate change adaptation, which are the same across all activities evaluated by the TEG
Regulation	A list of regulations and relevant guidance included in the technical screening criteria (particularly, the DNSH criteria for objectives 3 to 6)
BICS	A mapping of the NACE classification system to the Bloomberg industry classification system (BICS)
TRBC	A mapping of the NACE* classification system to the Thompson Reuters business classification (TRBC) system

*NACE codes are *the standard European nomenclature of productive economic activities*. They break down the universe of economic activities in such a way that a NACE code can be associated with a statistical unit carrying out the activity it designates.

Key Takeaways for Managers

"Taxonomy" and "mitigation" will be increasingly the subject of discussion in the years 2024 to 2030. After that, it is possible that these questions will be so embedded within normal corporate discourse that they no longer seem novel.

While, at this point, it is the European Union that is "making the running" in all this, it is to be expected that other trade blocs will adopt similar approaches. They may, in practice, essentially "cut and paste" the EU approach into their own Sustainability responses and associated legislation. Watch this space!

APPENDIX 6

The Business Case for ESG

Short-Termism?

At the time of writing this book, many organizations, particularly in the SME sector, were struggling with the impending "hike" in sustainability reporting, not to mention practical measures required to secure "wins" across the diverse areas of "E," "S," and "G" concerns. In developing a rational—and costed—responses to new demands, managers must build the internal *business case for action*. In reality, this is not as complex as it may at first seem. Beyond that, they need to ensure ESG issues are factored-in to individual business cases at the tactical level.

To determine ESG stance (see Chapter 5), senior managers carefully assess their business context and associated corporate plans and how ESG improvements will advance strategy. *We must consider how best to incorporate ESG factors into strategic and investment decision making.* Inevitably, there is something here about long-termism versus short-termism. What sort of company is yours? Are companies and investors too short term in their investment horizon, leading to business decisions that increase near-term reported profits at the expense of the long-term sustainability of profits? ESG theory assumes that the *true costs* of poor decisions are encountered in *externalities*, borne disproportionately by members of the workforce and by society at large.

The modern argument (and it seems a sound one) is that to prosper over time, an organization must not only deliver financial performance, but also demonstrate how it makes a positive contribution to broader society. Companies must benefit their direct stakeholders, including shareholders, employees, customers, and the communities in which they operate. In the absence of a clear sense of purpose, no organization, public or private, can achieve full potential—and ultimately may lose its *license to operate* from key stakeholders. Such organizations can succumb to short-term pressure to distribute earnings. But slavishly following this path, do they sacrifice advantages in employee development, innovation, and capital expenditures necessary for long-term growth[1]?

There needs to be recalibration of the relationship between public corporations and their major institutional investors. This might entail corporate governance evolving toward increased collaboration between organizations, shareholders, and other stakeholders, working *together* to achieve long-term value and resist short-termism. This is, perhaps, the essence of the "green movement" in terms of the COP process, but we should never forget that this is as much a political as an economic decision, and therefore subject to rational challenge and debate. Debate is always good and helps to build consensus over the long term.

Build the Business Case—Strategic Level

Forward-thinking businesses examine and evaluate ESG-related factors as part of their decision-making process. Some institutional investors have deepened engagement with companies around these issues, and this will expand in the decade following 2024. Comprehensive analysis of ESG factors can help build:

- An effective risk management framework
- A new focus for strategy development and growth opportunities
- Answers to demands of stakeholders such as customers, employees, and investors

Institutional investors seek to incorporate ESG factors into their process by (1) identifying relevant stakeholders and factors, (2) isolating and evaluating associated risks, and (3) supporting companies as they invest in their businesses to increase returns:

---

[1] Public sector organizations face analogous dilemmas: meeting short-term voter demands prior to the next election may be an equivalent pressure.

- **Identifying relevant factors**. The first step is to map the "ecosystem" of stakeholders associated with the organization and analyze their interests (i.e., their incentives, values, and viewpoints). Stakeholders typically include customers, suppliers, employees, regulators, the general public, shareholders, and even competitors. Once this ecosystem has been mapped, it is easier to understand which ESG factors are most relevant in your circumstances. Certain factors such as governance and human capital might apply broadly, while others such as environmental footprint may be more limited.
- **Isolating and evaluating associated risks**. Once relevant factors are identified, businesses can evaluate and quantify (to the extent possible) the organization's position and associated risk in each area. The active engagement by an investor with a significant stake and long-term perspective can promote a company's discussion of risk at the C-suite or board level, encourage corporate investment to mitigate risk (even at the expense of near-term profit), and provide support for the management team as it justifies its decisions to the broader investment community.
- **Supporting companies as they invest**. Beyond risk reduction, ESG *factor analysis* can assist identification of investments or activities that increase long-term returns. For example, an organization's investment in a more sustainable supply chain can (1) deepen relationships with customers (so promoting volume growth and premium pricing), (2) attract talent to the organization, and perhaps also (3) reduce costs. Such positive effects can build synergy and create a powerful impetus. To identify and capitalize on such opportunities, senior leadership evaluates *material ESG factors* as core inputs into strategy development.

Build the Business Case—Tactical (or Project) Level

Assuming the board has determined the organization's ESG stance, to build individual *business cases* relating to particular tasks, investments, projects, or contracts, it is necessary to identify and measure specific "E" or "S" or "G" implications arising directly. A standard subsection in the business case *template* for such factors will ensure this important element is not missed. Possibly, there will be threshold figure under which ESG considerations will require only cursory treatment and/or a materiality assessment (see Chapter 8 and Stage H1) that will trigger higher level approvals. But, these mechanisms are typical to all business cases; the ESG aspect is usually no more important than other aspects.

Building the business case involves relating ESG realities to our own business context. We need to recognize "E," "S," and "G" factors as they broadly impact our business sector. We need to evaluate, then, whether poor ESG performance is likely to (1) increase operational risks (insurance implications?), (2) reduce external investment support, or (3) damage our public image ("PR"). Within this, we need to attempt to put a figure on the "cost" of this, both now and potentially into the future. Understanding such costs, we can then evaluate the beneficial impact of efforts to improve ESG performance. *This is not an exact science, but the exercise improves understanding overall, and so confidence in the business case.*

Any business case will therefore (1) describe broad business context, (2) assess risks and opportunities, (3) assign a fiscal "cost" to inaction, and (4) assign an opportunity cost to improving ESG performance. After appropriate deliberation, the advantages—and disadvantages—of further ESG focus will become clearer. At the time of writing this book, an innovative technique is present to assist this process, specifically as regards "climate transition," called CTVaR (or Climate Transition Value at Risk). *See Appendix 2 for further insight.* This is an interesting development and will undoubtedly become more robust over time. It is possible that equivalent measures may be developed to provide a greater insight into emerging "social" risks and even for "governance"-type questions.

Does your standard business case template accommodate ESG questions?

The 39-Step ESG Roadmap

ESG—High-Level Roadmap

This high-level roadmap sets out 39 steps to deliver effective ESG management. Each step is "numbered" and should be considered an active *task* or even an active *subproject*.

Whether in the sub disciplines of "E," "S," or "G," the steps are identical. This means organizations can approach the problem with a common mindset, a common set of expectations, and a common project management style.

In the context of this book, despite the fact that the roadmap is identical for each ESG sub discipline, the *detailed guidance notes associated with each discrete step differ*. Navigation through the steps and through the associated discrete sub discipline notes is straightforward, however. Follow this simple approach:

In the "roadmap," where you see the relevant step number as 1, 2, 3, 4, and so on, then for the "E" part of ESG, the associated detailed notes are E1, E2, E3, E4, and so on. Similarly, for the "S" part of ESG, please associate with S1, S2, S3, and so on, and the same for the "G" aspect where you look for G1, G2, G3, and so on.

Relevant chapter numbers for the detailed notes are, respectively, Chapters 12, 15, and 18 for the sub disciplines of "E," of "S," and of "G."

The only exception is at "step" H8 to H11—reference here is to the separate "high-level" roadmap—see Chapter 8 for full details.

Review and understand business context **0**

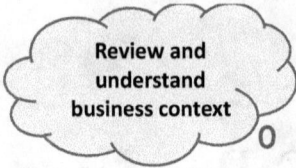

"E," "S," and "G" objective(s) documented **1**

What does this mean in practical terms? **2**

Board Exec nominated **3**

Stakeholder Engagement **4**

Data integrity **H8 to H11**

3 year horizon targeted (with metrics) **5**

Project Manager appointed **6**

Project management protocols enabled **7**

"E," "S," and "G" policy draft tabled **8**

"E," "S," and "G" policy draft socialised **9**

"E," "S," and "G" policy draft published **10**

Communications (internal) (external) **11**

Year 1 Plan
Year 2 Plan **12**
Year 3 Plan

* Internal

Comms Messages **13**
(website)
(marketing)

Associated filing systems **14**
created (audit trail)

Managerial and team **15**
targets devised and
promulgated

Review loop embedded **16**

Action phase **33**

* External

3PM workstream **17**

Know your customer **18**
(Sales)

Know your Supplier **19**
(Procurement)

Risk reviews **20**

Action phase **33**

* Procurement

Category Management approached agreed	**21**		Remedial action	**26**
Category Plan(s)	**22**		Comms messages (with suppliers) (with stakeholders)	**27**
Terms and Conditions (review)	**23**			
Review Progress at (periodicity)	**24**		Action phase	**33**
Feedback	**25**			

* Marketing

See Step 18 plus	**28**		Remedial action	**32**
Sales (Customer) materiality review	**29**			
Sales (Customer) risk review	**30**		Action phase	**33**
Sales – determine whether to enter dialogue with potential customer to remedy/address identified risks	**31**			

ESG—Establishing 3PM Links

Determine link to **34**
corporate strategy and
policy objectives
(5, 17, 21-27, 28-32)

Explore potential mutual **35**
interests and "wins" with
3P

Establish whether **36**
specific ESG targets are
best achieved in
combination with 3P

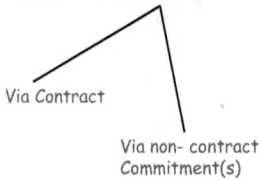

Via Contract

Via non- contract
Commitment(s)

Codify objectives **37**

Establish RAM measures **38**

Establish "project" plan(s) **39**
(6, 7)

Action phase **33**

About the Author

Peter Sammons, M-CIPS, a hands-on commercial specialist, whose career traverses private and public sectors. Author of *Right First Time: Buying & Integrating Advanced Technology* and *Contract Management: Core Business Competence*, he develops and delivers training seminars worldwide. With considerable practical experience of developing effective governance within the value chain (especially via suppliers and contractors), Sammons brings real-world solutions to the burgeoning ESG task.

Index

Note: Page numbers followed by "f" refer to figures and "n" refer to footnotes.

* 9 7 8 1 6 3 7 4 2 5 9 8 5 *